Praise for

"The AV8 Harrier-Straight Up and Out of Control"

MajGen Michael "Lancer" Sullivan, USMC (Ret)

"Straight up and Out of Control" is the finest and most compete book I've ever read about Harriers, squadron life and a military career for a Marine fighter/attack pilot. It is especially satisfying for me as John Capito was my instructor when I checked out in Harriers. Caps was the epitome of a Harrier pilot because he had mastered flying this more difficult jet, being able to perform magic with it, but he could also mentor others and train them to be very credible Harrier pilots. Caps' very strong reputation in the Harrier community as an early pioneer helped guide the Harrier program into the future with Short Takeoff and Vertical Landing (STOVL) jets being selected by the Marines to be its future. Today the Corps is replacing all their TacAir jet squadrons with STOVL F-35B Lightnings, save four squadrons of F-35Cs that will fly from conventional aircraft carriers, when required.

IT'S A HUGE JOY TO READ!

The AV-8 Harrier
Straight Up and Out of Control

A Few Observations and Confessions
of a Harrier Pilot

LtCol John Capito USMC (Ret)
31 October 1945 - 9 November 2020

TABLE OF CONTENTS

PROLOGUE

Glossary of Photographs

DISCLAIMER: The editors regret any errors made in credits for the photographs. Any errors brought to the publisher's attention will be corrected in subsequent printings of the book.

Cover design and background photograph   Capt. Gary Bain USMC (Ret)

Cover photo of Harrier Courtesy of Brad Silcott   BDS Aviation Photography

Book title courtesy of Hope Light, wife of Maj. Bobby Light USMC (Ret)

The Marine maintainers whose dedicated efforts kept the Harriers in the air and whom John loved.   Tim Hultine

LtCol John Capito   Author's personal collection

My dad, third Marine from the right, awarded a Silver Star and Purple Heart for his heroism on New Britain during WW II.   Author's personal collection

USMC Records copy of the citation for my father's Silver Star awarded for heroism in New Britain   USMC records

1stLt Capito (left) and 1stLt Steve Arps (white harness) with T-2B for Carrier Qualifications and aerial gunnery training at VT-4 at NAS Pensacola.   Author's personal collection

1stLt Capito in my VMFA-513 F-4B.   Author's personal collection

Our class trained with VMA-513 in the early Block 1 AV-8As seen on the VMA-513 flight line at MCAS Beaufort, SC.   Ted Herman

(L to R) Capt. Rocky Davis (in cockpit), Capt. Byron Trapnell, Maj Drax Williams, Capt. Joe Anderson, me, Maj G.O. Jensen, Lt Malcom Taylor (USN), LtCol Rocky Nelson, Maj Duke Savage, Maj Mike Abajian   Author's personal collection

(Above) The AV-8A cockpit - compact and busy.   Ted Herman

(Below) The AV-8A throttle quadrant: throttle with switches for radio and speed brake, nozzle lever in the forward position (nozzles aft), and the selectable "STO stop" on the rear of the quadrant used to pre-select a nozzle setting for take-off.   Ted Herman

DaNang Air Base, RVN.   My F-4B RIO. 1stLt Robinson and I, call signs Thumper and Bambi   Author's personal collection

Four VMA-542 AV-8s outbound from MCAS Yuma, AZ, to the Chocolate Mountain ranges   1974 photo courtesy of British Aerospace

(Above) (L to R) John Halloran, Wayne Peterson, me, Mike Ryan, Mickey Taylor, Marx Branum (in cockpit), Dale Heely, Larry Wahl, P.J. Lowery. Dale Heely

(Below) An AV-8 comes to a hover alongside LPH-9, USS Guam. The lead aircraft has already landed on the fantail. 1974 photo courtesy of British Aerospace

AV-8s operating at LZ Bluebird, Camp LeJeune, NC during Exercise Solid Shield. Steve Torrent

Landing on 30 ft-wide Lyman Road at Camp LeJeune, NC. Kyle Andrews

An AV-8 lands on a 96 ft by 96ft pad at LZ Dove, Camp LeJeune, NC. Steve Torrent

Capt. Joe Gallo getting ready to launch from LZ Bluebird at Camp LeJeune, NC. Dana Gallo

Approaching the LZ located among the 90-ft high trees required concentration and the help of the Landing Site Supervisor to come in to a hover and vertical landing. Steve Torrent

Capt. Bobby Light greeted by BGen K. Smith USMC after landing at a new forward site in Korea. Bobby Light

(L to R) Bill (Few) Callahan, Jim (Stranger) Sabow, and me. Author's personal collection

VMA-513 maintainers, working through the night, remove the wing to change the engine. Ted Herman

VMA-513 cruise plaque on display in the Naval Aviation Museum, NAS Pensacola, FL Ted Herman

(L to R) Win Rorabaugh, Jim Sabow, Bill Callahan, Mike Siepert, and me on the ramp at MCAS Yuma after our return to CONUS Author's personal collection

CPL Way (facing) and his crew on the frigid Cold Lake, Canada tarmac advises SSgt Swatosh (right) a jet is ready for a sortie. Charles Way

Me, Major Art Nalls, Col Duke Savage, and McDonnel Douglas test pilot Jack Jackson (Col, USMCR) after my familiarization flight in the new TAV-8B. Author's personal collection

Representatives from McDonnell Douglas and NAVAIR and I discuss issues with the new AV-8B. Author's personal collection

Commanding Officer VMAT-203. Author's personal collection

BGen Chuck Yeager flies a TAV-8A to familiarize him with Harrier flight characteristics for the introduction to the Italian Navy. Author's personal collection

Flanked by a graduating class of new AV-8B Harrier pilots. Author's personal collection

Leading, instructing, flying…it doesn't get any better. Author's personal collection

Background photo under "Semper Fidelis … Caps Brad Silcott BDS Aviation Photography

Straight Up and Out of Control

Dedication and Acknowledgements

Linda Penn Capito

To all of John's fellow pilots, aircraft maintenance personnel and those sharing their lives as Marines during the period that John wrote about.

John and I, best friends for life, were married the 10 years before his death. In our travels we visited many Marine friends, sharing old stories and laughter that was priceless. Many said to John, "Caps, you've just got to write it down". So here it is in his book, one that brought him smiles, laughter and tears while writing it. Enjoy.

Acknowledgements

John's father, John E Capito, a former Marine who inspired John through most of his career in the Corps.

Joe Gallo, for his early and fervent inspiration to put this story in to words.

Thanks to Linda Loyd Hill Vanhooser, for her preliminary editing, and to Capt. Gary Bain, USMC (Ret) and LtCol Ted Herman, USMC (Ret) for their efforts in final editing and publishing.

And finally, for the Marine enlisted maintainers and officers whose dedicated efforts kept the Harriers in the air and whom John loved.

From the editors

Capt. Gary Bain, USMC (Ret)

John and I shared a long and enduring friendship from the time he first started flying the Harriers. For the past few years, we both pursued writing books about our life in the Corps. He completed the first draft of his book and because of me being one of the first ten original Harrier pilots and for my editing experience he asked me to edit his book. I was quite honored and took the task on, not realizing that I would need to complete the job for him.

As a note the original manuscript in Caps' own words has not been changed. Only minor typos, grammar, and historical corrections were made.

Thanks to Steven Capito, John Capito's son, for his cooperation and enthusiasm for seeing that his father's book was completed and published.

I would like to thank Linda Penn Capito for her assistance in gathering his personal photographs and providing contacts, names and places where he served.

Many thanks to his fellow pilots and those Marines that served with him, and maintained the aircraft; for their support in providing photographs, dates, names, and places where the photos were taken.

Thank you to Richard Benjamin and Ray Surface, owners RBA Marketing and Media for photographic and book cover template assistance and to Linda Loyd Hill Vanhooser for proofreading my work and assisting with the initial structure and format of the book. Her contributions and guidance were most professional and very much appreciated.

A very special thanks to LtCol. Ted Herman USMC (Ret) for bringing the book to a state of fruition. Ted was one of John's best friends in the USMC, a Harrier pilot and squadron mate during the time Caps served in the Corps and has a vast knowledge of the Harrier, its history, and the pilots that flew the aircraft. His expertise in writing professional articles as well as authoring books really added continuity and a professional touch that was instrumental in completing this work.

John Capito was a special person and I take a lot of pride being involved in bringing his words to life in his dream of writing this book.

Semper Fidelis, Caps

LtCol Ted Herman, USMC (Ret)

I first met Caps in 1968 at NAS Pensacola as we both began pre-flight in the Naval Aviation Training Command - *what a character*!

Although we fell out of sequence in our training and first assignments, our paths continued to cross randomly until 1973 when he arrived at VMA-542 in MCAS Beaufort for Harrier training. For the next six years together, we experienced life in the fast lane; sometimes too fast, but never dull. Our careers took different paths in 1979, but we never lost touch.

Caps lived large and infused us with enthusiasm, esprit, and a common-sense approach to many of the challenges we faced in those early days of the Harrier. He found learning and advice in just about everything that happened around and to us. While many of us griped about circumstances or people, Caps used the experience to move on in his growth as a leader.

This, his final work, a compendium of his experiences, fun, learning, leadership, and love of life and people, is a worthy memorial to a true man and a dear friend.

Adios, my friend...

Straight Up and Out of Control

PROLOGUE

A few years ago, Vince Murphy, a former Navy pilot and close friend, looked at me one day and said, "You know, Capito, you and I are incredibly average." I had to agree with him!

As I near the end of my days, I feel compelled to share this story. The life of a United States Marine is anything but normal; couple that with being a Marine aviator and you have a combination that would challenge even the most talented of individuals. There is no finer camaraderie than that which exists among Marine aviators and I believe that will be explained in no uncertain terms in the following story.

To me, there is no greater exhilaration than taking flight in a jet aircraft and soaring to the heavens. This is best described in the following poem written by John Gillespie Magee, Jr.

High Flight

Oh! I have slipped the surly bonds of Earth
And danced the skies on laughter-silvered wings;
Sunward I've climbed, and joined the tumbling mirth
Of sun-split clouds, — and done a hundred things
You have not dreamed of — wheeled and soared and swung
High in the sunlit silence. Hov'ring there,
I've chased the shouting wind along, and flung
My eager craft through footless halls of air . . .

Up, up the long, delirious burning blue
I've topped the wind-swept heights with easy grace
Where never lark, or ever eagle flew —
And, while with silent, lifting mind, I've trod
The high untrespassed sanctity of space,
Put out my hand, and touched the face of God.

Pilot Officer John Gillespie Magee, Jr
No.412 Squadron RCAF
KIA 11th. December 1941

Straight Up and Out of Control

PART 1 (1973-1974)
MCAS Beaufort, South Carolina

Straight Up and Out of Control

1: Getting there

My dream of becoming a United States Marine Corps Naval Aviator started when I was around the age of six. I was greatly influenced by my dad, who served as a Marine in World War II at the famous battle of Guadalcanal in the South Pacific. He was in an engineer battalion that worked on Henderson airfield and later at Cape Gloucester, New Britain. His heroes were Marine pilots. That is all I needed to hear. From that point on, I was determined to become a Marine pilot.

My dad, third Marine from the right, awarded a Silver Star and Purple Heart for his heroism on New Britain during WW II.

S25010
DGP-298-age

CombevFlt
Spot Award
Serial 01004 NOV 29 ███
Signed
_____

The President of the United States takes pleasure in presenting the SILVER STAR MEDAL to

CORPORAL JOHN E. CAPITO, USMCR.,

for service as set forth in the following

CITATION:

"For conspicuous gallantry and intrepidity as Operator of a Bulldozer while serving with the First Marine Division during action at Cape Gloucester, New Britain, on January 3, 1944. The first to arrive at a stream crossing which had stopped a platoon of tanks supporting the advance of our troops, Corporal Capito braved heavy Japanese machinegun fire from pillboxes less than fifty yards away as he maneuvered the bulldozer down the bank of the stream. Wounded during this operation, he was assisted to a nearby defilade for first-aid treatment and, promptly returning, rendered further service by aiding the relief bulldozer operators and remaining in action until the advance of our tanks and troops was assured. Corporal Capito's courageous devotion to duty was in keeping with the highest traditions of the United States Naval Service."

For the President,

JAMES FORRESTAL

Secretary of the Navy.

R--Bradford, Kentucky
B--Bethlehem, Kentucky

USMC Records copy of the citation for my father's Silver Star awarded for heroism in New Britain.

After applying for the Marine Aviation Cadet (MarCad) program in late 1964, the Marine at the Officer Selection department told me the program was going to be closed down. In order to become qualified to be accepted and to attend flight school, I would need to join the Platoon Leaders Class (PLC) while I was in college, attend two, six-week long summer camps, graduate, get commissioned, attend Basic School after commissioning and then go to flight school. That was the route I ultimately took to earn my Naval Aviator wings, except that I was able to avoid Basic School.

While I was in flight school, many of my new-found friends wanted to fly helicopters. After initial flight training, there were two pipelines, helicopters or jets. My best friend, Joe Rowland, and I, along with many other good friends had too good a time being Marine officers while we were in flight school. We expected to fly helicopters. To get assigned to jets, a student needed to study a bit more than we were doing at the time.

We finally completed pre-flight academics and then started initial flight training in the Beechcraft T-34B Mentor, a propellor-driven, single-engine, fully aerobatic, military trainer aircraft. Once we completed that training and prior to the date that the aircraft pipeline selection arrived, Joe and I and many of our friends had already changed our mailing addresses to Whiting Field near Milton, FL to fly the North American T-28 Trojan in preparation for helicopter training.

Selection day finally arrived, and the class went to the student control building to find out who was selected for each pipeline. There was a lot of tension in the room as we were going to find out what our aviation life's work was to be during our time in the Marine Corps. The names were called, and our friends were all smiling. Joe and I were not called for either pipeline. We were shocked and a bit nervous. After the selection announcements were completed, a Navy Commander called us to the front and told us to go in a room on the second deck at one p.m. It was about eleven a.m., so we went to the cafeteria to drink Cokes and coffee for two hours with a few of our friends. Everyone was excited talking about their futures, and at the same time we were wondering what was in store for the two of us. Joe and I were not excited at all. We were becoming a bit scared.

We both were sweating as we entered the room at one p.m. No one was there. Now we really started to worry. We asked ourselves a hundred times what we could have done to not get selected for either pipeline. We knew our grades were not great, but they were not that bad. They were equal to or even higher than all our soon-to-be helicopter buds. We had no answer for our predicament. The Commander arrived a few minutes later. We snapped to attention. He was not particularly friendly. He threw a clipboard at the blackboard on the front wall to get our attention. That was a wasted move on his part; he already had our attention. He called us a couple of unprintable names and we were shocked. Then he gave us a lecture about our flight school grades, our partying and lack of effort. We had no idea who this guy was and why he was after the two of us. After chewing us out for what seemed to be a long time, he told us we were the two luckiest people in the room. We looked at each other and waited for the news. Then he said we were the two dumbest students he had ever assigned to the jet pipeline in Meridian, MS.

As it turned out, out our good friend Steve, who was going to fly jets had put our names in for jet selection so we could stay together in flight school. We had no idea he had done that and even had we known; we would not have expected to be selected. The Commander told us he had canvassed our instructors and was told if we worked a little harder and partied a little less, we would make good jet pilots. We were being assigned to the jet pipeline based upon "the needs of the service." He also told us if we did not get through the jet program, he knew enough Marine Colonels to make sure we would end up in Vietnam as untrained grunt 2nd Lieutenants with a three-day life expectancy. He dismissed us and we walked out of the student control building looking pretty ragged. Our helo buddies had all headed off to Whiting Field to check in. There was no one around for us to share the good news with.

We took him up on his offer to work harder, and off we went to Meridian, MS for basic jet training. There we flew the North American T-2 Buckeye jet trainer. It was a turbo jet capable of reaching over 500 mph as well as conducting carrier operations. We learned instrument flying, how to fly formation, and conducted aerobatics training. Once we figured things out up there, we would drive to either New Orleans or Pensacola at least twice a month to party or just take a sanity break.

1stLt Capito (left) and 1stLt Steve Arps (white harness) with T-2B for Carrier Qualifications and aerial gunnery training at VT-4 at NAS Pensacola.

We finished basic jet training in Meridian, then went to Pensacola for carrier qualification. Landing on a carrier for the first time was a real challenge. That required very precise and professional control of the aircraft. Any student that did not successfully complete the carrier qualification course was dropped from flight school. Having qualified for carrier landings, we then departed for Beeville, TX to complete advanced jet training. There we trained in both the Grumman TF-9F Cougar, a two-seat trainer, and the F-9F single-seat model.

After meeting some of the instructors in the "jet" pipeline, it did not take us long to figure out we were not the two dumbest students to ever be assigned to jets.

When we were close to finishing flight school, Steve, Joe, our roommate Hugh, and I decided we wanted to fly the world's most modern and sophisticated jet fighter aircraft, the famous McDonnell Douglas, Mach II, (twice the speed of sound) F-4B Phantom II. At that time, the Marine Aircraft Wing (MAW) to which you were going to be assigned chose the aircraft you would fly. One of the Marine instructors gave me the name of his friend who was the training officer at the 2nd MAW. I was nominated by my "good friends" to give him a call. We wanted to let the good captain know our plane assignment desires. He told me he had our requests and not to call him again. As our completion date became closer, I called him again. He told me not to call anymore and hung up the phone. That was definitely disconcerting.

We finished flight school during August 1969. To be sure we would be assigned to fly the Phantom, we all drove straight to the Marine Corps Air Station (MCAS) at Cherry Point, NC from the flight school in Beeville, TX, proudly wearing our coveted Naval Aviator wings of gold. We went to the 2nd MAW training office to check in with the training officer. The captain I spoke with had just been released from the Marine Corps. I introduced myself to his replacement, also a captain. He started laughing, opened the center desk drawer and gave me a folded piece of paper to read. The note was from the captain that I had spoken with and said something to the effect that perseverance is the way to get anything you want in the Marine Corps. Joe, Steve and I were assigned to Phantoms and Hugh was assigned to C-130s. Needs of the service, once again.

•••

In the late spring of 1970, Joe and I were pilots in VMFA-513, a Marine fighter attack squadron located at the MCAS Cherry Point, NC. We were flying the Phantom F4B's. At that time, the Marine Corps had made the decision to purchase the Hawker Siddeley AV-8A Harrier aircraft off the shelf from the United Kingdom. While in the squadron, a British admiral visited with us and presented a brief concerning the Harrier aircraft capabilities. We enjoyed the lecture, but it was of little importance to most of the pilots. The majority of us had orders in hand as replacement aircrew being assigned to the Western Pacific (WESTPAC). We were going to either Japan or Vietnam. The Harrier sounded like a fun airplane, but it was not relevant to us as we headed off to our next duty stations.

1stLt Capito in my VMFA-513 F-4B

During the summer of 1970, VMFA-513 stood down to relocate to MCAS Beaufort, SC. It stood up one year later as the first Marine Corps AV-8A Harrier attack squadron now designated VMA-513. The Harrier was the world's first Vertical Short Take-Off and Landing (V/STOL) jet aircraft. The squadron mission was to pioneer this unique and controversial aircraft to prove its viability for the concept of ground support for troops in the field. Ten pilots were selected from throughout the Corps to validate the aircraft as well as the concept.

• • •

I worked the phones to get into Vietnam. There were way too many 1st Lt Phantom pilots in the Marines. I asked the same air wing training officer how to get in country (meaning orders to Vietnam). He told me he had a buddy in Hawaii at Fleet Marine Force Pacific (FMFPAC) and that I could call him for help. The captain gave me the Commanding General's phone code for the Automatic Voice Network (Autovon) (worldwide American military telephone system), so that I could get priority for the call. Once again, I spoke with another captain, confirming my belief that captains ran the Marine Corps. He put my name down and told me I would need to have the Commanding Officer (CO) of my squadron confirm my designation as an F-4B pilot and to put that in my record book. I had flown F-4Bs for the most part, but I was designated for some reason as an F-4J pilot. There was not much difference in the F-4B and F-4J models. I convinced the CO to give me a dual designation. Nobody cared, and with that accomplished I was headed to Vietnam. Joe, Steve, and most of my 513 pilot buddies went to Iwakuni to keep the Russians from attacking and patrol the Far East from the Philippines to Misawa, Japan to ensure it was safe from any other intruders.

. . .

I was headed to Vietnam to follow in my dad's footsteps serving in the Marines during a war. My dad was not all that happy about my decision. I also wanted to be in Vietnam to avenge the death of one of the finest people I ever knew. That was my grade school, high school and college friend, Johnny Miller, a Marine who was killed in 1966. Johnny Miller's death weighed heavily on my dad. I was looking forward to killing a bunch of Viet Cong (VC) and North Vietnamese troops while supporting Marine grunts in the field flying two or three flights a day, just as the instructors in the training command said we would be doing. There was even a possibility of getting to shoot down a MIG. Unfortunately, I was woefully unprepared to actually do that. It did not take me long to realize that these were the misplaced dreams and wild expectations of a newly minted Marine 1st Lt Phantom fighter pilot.

I arrived in Vietnam too late to participate in the number of missions they were flying earlier, which was two or three bombing flights per day. Those days were over for the F-4 community. Marine squadrons were not involved in air-to-air engagement opportunities, only air-to-ground. My squadron, VMFA-115, had limited aircraft availability and lots of aircrew, but I was fortunate to have a few good flights. I arrived in July 1970 and the squadron left Vietnam in February 1971. I stayed behind to work at the 1st MAW General Staff Level for Operations and

Plans (G-3) for Major Rich Hearney. All things considered, based upon what I had hoped I would get to do, versus what I actually did accomplish, my Vietnam tour was a very disappointing year for me, having flown only 105 combat missions. Rowland, Steve, and the rest of my buds were in Japan flying two to three times as much as I was flying in Vietnam. The Phantoms in Japan had good aircraft availability. The squadrons worked with Okinawa-based Marine ground units and flew a lot of air-to-air flights. They flew cross-countries on the weekends and visited all the Officers' Clubs (O'Club) in WESTPAC that were populated with Department of Defense (DOD) schoolteachers. They were having a great time.

Lesson learned: Be careful what you ask for!!!!

...

Returning home from Vietnam in 1971, I was stationed at the Marine Aviation Reserve Training Detachment (MARTD) in Dallas, TX. I had just been married and had not yet decided about a career in the Marines. The Harrier was now flying in one Marine squadron, but I still had little knowledge of the plane. In early 1972 Headquarters Marine Corps (HQMC) sent an All Marine Message (ALMAR) to commands requesting volunteers to train to fly the Harrier. My boss, Major Rich Hearney, and I both had transferred from Vietnam to MARTD Dallas. We decided to apply for the Harrier program at the same time. There was a selection process involved, so we assumed there would be serious competition for the small number of slots.

When the ALMAR came out requesting volunteers for the Harrier, there was a major in the reserve squadron who told me he could make a phone call and get both of us selected for the Harrier program. Admittedly, I took that with the proverbial grain of salt. A couple of days later he told me the two of us were in. A few weeks after that, HQMC confirmed that we had been selected. It was a good example for me of the close-knit Marine Corps Aviation community.

When we were selected, the Harrier community had one fully manned squadron, VMA-513, and a second squadron, VMA-542, that was growing to full strength; both were located in Beaufort, SC. By the time I arrived for training, the third squadron, VMA-231, was beginning to stand up in Cherry Point, NC.

Major Hearney left Dallas ahead of me to join the other pilots in his class. Their class trained in England to fly the Harrier. I transferred to MCAS Beaufort, SC, during August 1973, to be assigned to VMA-542.

Our class trained with VMA-513 in the early Block 1 AV-8As seen on the VMA-513 flight line at MCAS Beaufort, SC.

MCAS Beaufort was not a well-kept secret. Beaufort is a beautiful town. The entire area says "OLD" in capital letters. Water practically surrounds Beaufort, and the Intracoastal Waterway passes through on the east side of downtown. Homes built before the Civil War and many old live oak trees lined the streets. Beaufort was occupied by Union troops during the Civil War, so there had not been much damage inflicted there. It has had a significant Marine Corps presence for many years. Parris Island Marine Corps Recruit Depot (MCRD) became active in the Beaufort area in 1915; the air station opened in 1943. Of historical significance, Jean Ribault led an expedition to the New World in 1562 and founded the outpost of Charlesfort on Parris Island.

· · ·

When my wife and I arrived, Beaufort, we discovered, turned out be a wonderful place. The air station was small and well planned. The runways and close-by tactical working areas over the ocean made MCAS Beaufort an optimal place for aircraft to operate. Base housing, located about three miles from the airfield, on the banks of the Broad River, was some of the best in the Marine Corps. We looked forward to calling it home.

I suspect most new Harrier pilots arrived in Beaufort without a clue as to what to expect. Each of us was "selected" to fly the Harrier, so we had a pretty high opinion of ourselves prior to arrival. We had no advance notice concerning our training plan. At the time, all the Marine Chance Vought F-8 Crusaders, F-4 Phantoms and the Grumman A-6 Intruder pilots learned to fly without the benefit of a two-seat trainer. Only the Douglas A-4 Skyhawk had a two-seat trainer, the TA-4F. The Marine Corps had no two-seat trainers or simulators for the AV-8A Harrier. The prospect of flying a single-seat aircraft for the first flight seemed business as usual for most of us.

· · ·

I reported to VMA-542 in early August. I had met my future CO, LtCol Stan Lewis, a few months earlier. At the time, he was assigned to the 4th MAW Headquarters of which Marine Aircraft Group (MAG) 4 was a subordinate command. One of our pilots had ejected from an F-8 Crusader on a wet runway at the Naval Air Station (NAS) Olathe, Kansas. After touchdown, the pilot reported a control problem and shut down the aircraft's engine before he ejected during landing rollout. The plane drifted off the runway into the wet grass and mud and stopped with no damage. The pilot was fine. We were told the plane was intact, missing only an ejection seat and canopy. I was the MARTD Aircraft Maintenance Officer (AMO). The MARTD Commanding Officer (CO), Col Stiver, sent me to Olathe to find out what happened.

The weather enroute was rough and certainly no more than minimum requirements for landing when I arrived. I landed my F-8, taxied to the visiting flight line, and pulled in next to a Lockheed T-33 Shooting Star aircraft. A squared-away LtCol walked up to the F-8 as I was climbing out. Once I was out of my flight gear, he looked at my nametag and asked, "Captain Capito, what was the weather when you landed?" I replied, "two hundred and a half, sir." That would be a ceiling of two hundred feet and one half-mile visibility. Those were the minimum landing parameters for a Navy/Marine aircraft. He shook his head and said, "We just landed in the T-33, at minimums, and the weather seemed to be getting much lower as we landed. Then you show up." I replied, "two hundred and a half, sir." He then asked, "You know, I am soon to be your CO in VMA-542?" I replied, "Yes, sir!" We talked some more about the crashed F-8 and he stayed for the rest of the day to investigate the accident, returning later to NAS Glenview, IL.

We towed the plane out of the grass, and I had my maintenance guys fly in from Dallas in a helicopter. They put a new ejection seat and canopy in the "crashed" F-8. I performed a high-power engine turn up on the plane to make sure the engine was working and to determine if it was flyable. It was. Col Stiver came to Olathe to pick it up. We flew back to NAS Dallas together as a flight of two. During the flight home, I wondered if I might have gotten off to a bit of a bad start with my future CO, Col Lewis, whom I had met earlier.

2: Checking in
MCAS Beaufort, SC

The first day of check-in at Beaufort, I met a fellow student, Capt. Byron Trapnell, and his wife. We became close friends that night, consuming a bottle of his Scotch until around three in the morning, all the while discussing our past, present and future. Our families rented trailers next door to each other while we were looking for space in base housing. Trapper was short, built like a fireplug, and sported a mustache which encroached upon the limits of official Marine Corps grooming standards.

Trapper and I talked about the rumor that competition was fierce to be selected to become a Harrier pilot, i.e., "The Marines selected only the best pilots they could find to fly the Harrier." We figured being selected meant we must be among the best. However, as we were talking, we realized there were more than 40 "best" pilots in the two squadrons that were already flying Harriers. And 10 more pilots were being assigned to our class. During our long night, Trapper and I figured out that we were probably just lucky as hell to be there. For Trapper and me after that initial night of Scotch consumption, as the line in Casablanca goes, "It was the beginning of a beautiful friendship!"

The next morning, we began checking in to the squadron. The office spaces were temporary buildings. The hangar looked like it had been there for some time.

The first person we met was the squadron Administrative or S-1 Officer, Major Jim Sabow. My first impression of him was that of a squared-away, possibly a bit aloof, or even a bit standoffish, all business, Marine major. He was about five nine or ten, sandy hair and looked to be in great shape. A professional officer if I ever met one. He welcomed us aboard but seemed a bit too busy to talk with us.

Then we met Major Tod Eikenbery, the Operations or S-3 Officer. Major Ike, as he was called, was easy to talk with, a friendly person who welcomed us to the squadron. He actually seemed excited to have us there.

He was about average size and didn't look like he was a Physical Fitness Test (PFT) poster boy. He certainly let us know he was in charge of the operations department. On our first impression, he was easy to like.

Next up was the Executive Officer (XO). Major Marx Branum was a slow-talking Alabama boy who was a Naval Test Pilot School graduate. He had been prominent in the early testing of the Harrier and was the knowledge base for the plane in our squadron. He was a couple of inches taller than I. He did not strike me as a jock. He had red hair and his call sign was Carrot. He was also easy to talk with and seemed genuinely happy to have us onboard. When I was in Dallas, I had known two famous test pilots who worked for General Dynamics who had flown the F-16. Major Branum seemed to have that same low key, unflappable demeanor. I liked him the first time we met.

On that day, I had no idea these three men would be very important in my life for the next three-and-a-half to five-and-a-half years. Along with most of the captains in the squadron, we would become best of friends and maintain these friendships for life.

Finally, we met the CO LtCol Stan Lewis. He was a leader of men. It took zero seconds to figure that out. He was probably six feet or so in height. He was a good-looking Marine officer of easy disposition and all professional. If he remembered meeting me, and I am sure he did, he didn't address it. After our introductions, as we left his office, Trapper and I knew we were joining a winning team. So armed, off we went to become VMA-542 Harrier pilots.

(L to R) Capt. Rocky Davis (in cockpit), Capt. Byron Trapnell, Maj Drax
Williams, Capt. Joe Anderson, me, Maj G.O. Jensen, Lt Malcom Taylor
(USN), LtCol Rocky Nelson, Maj Duke Savage, Maj Mike Abajian

We were in a standard class. Four were assigned to VMA-542. The
other six would go to VMA-231 to become the core of that squadron.
In later years two members of our class became general officers, and
two were selected for colonel. One of the pilots coming to 542 was a
Navy exchange pilot to replace the one currently assigned to the
squadron.

We began ground school, taught by squadron pilots who had Harrier
flight time. We also had a British Royal Air Force (RAF) pilot,
Squadron Leader Bruce Latton, who helped with the classes and flights.
We had good lectures, were well briefed, and our confidence in the
"jet," as it was called by many pilots, grew every day.

With no simulator, we spent a lot of time in the cockpit learning
switch locations and functions. The Harrier design was of a 1950s'
vintage, so ergonomics and pilot comfort were not considered to be of
much importance, although there was a parasol (umbrella) to shade you

from the sun when standing alert. It did have a Head-Up Display (HUD) that was new to us. The HUD contained some essentials for flight. You could see your flight attitude, airspeed, altitude, angle of attack and sideslip in the HUD by looking through the front of the canopy, thus maintaining your visual contact with the outside environment and at the same time monitoring your instruments. This was a real boon for flying Close Air Support (CAS) missions. The canopy was called a hood and there were other terms foreign to us, even though they were in English – that would be the Queen's English!

The Harrier at first glance was a conventional jet fighter. Up and away, it flew like an A-4 or any airplane we had flown previously. But its design and takeoff and landing characteristics were quite unique and challenging.

The airframe was optimized for lightness; hence it had unique maintenance challenges beyond our having to translate all the instructions and publications to American English.

The nose and center-mounted main landing gear was described as, "bicycle landing gear." It had a shoulder-mounted swept wing that drooped down at the wingtips to enhance maneuverability and also to allow the wingtip-mounted outrigger landing gear to touch the ground. We jokingly called them "training wheels." The landing gear setup provided unique ground handling advantages – and challenges – that were in our best interest to learn to master.

The Rolls Royce Pegasus engine was a highly responsive fanjet that put out 21,500 pounds of thrust through four rotatable nozzles mounted two to each side of the fuselage. This in turn supported the airplane on four "posts" of downward blowing thrust when hovering. The front nozzles blew "cold" air from the first stages of the fan and the rear nozzles blew "hot exhaust." The pilot controlled the nozzle movement using the nozzle lever in the cockpit. Water injection, when used, could add another 2,000 pounds or so of thrust.

To control the aircraft in other than wing-borne or conventional flight, there were ingenious "reaction controls" at the nose, tail and wingtips that utilized bleed air from the 8th stage of the engine compressor. High-pressure air sent to these reaction controls provided thrust required to move the Harrier either left or right, forward, or aft and to raise or lower the nose or tail for pitch control while in the hover mode of flight. The reaction controls were interconnected with the aerodynamic controls (ailerons, stabilator and rudder). Transition from full aerodynamic flight control to reaction control flight was transparent to the pilot. These controls were very much like those used in spacecraft.

The handling of the aircraft in jet-borne flight was the crux of our training and the uniqueness of the Harrier experience. The cockpit was literally the front end of the engine. Ambient noise in the cockpit was so extreme we were equipped with special-order, form-fit helmets. The huge engine intakes on either side of the cockpit required huge amounts of air that could cause yaw control problems if the nose of the plane was allowed to rotate sideways out of the relative wind.

To help the pilot keep the nose in to the wind, there was a small weathervane mounted on the nose just in front of the windscreen. Any movement of the nose too far out of the wind coupled with an excessive nose-up attitude, Angle of Attack (AOA), could cause the airplane to roll uncontrollably with fatal results. We called that the "death equation." This was an oft-repeated discussion in the training syllabus.

The most obvious difference in the Harrier cockpit from other aircraft we had flown were the three "levers" on the throttle quadrant. The outside lever was the throttle. The next lever, closest to the pilot, was the nozzle lever. The third lever, really a movable stop to govern nozzle lever movement, was the Short Take Off (STO) stop. There was also a hard stop at 82 degrees in the nozzle lever arc for hovering, (called, you guessed it, the "hover stop"), and another at 97 degrees, called the braking stop. The braking stop allowed the nozzles to rotate 17 degrees forward of vertical to help slow the aircraft or back up. The squadron mounted a throttle quadrant on a piece of wood so you could sit at a school desk chair to practice working those three very busy levers.

(Above) The compact and busy AV-8A cockpit.

(Below) The throttle quadrant consisted of the throttle with switches for radio and speed brake, nozzle lever (seen in the forward position (nozzles aft), and the selectable "STO stop" on the rear of the quadrant, used to pre-select a nozzle setting for take-off.

The throttle was familiar to all of us. The nozzle lever and the STO stop were new. Together, these two made the Harrier the Harrier! Short takeoffs, vertical takeoffs, slow landings, and vertical landings all were accomplished utilizing these two additional levers in some fashion.

For example, if you wanted to do a vertical takeoff, you made sure the STO stop was pulled full aft, out of the way of the nozzle lever. For the takeoff, you would complete engine checks at 55% thrust with the brakes on. Then at a 40-degree nozzle position to verify there was reaction control power, you would rapidly pull the nozzle lever aft to the 82-degree hover-stop and add full power. You would quickly be airborne.

For a short takeoff, using a 65-degree nozzle setting, you would place the STO stop at the 65-degree position and ensure it was secured. When you completed your checks, added full power for takeoff, and approached the computed airspeed, usually 65 knots, you pulled the nozzle lever aft until it hit the STO stop at the 65-degree position. Once airborne, after raising the landing gear and flaps, you had to manually clear the STO stop by putting it in the full aft position. That was an important checklist item.

Here is a quick note about the STO speed. If you did not anticipate the end speed and waited until the airspeed indicator hit 65 knots, you would probably be doing 70 knots when the nozzles were lowered. This would result in the nose tucking downward on takeoff, which would definitely catch your attention.

When these levers were properly positioned, the Harrier functioned as advertised. On the other hand, if you were planning a vertical takeoff, and the STO stop was on the wrong setting, it could block the desired movement of the nozzle lever and it cause the plane to scoot forward instead of going straight up. Although you could override the STO stop by pulling up the spring-loaded nozzle lever, it was imperative to put the STO stop in the proper position prior to takeoff or landing and to remember to place/confirm it stowed full aft, once airborne; things happened very quickly during takeoff and landing. Learning these procedures required a good bit of time sitting at the desk and practicing with the unfamiliar pieces of the throttle quadrant. This was as close to a simulator as we could get.

After a few days in the squadron, Friday rolled around. Trapper and I, along with others assigned to our class went to the Officers' Club (O-Club) Friday afternoon for happy hour. I knew a couple people in the squadron. Capt. Ted Herman and I had been in flight school together and, unlike me and my buddy Joe Rowland, he read all the books and studied hard to get assigned to the jet pipeline. We visited when he flew his EA-6A Intruder into Vietnam. He knew quite a bit about the Harrier.

Capt. Dale Heely and I served together in Vietnam in VMFA-115, flying F-4 Phantoms. He was a good pilot when we were in the Republic of Vietnam (RVN) and he was good in 542. I looked forward to being in the squadron with both of them.

Attending classes at the squadron and socializing at the O'Club, you got to know other squadron pilots. One of the captains was Larry Kennedy (Slug), one of the senior flight instructors for our Familiarization Class (FAM). He was good at it. Slug was a person you wanted to have for an instructor; always calm, and he made sure you were mentally and academically prepared for each flight. John Halleran (Filthy), possessed a great sense of humor, was a good pilot and easy to talk to about any subject. Mike Ryan (Rook) was the consummate Marine. He was a good officer, pilot, and friend. We all thought he would become a general, and he did. Greg Kusniewski (K-9) was a high-energy person who had a knack for organization. He was a good flyer and easy to get along with in any circumstance. Vic Taber (Buc) was a top-notch pilot. He had a good sense of humor and the ability to let things play out and enjoy the results. Bob Snyder (Diamond) was usually called Snyds and became a great friend, was a good pilot and could take over almost any situation. Wayne Peterson defined laid back and low key. He was very reliable and a good person to know. PJ Lowery was a good friend and a non-drinker in a drinking world. He was a perfect fit for the squadron and could fly really well and do his job with the best. PJ was a very solid officer. Rob Robitaile was a person I did not get to know very well, but he was smart and a good aviator. Our Navy exchange pilot, Larry Wahl (Squid) had a great personality and, like Snyds, could take over a room. A good pilot with a lot of experience, he would help anyone who asked. Ross Hieb had a lot of Harrier time when I arrived. He seemed to be a well-rounded Marine officer. Dave Beard was another smart guy who was a good pilot and Marine officer with a sharp wit. Denny Snook was also there. We had been in 513 flying Phantoms together. Denny was a solid pilot and a good source of flight information.

As for call signs, you did not give yourself a call sign. Trapper's call sign was Whiskey and mine was Bambi. People were kind to me and called me Caps, unless I was flying. A pilot was usually awarded a call sign by his squadron mates. I received my call sign in Vietnam. One of my drunken pals was sitting behind me watching an outdoor movie in Chu Lai, the MCAS located in South Vietnam. I have ears that tend to stick out a bit. He started giving me a hard time because he claimed he could not watch the movie because of my ears. He wanted to call me Dumbo but could only think of Bambi. It stuck. It takes a brave or crazy person to show up to a Marine fighter squadron with a call sign of Bambi! I did not carry a weapon in Vietnam when I flew. I figured if the VC caught me, with a call sign of Bambi and no weapon, they would think I was crazy or one really badass Marine. In reality, I was neither.

DaNang Air Base, RVN. My F-4B RIO. 1stLt Robinson and I, call signs Thumper and Bambi

...

The Beaufort O-Club offered a chance to meet not only the 542 pilots, but also some of the original 513 pilots. Those 10 pilots paved the way for us and already had a lot of Harrier flight time. They had been on many weapons deployments and shipboard operations during the first two years. For us new guys, it was not the time to talk. It was a time to listen. The time for us to talk would come soon enough. At the club, there was always a lot of drinking, along with the usual bragging, talking flying, good-natured harassment and just having some crazy fun. Friday afternoon happy hour was a squadron ritual week in and week out. During the seventies, alcohol was very prominent in Marine aviation.

3: Settling in

After a couple weeks of ground school, and about three weeks prior to our first Harrier flight, we went to MCAS New River, NC, to fly a Boeing Vertol CH-46 Sea Knight helicopter. They gave us lessons to learn the techniques of accelerating and decelerating transitions and the visual cues for hovering. The first attempt to hover was a trip. I was heavy-handed and it took a bit of stick time to figure out the visual cues required to position the aircraft over a spot on the ground without moving. After about three hours of helo time, we returned to Beaufort. Hovering took a few skills some of us had never tried or at least not mastered, so it was very beneficial to learn to hover the CH-46. We were required to fly it with the Stability Augmentation System (SAS) off because the Harrier did not have that system incorporated yet.

During the week, when we were not studying or getting settled in base housing, we had time to watch the Harriers flying around the landing pad. Those pilots were from both squadrons coming and going. Trapper and I saw an airshow almost every time a pilot came in for a landing. We knew it took a lot of flight time to get that comfortable in the plane. The 513 pilots probably had 300-500 hours each in the Harrier. They were good. There were a few 542 pilots with 300-500 hours as well. It was both fun and educational to watch some of these guys come in to the field to land.

One pilot in 513, Major Del Weber, made the Harrier perform maneuvers that defied logic. From his hover of 50 feet, we watched him do a braking stop descent, which meant the nose was pointed toward the ground in approximately a 17-degree, nose-down angle. But that was not all. He rotated the aircraft around the nose, centered over the pad, scribing a full circle. He came to the landing attitude at the last possible moment and touched down. I thought that was the coolest thing I had ever seen. But his show was not over. He immediately performed a vertical takeoff and began to slowly turn the Harrier 360 degrees, over the exact spot, as he climbed to the hover altitude of 50 feet or so. I was totally amazed. When I told someone in the squadron about it, they said, "Yeah. That's probably Weber." It was.

I was soon to learn we had pilots in 542 able to fly the Harrier like that. Bob Snyder, Jim Cranford, and Buc Taber were very capable in the "airshow mode." Being able to fly the Harrier like that and attempting to duplicate those precise maneuvers was a good goal to shoot for once you had some flight experience. Everyone seemed to encourage those maneuvers when coming back to land. Apparently after you completed FAM no one paid much attention to what you did, as long as you didn't harm yourself or the aircraft.

• • •

Well before we started flying, we soon found out being stationed at Beaufort offered many advantages. The biggest advantage for flying was location. We were about 400 miles south of the 2nd MAW Headquarters at Cherry Point, NC. The commanding general and his staff lived at Cherry Point. Occasionally, the general came to visit and then went back to Cherry Point. There were two air groups in Beaufort, commanded by colonels. The base commander was also a colonel. These guys loved to fly, and Beaufort was the best place to fly on the East Coast. The message for all was that Beaufort was an air station where flying was a priority.

• • •

During the week, until we started flying, it was not all work and no play. After Trapper and I were able to move our families to base housing, our wives were happy and therefore we were happy.

The military housing complex was located on the Broad River. We both bought powerboats and went crabbing and picking oysters during our afternoons off and on the weekends.

One Saturday, before we started flying, we decided to catch some shrimp, so we went to the Post Exchange (PX) and bought a shrimp net. We were full of confidence as we headed to the boat ramp, ready to cast our net upon the waters. Nothing could be simpler than to throw a net and pull 'em in! When we arrived at the ramp a kid about 10 years old or so was there also. He looked at our new net, still wrapped in plastic and, either because of envy or pity, he asked, "Hey Mister, want me to show you how to throw that net?" Of course, two F-4 fighter pilots, soon to be Harrier pilots, did not need any guidance from a fourth grader about casting a shrimp net. We declined his help.

Trapper removed the net from the plastic. He handed it to me. I shook it loose, or thought I did, and cast it into the water. It remained in a fairly loose ball, did not open, and sank. I did get one shrimp. It was probably knocked out by a direct hit. We sat down, drank a couple of beers, and carefully studied the situation while watching the kid as his net blossomed like an umbrella opening, a thing of beauty every time he threw it out. He hauled in a load of shrimp, cast after cast. Trapper finally decided it was his turn to catch some shrimp. He positioned himself like the kid, cast away, confident of success. The net opened to about one-third of its circumference. No shrimp. We finished our beer and decided some things take a talent we did not possess. Shrimping with a net might be one of 'em. I kept that shrimp net for many, many years. The memory of that day with Trapper has remained with me long after the taste of shrimp would be gone.

· · ·

You could tell from spending time in the squadron that it was a serious place. Many people were working hard to get our pilots safely trained. Trapper and I were soon to find out just how serious it was. We were studying in the back room of one of the temporary office buildings, seated behind two bookcases blocking us from view. If you looked into the building from the front door, we were not visible. We were reading our flight manuals when the outer door opened and closed. LtCol's Lewis and Nelson, the CO of VMA-231, and a member of our class, came into the front room. They started speaking. Trapper and I stopped reading. We were all ears and made no sound. They were both good leaders and they were serious about something. The final portion of their conversation went something like this. LtCol Lewis asked LtCol Nelson about a student who was scheduled to show up for the class to be assigned to VMA-231. He was apparently going to arrive very late to start with us. He was also a major selectee, which Trapper and I thought was a big deal. LtCol Nelson said, "That pilot has a cavalier attitude. He can come to the next class. I don't want him here now." LtCol Lewis concurred. They left the building.

Trapper and I, after figuring out what the cavalier attitude comment meant, realized for the first time that failure was a real possibility. We had never considered that to be a possibility until we heard their discussion. We looked at each other and promised ourselves to do our best to tighten up our efforts.

4: Flying Time

September 20, the day for the first Harrier flight, finally arrived. As a class, we were well prepared, confident, and ready to fly. I am sure there was some tension and nervousness for both new pilots and instructors, but we were ready.

First, we had the "acceleration hop." The first sortie, staying on the runway, consisted of three acceleration runs. You taxied on to the runway, set the power to 55% to do engine checks and then went full power. At 100 knots (in about 1000 feet), you pulled the power back and used the nozzle braking stop position, aided by wheel braking, to stop the airplane. This really gave you a feel for two things. One was the rapid, almost explosive, acceleration of the Harrier, and two, the amount of concentration needed to fly the plane all the way to a full stop.

On our first two flights, our class performed a conventional takeoff and landing, just like other aircraft we had been flying. We started hovers on our third flight. The Harrier training syllabus was essentially a work in progress.

I went last. The takeoff was awesome. So much power! The F-4 had two afterburners. The F-8 had a one very loud afterburner. Those planes made noise and had awesome power but did not deliver the acceleration of the Harrier. I think you could compare it to the acceleration of an electric vehicle versus a gas powered one or a Funny Car dragster. When you slammed the throttle forward, you were shoved back in your seat. The engine noise was tremendous, the instrument panel seemed to vibrate, almost to a blur, and the acceleration caught you off guard. Gear up, flaps up, nozzles aft, STO stop cleared and you were soon passing 400 knots. This was just too much fun! And as a note, with a lightly loaded Harrier, it could accelerate from the hover to 600mph in one minute or climb to 43,000 feet in two minutes!

· · ·

Bob Snyder, Diamond, was my flight leader. We went to the working area, which was offshore, to allow me to get familiar with handling the jet; pull some "Gs," level turns, wingovers; fun stuff. We started home and it was getting dark.

There was an Inertial Navigation System (INS) in the Harrier with a moving map display, about the size of a four-inch crystal ball. It was in front of the control stick and low down on the center panel. The light in the map was turned on full bright and was very distracting. I had no clue how to turn it off. I asked Diamond how to turn it off, but he too had no answer. I put my flight gloves over it with marginal success. My first Harrier landing was uneventful. But, for bragging rights, my logbook has one-half hour of nighttime on my very first Harrier flight.

The second flight consisted of two conventional takeoffs and landings with additional air work. The overall goal of that flight was to help us familiarize ourselves with the cockpit layout and handling characteristics of the plane.

The third flight, we did press-ups, which is a vertical takeoff to a 30-50- foot stabilized hover. Then, reducing power slightly you make a vertical landing.

Wives and kids came to witness our first hovers. It was a casual atmosphere. The squadron joke was for families to bring marshmallows and a stick to roast them on in the event of a crash. There was lots of noise, fun and certainly a few anxious moments for the new Harrier pilots and observers. You did not want to screw up in front of your family.

FAM training included 15 flights and lasted for eight days. By the 28th of September, we all had about 10 or so hours in the Harrier. It was a great feeling. You knew you had accomplished something wonderful!

The VMA-231 pilots departed to Cherry Point. Mickey Taylor, the Navy exchange pilot, and one other pilot and I stayed in 542. It turned out Trapper was still with us for a bit longer but was to be transferred next door to VMA-513 as they worked up to deploy to Iwakuni, Japan.

5: Squadron Life

After completion of the initial FAM syllabus, Trapper and the three 542 pilots flew instrument flights, navigation routes, bombs, and rockets, and were immersed into the squadron daily operations. Flight training was fun. We completed a large part of the initial flight syllabus in a month; pretty much all the basics, in two months.

While we continued to fly during this time, we did not yet have collateral duties as we remained in a quasi-student status. We did have to run the semi-annual Marine Corps PFT.

The day of the test, all squadron officers gathered in a small grassy area behind the squadron office buildings. The PFT was fairly simple. It required six pull-ups to pass: 20 for a perfect score. The run was three miles in gym gear, requiring 30 minutes or so for a passing score: 18 for a perfect score. We also did sit ups. It required 35 to pass and 80 in two minutes for a perfect score.

We were told in advance that failure to pass the PFT could be grounds for dismissal from the program. Trapper and I were not exactly jocks, but we could always pass the PFT. We started that day with sit-ups. One officer held the other's feet and counted; then you traded places. Trapper went first. At number 18, he froze in place, stuck almost upright. He could not move, neither further up nor all the way down. I tried to get him to relax, to keep on going. He could not. The look on his face was one of total terror! It was very difficult for me to look at him without laughing, which would have brought unwanted attention to our plight. He was stuck, and no amount of prodding or cajoling was going to get him to relax. I looked around and kept counting. He made it to 35 without moving his body past number 18. When it was my turn, he fell backwards and was able to get up to hold my feet and count for me. We finished the other events and completed the PFT - still in the program.

· · ·

Trapper and I did get to take one weekend cross-country prior to his leaving the squadron. A few days before we took that flight, my wife

31

and I had a Royal Navy Officer, Lieutenant Commander Chris Wheal, over to the house for dinner. He was on a tour as an exchange officer with the Naval Safety Center in Norfolk, VA. He had flown the Harrier a bit and was very familiar with the plane. We discussed some potential "gotchas."

There was an urban legend going around the squadron, from the old guys, saying you could expect a 50-hour scare. I asked Commander Wheal about that and he agreed. He told me one thing was guaranteed to happen, that many of us would forget a flight procedure. He said you could become momentarily brain dead in the airplane, and it happened to many people. He cautioned me to be heads-up about it.

On our cross country, Trapper and I flew to NAS Pensacola for fuel. We left there and landed at NAS Key West for the night. The next morning, we were going to do some local flying. We briefed our flight to go to the offshore working area and come back to do takeoffs and landings until we were low on fuel.

After we returned to the field, I was performing a vertical takeoff to turn downwind and then return to the same spot for a vertical landing. I did the takeoff but forgot about moving the nozzles to accelerate to wing-borne flight. Instead of pushing the nozzle lever forward to rotate the thrust from down to aft while maintaining a constant nose attitude, I dumped the nose of the plane like flying a helicopter. It was an odd feeling. I knew something was amiss as I was going down the runway with the nose pointed downward and beginning to fishtail. It dawned on me I needed to nozzle out (rotate the exhaust nozzles aft). I slowly pulled the nose up to the proper attitude and began to nozzle out and accelerate. Then, safely airborne, I came back around for a couple of vertical takeoffs and landings.

When Trapper and I finished a few more of these circuits, we went to base ops to file a flight plan for takeoff. When we walked to base ops, Trapper could not stop laughing at me because of the unusual airshow I put on. I told him about the warning Commander Wheal had given me, and I did exactly what he said I could or would do. We both learned a Harrier flight lesson at my expense.

Trapper left the squadron shortly after we returned from this flight.

We stayed close friends while in Beaufort and were stationed together again later in Yuma, AZ, and much later at Cherry Point. Trapper could make a person smile about as quickly as anyone I ever knew. We remained the best of friends.

6: Daily Routine

Once my training was completed, I was assigned to be the ordnance officer. The Harrier is an attack aircraft. It could carry bombs and rockets in the US Navy and NATO inventory. The Harrier also carried two Aden 30-millimeter cannons, mounted in two pods underneath the belly of the aircraft. This gun was awesome. It was accurate and deadly. It seemed to be the perfect weapon for our mission of Close Air Support (CAS).

Actual ordnance loads depended on the type of takeoff to be utilized. For a vertical takeoff, fewer weapons could be loaded due to takeoff weight restrictions. For a short takeoff, a much larger weapons payload could be loaded on the Harrier and a maximum load when able to perform a conventional take off.

...

I spent most of my time around the maintenance area when not flying. In a squadron, that is where most of the work is performed. You could find troops putting in long hours to have aircraft ready to make the day's schedule; in the evening, a night crew would arrive to get aircraft ready for the next day.

New Harriers were still arriving from the UK, having been flown over in large transport aircraft in boxes and put together by 542 Marines. The Brits showed class; the boxes were made from mahogany and teak. Those of us with some forethought hoarded some of them and are to this day prized possessions of the former members of the Harrier community. Prior to my arrival, a passenger was found in one of the crates opened by the troops; a kangaroo rat. It took a couple days for the troops to track him down.

The Harrier was a bit difficult to maintain. Just as pilots had to learn to fly the Harrier, maintenance troops had to learn how to work on it. Instructions and maintenance publications from Hawker Siddeley, the Harrier manufacturer, for some items were late in arriving, and modifications to the airplanes were seemingly randomly installed at the factory. Given the challenges, the troops did a great job.

One of the things I noticed in the maintenance department was the large number of civilian technical representatives (tech reps) helping out with maintenance tasks, education, and support. Some were from the US, and more from the UK. In Vietnam we had of a couple of F-4 reps, but nobody ever saw them around. In Dallas, we had none due to the age of the F-8. Harrier reps in Beaufort were invaluable for all of us. The senior rep was Des Grout, a genteel British gentleman from Hawker Siddeley. The others who became our friends and essential squadron members were Dave Clegg, Cliff Olsen, Marty Boone, Duncan Hastie, and Steve Sage. We learned their quirks and they learned ours.

. . .

On the flying side, we four "new guys" were quickly integrated into the squadron flight schedule. One leadership lesson learned from Col Lewis occurred at the expense of a fellow classmate.

The ready room is the center of the squadron and, as such, it is very important in a pilot's life. Usually, this is a large room in a hangar equipped with shipboard-like chairs that is set aside for the control of the flight schedule, flight briefings, and All Officer Meeting (AOMs). In 542's temporary buildings, it was a large room adjacent to the operations office building. The Operations Duty Officer (ODO) was stationed in the ready room. The ODO controls ongoing flight operations and is usually a junior pilot. There were both UHF and VHF/FM radios at the desk so the duty officer could communicate directly with pilots or maintenance when required. The Harrier was unique to me at the time with both UHF and FM radios.

One afternoon the duty officer received a phone call from base operations. A farmer had notified them the radio antennae on his farm had been clipped. He thought it had been damaged by a Harrier flying in the local area. The antenna was probably no higher than 200 feet. About the same time, the maintenance officer came in to tell the ODO a recently returned airplane had some damage underneath the wing. The pilot flying the Harrier was already in the ready room when the news came in.

The pilot told all of us in the ready room, in no uncertain terms, he never flew below 500 feet. He was adamant. Col Lewis stepped out of his office to find out what was going on. He then asked the pilot to come in so they could discuss the situation. As I remember it, the pilot went into the CO's office for a short time, then came out of the CO's office and departed the squadron area. I never saw this Marine again.

* * *

Col Lewis, the Skipper, (an informal title for the CO of a Marine unit), held an immediate AOM to discuss the incident with the rest of us. We were all anxious to hear what had happened. He explained to us that the pilot would not be returning to the squadron. The pilot was not leaving because of his low flying, but because he lied to the Skipper. Col Lewis told us had that pilot told him the truth about his altitude, he could help him justify what happened by explaining to others in the chain of command just how difficult it was to fly the Harrier during high-speed, low-level flight involving high workload scenarios. We all left the ready room realizing what we had just been taught. Tell the truth!

* * *

The next couple months after the initial syllabus training was completed, we were flying tactical sorties designed for pilots so they could become combat qualified. Increasing proficiency in bombing, navigation, air refueling, landings, and air combat maneuvering for each pilot was the goal of Major Ike's operations department. The driving force for the daily flight schedule was to get each pilot combat qualified as soon as possible.

* * *

On the social scene during this period of time, Col Lewis would schedule family outings in the Beaufort area. One favorite involved loading our boats and cars with wives to eat lunch at Hilton Head Island. The skipper's wife, Faye, did a great job keeping wives involved with squadron life. On one memorable squadron excursion, Capt. K-9 chartered the largest boat available at the base for an offshore fishing trip. At the point where this fine fishing vessel entered the Atlantic the seas were very rough, but we pressed on. Very soon, fishing took second place to not getting seasick. Not throwing up on that trip became a point of pride for some of us. More than a few were sick, and the return trip was a hoot.

It is amazing how small events in life, like these, become touchstones for strong friendships. All officers and wives were involved in the life and times of VMA-542 under the leadership of Col Lewis, and Majors Branum, Eikenbery and Sabow.

I felt I knew Major Ike and Major Branum well. I did not yet know Major Sabow very well. One Monday he asked me to accompany him to go on a cross-country flight. We departed Friday morning and had a great time. We got to know each other better through our flying and at the bar Friday night. He was a unique individual and lots of fun to be around. When we returned home, I submitted my cross-country expense report to admin and received $12. That covered one meal and two nights in a Bachelor Officer Quarters (BOQ) room. Major Sabow filled his out and he received over $40. He took me under his wing to show me how to properly fill out an expense report. This was the beginning a long friendship with Stranger, or "Sabs" as I called him.

• • •

One other social event we had was an Officers Mess night. According to some sources, this event dates back to the Middle Ages. In the Marine Corps it is a gathering of the officers of a unit, usually at the Officer's Mess, (an area where officers eat and socialize), in this case we held it the O'Club. It is also called a Dining- in. Formal uniform attire is required. This event is ripe with protocol. Examples of a breach of etiquette might be a request to leave the table for a head call (go to the restroom) or permission to loosen your collar. These are met with disdain from other officers. Although these are "formal" dinners with strict protocols, there is usually a time when things break loose. The president of the Mess Night would invite the guest of honor to speak, and the smoking lamp would be lit. Cigars are the preferred smoking choice. As an example of "breaking loose," a very common incident for a mess night would involve rolls, dipped in red wine, thrown at the guest speaker, who also would be attired in a formal dress uniform.

There are many wonderful stories of things going awry during a Navy or Marine Mess Night. The most famous Mess Night Marines of my era happened during flight school. This particular incident involved a Navy admiral in charge of the Naval Aviation Training Command (NATC) and LtCol Ish Lawrence, a Marine on the staff. Col Lawrence convinced the admiral to participate in a three-man lift.

That event entails a bet that a certain person can lift three men from the floor. It requires a gullible non-believer, in this particular case, the admiral. He would be interlocked together with two others, sitting flat on the floor. While the disbelieving target sits down to get into the proper position, his accomplices begin to interlock their arms and the rest of the observers fill their beer mugs. At the count of three, the "lifting" officer jumps back and everyone pours beer on the remaining victim as the two other men roll away from the beer bath. Everybody laughs, except maybe the person getting beer poured on him. It is all in good fun; however not everyone sees it that way. The best part of the story about Col Lawrence was the admiral relieved him of his duties the next morning. The Marine Corps immediately transferred him to Beaufort where he was given command of an A-4 squadron.

While the 542 Mess Night was absent those types of events, we had lots of fun in keeping with the finest traditions of the Marine Corps.

...

Squadron pilot makeup was a mix of civilian society. Everyone had good stories to tell about their previous careers prior to flying the Harrier. Most pilots were athletic, some played racquetball or handball, some were runners and a few lifted weights. We had fishermen, boaters, car guys and motorcycle guys. Some were very religious; some were not. A few were serious by nature, and some were hell-raisers. Larry Wahl, our outgoing Navy exchange officer, was truly a fun person to be around. Capt. Bob Snyder was the larger-than-life character in the squadron.

Snyds was a good looking fellow and knew his way around our world fairly well. We flew together on a couple of flights and got along great. We were both practical jokers, big drinkers and egged each other on to the next adventure. Both of us could laugh at ourselves and get people around us going. He was the master of that art, and I was still under training.

One night in early October, Snyds had a squadron party at his house. Everyone had a few drinks and started talking about finding the perfect speaker for the Marine Corps Birthday Ball. The Marine Corps birthday is November 10, and the Marine Corps Ball is a celebration of the tradition and history of the Marine Corps. We had a good crowd, and after a few beers and some discussion, the vote was for Ed McMahan to be our guest speaker. He was a retired Marine colonel, fighter pilot, and Johnny Carson's sidekick. We had just enough to drink to believe we could call the studio and actually speak with him.

We called some numbers and managed to get the NBC studio where the Carson show was taped. We spoke with a couple more people, and Ed came on the line. Snyds and I were stunned at our success. Since we were Harrier pilots, we thought anyone would be honored to be our guest speaker. After a quick hello and some small talk, we told Ed about our request. He agreed to do it. We were ecstatic! Then he told us the charge for him to come to Beaufort to be our guest and speak at the Marine Corps Ball would only be $10,000.00. We were stunned for the second time in less than five minutes. Needless to say, a bunch of Marine captains were not capable of funding his trip. We signed off and spent more than a few minutes badmouthing the good colonel, then returned to the party.

7: Yuma Deployment

Four VMA-542 AV-8s outbound from MCAS Yuma, AZ, to the Chocolate Mountain ranges

Our squadron goal was to get all the pilots fully combat-qualified. Major Ike kept moving us forward at a steady pace. The fastest way to decrease the calendar time required to complete the syllabus was to deploy to MCAS Yuma. Yuma was the most flight-friendly base in the Marine Corps. There were many targets, ranges and working areas just a few minutes as the crow flies from the base. We were also able to drop live ordnance there...AND...the flying weather was always perfect! It was the ultimate opportunity to increase the proficiency of both pilots and maintainers.

In terms of Harrier flight time, I was the junior pilot going on the Yuma deployment. I was a last-minute addition and very excited, to say the least. This was really my first-ever squadron deployment. When I was in Dallas, I would visit the Reserve squadrons when they were deployed, but that was not the same. Deployment flight operations are completely different from home base ops. There is an even greater sense of excitement about flying in a cohesive and professional active-duty squadron. Families were not around so we all stayed in the BOQ.

That gave us a chance to get to know each other much better, fly together, drink and party together, and build on our friendships.

Some squadron pilots flew the aircraft to Yuma. There were more pilots than planes going west, so the maintenance troops, parts, and the rest of the pilots flew out in C-130s.

The airplanes parked at the flight line of the visiting hangar when they arrived. The maintenance troops set up shop in the hangar. The visiting hangar at Yuma was bare bones, only utilized for deployed squadrons. After getting the planes squared away, the troops moved into their barracks; then the night crew returned to the hangar to get the planes ready for the first day's flight schedule.

When a squadron arrives at the deployment location, there is not a moment to lose. You are there for a short period of time, and the goal is to maximize usage of range and target availability. Marines from the MCAS Yuma Station Operations Department held briefings in the ready room soon after the squadron arrived. These briefs familiarized squadron pilots with the course rules, target areas and essentially gave squadron pilots the information to live by while flying in Yuma. After finishing the welcome aboard briefings, the pilots moved into the BOQ.

• • •

For many years, the restaurant of choice for most Marine squadrons deploying to Yuma was a Mexican restaurant called Chretin's. Joe Chretin, the owner of the restaurant, was truly a friend to Marine aviation. Many nights, the entire squadron went there to eat dozens of nachos and drink copious amounts of his famous margaritas. While flight training was the ultimate goal of any deployment, squadron camaraderie was very high on the training list.

As the new guy, I did not get to fly many flights. I stayed around the maintenance department, working with my ordnance troops. I worked for Major Palmer, the AMO. Having been a maintenance officer in Dallas I wanted to better understand the overall maintenance effort for the Harrier. The Assistant Aircraft Maintenance Officer (AAMO) was Capt. Jim Cranford, call sign Snacks. Capt. Cranford and I had a similar vision of the maintenance tasks required to meet the daily flight schedule. Snacks and I became good friends on this deployment.

Every squadron maintenance department needs good senior Staff Non-Commissioned officers (SNCOs). Those gents were the basis of management of the maintenance department. The better Marines you had in these positions the better product you were going to put forth. We had some good ones with us, Master Sergeant Mayo, Gunnery Sergeants Selander and Wright. We also had the tech reps with us, and they continued to help aircraft availability and became civilian squadron members.

As a new squadron pilot, you try very hard not to screw up. There's nothing you can do that does not get noticed by somebody or everybody. Harrier squadrons were having two issues during that time frame which grabbed the attention of the generals: something to be avoided at all costs. One issue was pilots pressing the target in a gun run and having a ricochet hit the plane during a low altitude pullout off the target. The second one seemed a bit odd. When the Aden gun was fired, the shell casings left the gun pod going aft, along the lower fuselage. The speed brake was located to the rear underside of the fuselage and was actuated by an easily accessed button on the throttle. If the speed brake happened to be lowered when the gun was fired, the expended shell casings would happily punch holes in it. That required removal of the speed brake and extensive metal rework. These two issues had recently happened more than a couple times and were high visibility incidents in the fledgling program. The CO, XO, Operations Officer (OPSO) and the AMO briefed us on these two items, almost daily, or so it seemed. In Yuma we were firing the guns all the time.

. . .

On one of my flights, I was dash two, (normally to the right of the lead aircraft), on a four-plane flight going to the Chocolate Mountain Aerial Gunnery Range (CMAGR). We had live guns and rockets. I was excited because I had not fired or dropped live ordnance since I left Vietnam, more than two and a half years earlier. LtCol Lewis was the flight leader. Since I was still a 100% new guy, I was overly attentive during the briefings, pre-flights, etc., just to make doubly sure I would not miss anything in the brief or do anything wrong on the flight.

The takeoff and rendezvous were normal, and we had a nice flight to the target area. As we entered the target area, the Airborne Forward

Air Controller (FAC) gave us our target brief. We were assigned a right-hand racetrack pattern. The four planes flew past the target for a short period of time, then the first pilot turned right, the next pilot took his interval then turned right to follow the lead aircraft. The lead pilot completed the racetrack pattern by rolling in toward the target on the attack heading. He then pulled up off target and turned right in the climb to do it all over again. Each of us had flown these patterns many times both stateside and in Vietnam. This was old hat for the four of us.

When the FAC gave us the target brief, he called for a right-hand pattern. LtCol Lewis acknowledged the direction of the pattern, then immediately turned left. As dash two, I am thinking, "What should I do?" Trying to be discreet, I asked the FAC for the direction of the pattern, he again replied, "right-hand pattern." I turned right, unsure of that move, but fully expecting the CO would correct after his first run. He was starting his run from the left entry, so I watched him carefully to gauge the appropriate separation needed before I started my run. He fired his rockets, and I followed him in to fire mine. I looked up, and as he pulled off the target, at altitude, he turned left again. After I fired my rockets, pulled off the target and climbed to altitude, once more I asked the FAC for the direction of the pattern. The CO quickly came on the radio and said something to the effect, "If you can't figure that out, you don't need to be here." We finished the rockets with one plane going left and three planes going right. The other two pilots in the flight kept quiet.

Now it was time to fire guns, and I was pumped! I had never strafed very much before. The F-4 had a gun pod that was unreliable and almost unusable, even in Vietnam. On my first roll-in I was cleared hot, meaning I had permission to fire my weapons. It was great … until the windscreen shattered. It looked like a spider web, and it happened so fast! I can still see it as I write this. At the time, I thought, "What to do? What to do?" The plane seemed fine to me, the engine was running smoothly, the windscreen is very thick, I still had ammo left … so I decided to finish my runs. I had no other problems.

We were heading back to Yuma, performing a running rendezvous to get the flight together. During that type of join-up, the leader heads toward home while the rest of the flight catches up to him. Dash four,

Capt. Mike Ryan, was having trouble catching up. We slowed down so he could join on us. Then someone in the flight came up on the radio, and said, "Check your speed brake!" Mike retracted his speed brake and quickly joined up with us.

Once together in formation, we inspected each other's plane to check for hung ordnance (rockets that had not come off), report any damage and our fuel state. When asked to report my status, I squeaked out my fuel state and said, "I had a frag hit my windscreen." That was a very quick and terror-filled transmission. The rest of the flight home was very quiet and uneventful, but my mind was on the debriefing yet to come. We landed and everyone headed toward my plane. That was not good. The new guy had really screwed up!!!

Then about the same time, someone on the flight line yelled, "Hey, Ryan's got shell casing holes through his speed brake." The two things we were warned not to do, we did on that flight. I did not yet know Mike very well, but since he had the speed brake problem, the heat was gonna be shared. I owed him big time for that.

In the ready room, I was immediately accused, by a couple of the higher-time pilots, of pressing the target - going too low before, or during, firing the guns. I was fairly certain I had not done that, but I had no way of knowing for sure. Anyway, it would be my word against theirs, and I was the new guy. Fortunately for me, someone suggested watching the gun camera film. That thought never entered my addled mind.

The Harrier had a gun camera that recorded the information in the HUD when you engaged the trigger. The couple of minutes it took to get that film developed, coupled with the thought I may have screwed this up, had me on pins and needles. Me, the new guy, the last one chosen to come along, etc., etc., was all playing in my mind. Shortly after the projector began, the spider web instantly appeared. Fortunately for me, the film confirmed my release altitude was fine. When the ricochet hit the screen, I was well above the minimum release altitude. Nobody in the ready room said anything, but they all probably heard my sigh of relief. It turns out, the ordnance shop conclusion was that a bullet had fragmented on exit from the barrel and splattered my windscreen.

LtCol Lewis, ever the teacher and leader, discussed both of these events at an AOM. I felt certain he took some heat from on high, but never said anything else about it to Mike or me.

• • •

We flew a few more days in Yuma then started to plan the return trip to Beaufort. The maintenance and logistics folks were packing up to be ready for the long C-130 flight home. Our Supply and Logistics officer (S-4) was Warrant Officer Jack Whitaker. We had been stationed together at Dallas and were good friends. The Skipper let him drive his motor home to Yuma to be the advance party officer. Jack had a half-day head start on us as we were leaving Yuma. When we took off in the planes, early afternoon, we saw his motorhome parked on the side of the road only a few miles from Yuma. We knew he was catching a well-deserved nap before he finally made it to Phoenix for the night. He was emblematic of the way we all had worked, flown, and played hard on the deployment to Yuma!

Since I did not fly out, I would have killed to get the chance to fly a Harrier back to Beaufort, especially after my recent windscreen incident. Snacks was scheduled to fly one back. To my surprise, Major Ike put me on the flight schedule to fly a bird home.

All the airplanes were flight worthy, but each had some discrepancy that could prevent them from being 100% ready for all flight missions. The CO, XO and Major Ike reviewed each airplane issue and assigned the planes to each pilot based upon his respective experience. LtCol Lewis had us review the gripes on the plane we were assigned to. He told us we did not have to fly that plane if we did not feel comfortable with it. He gave us a choice to make a decision, as a pilot and Marine officer, to either accept the plane or not. He told us there would be no repercussions if we decided not to take the plane assigned to us.

I believed him completely. He was truly a man of his word. To me, that was a wonderful thing to do. It was the second leadership lesson I learned from Col Lewis. Be honest, tell your officers and troops what is at stake. Respect them and know them well enough to believe they will understand what is required, and then do the right thing!

8: More of the Same

Sometime after we arrived in Beaufort and returned the planes to tip-top condition, Snyds and I flew a cross country to Dallas, my former duty station. We hit Friday night happy hour at the Dallas O'Club and had a big time with some of my reserve buddies. We went with some of them to a restaurant in Dallas called Bobby McGee's. After a couple of more drinks, my buddies headed home. Snyds and I decided to get something to eat at the restaurant. When you walked in from street level, you faced a long bar with a mirror behind it. There were some dining tables scattered around to the right, an old-style bathtub on the left filled with ice to keep the salad bar cold, and all of that was overlooking the lower level of the restaurant. There was additional space for a band and a dance floor on the first floor at the entryway in front of the bar. Downstairs, in a basement-like setting, there were tables seating either two or four patrons along the walls, with curtains for privacy. There were numerous other tables scattered around the room with toilet seats for seating. It was something Snyds and I had never seen before.

We ventured downstairs to eat, and Snyds ordered escargot. The waiter was totally flustered, and we took full advantage of that fact. He went upstairs and returned to tell us they did not serve that here. Snyds started laughing loudly, the waiter became nervous, and then we ordered our food. We had to go upstairs for the salad bar. When we got there, there were lots of cherry tomatoes. As attack pilots, we decided to see if we could toss a tomato into the toilets from upstairs. We hit a few and missed a few. Snyds and I started inviting others to try their hand at being attack pilots. Soon we had a quite a few people tossing tomatoes from the salad bar toward the open toilet seats. The energy in the place just exploded. The band arrived while we were doing all this. As they were setting up, Snyds went over, grabbed the mike to announce once the music started, he expected everyone to get up and dance.

We ate quickly and headed back upstairs to the action. I kept looking over my shoulder for either the bouncer or the manager. Neither showed up. We went from table to table, up and down the stairs, getting people to start dancing. The bar was packed; people who came to dinner decided to stay for drinks and dancing. Nobody was leaving. People were coming up to us, and we told them we were Marine Harrier pilots from North Carolina. I do not know if they believed us, but it was an unbelievable evening. We knew we needed to get out of there to find our way back to the base. We went over to pay our bill and the manager finally showed up. He comp'd our bill. He wanted us to return next week. He said it was the best crowd experience and energy he had ever seen in the restaurant since he began working there. We found a ride and got of there before he changed his mind. It was a fun night!

The next morning, we filed a flight plan to return to Beaufort. There was a line of scattered thunderstorms to the east of Dallas. Once airborne, we asked center for a vector around the weather. They denied us a change to our route. We were doing fine until a bolt of lightning hit Snyds' pitot tube (used to determine airspeed) on the very front of his Harrier. I watched it happen and it was something to see. Snyds kept flying and I stayed in position to keep him in sight. I glanced at my gyro and we were inverted. I called Snyds on the FM radio and said, "Snyds we're upside down!" He replied, "I finally have my instruments back. They went out for a few seconds. I got it (aviation jargon for, "I'm in control"). I'll keep rolling until we get upright." The rest of the flight was uneventful. When we landed, his plane did have a nice size burn mark on the pitot tube.

· · ·

Once home, we continued the squadron social life. This allowed all of us the opportunity to get to know each other better. Col Lewis continued to lead the way in squadron events. He really impressed my dad, a WW-II Marine, when my parents came down to visit. We had been out on our boat and were coming back to the ramp to load it up on the trailer. The Skipper had just finished putting his boat on his trailer. He grabbed our boat, helped get it on the trailer and load our car. I introduced the two of them, they had a quick conversation and we headed home. My dad was surprised any LtCol would help us out like that. He said the ones he knew in WW-II were much different.

The leadership in the squadron was evident both at work and play.

Marx Branum and Ike were always accessible and ready to work on any issue. To a person, we were all proud to be pilots in VMA-542. In my short time in the squadron, I never sensed any drama, backstabbing or maneuvering among the company grade officers.

I had made some good friends by this time - Ted Herman, Dale Heely, Larry Wahl, Jim Cranford and, of course, Bob Snyder.

In January, the next FAM class reported aboard. They were Mike Siepert (Mammal) Joe Gallo (Cobra), Win Rorabaugh (Bag), Mark O'Conner (Nods), Al James (Uncle), Bill Callahan (Few) Bill McDougal, Jim Eicher, Rick Briggs, Mike Regan (Rags), and Randy Balara (Banana). The entire class was to remain in 542, except for Randy Balara who was going to 231.

Call signs must be earned, like I said, but they can be changed. One example was Capt. O'Conner. He became known as Nods because he had the habit of falling asleep during lectures scheduled right after lunch. The few people I knew who chose their own call signs usually found them changed by a fellow squadron pilot.

Mike Siepert had a different experience. We were at happy hour soon after Mike joined the squadron. Mike was a first lieutenant when he joined 542. He walked to the bar to introduce himself to Capt. Snyder. They began to talk, and Snyds reached over and pulled the pocket off the front of Mike's shirt. Mike took that good-naturedly, but a bit later Snyds pulled the other pocket off his shirt. Mike reached over, grabbed Snyds by the collar of his T-shirt and started swinging him around in a circle. Snyds eventually landed behind the bar along with some newly broken bottles of booze. When he was climbing up from the floor, he wanted to call Mike "Animal," but we all heard "Mammal." That became Mike's call sign.

Almost all the "old guys," meaning squadron pilots who had flown the Harrier, were involved in some manner during this FAM class. One big difference in their syllabus was to have the pilots perform press-ups on their first flight. Once again, families were invited to observe those first hovers. All went well until one of the pilots, after a nice Vertical Take Off (VTO) and a stable hover, dropped a wing down during the descent for landing and broke an outrigger landing gear. The aircraft was shut down and there were no major issues. After that mishap, family viewing was no longer part of the syllabus. The plane did not catch fire, so they would not have been able to cook the marshmallows, anyway.

While we were working the new guys up (it is amazing how quickly one can transfer the new guy designation to someone else), the squadron was busy flying numerous required sorties in support of the grunts (Marines of the ground forces) from Camp Lejeune. We also flew airshows, static displays and other assorted tasks from higher headquarters. There was never a shortage of tasks from higher headquarters for Harrier squadrons.

9: USS Guam (LPH-9)

In March of 1974, the squadron was tasked to work with the Navy to determine if the Harrier could be a potential platform to drop sonobouys. A sonobouy is an expendable small buoy that contains a tactical sonar system for searching for submarines. The theory being that Harrier response time to reach a possible submarine contact would be significantly faster than either a helicopter or a Lockheed P-3 Orion, an airborne sub chaser aircraft. VMA-513 had previously flown the same mission the year before.

This was another opportunity to showcase and utilize Harrier capabilities. I could not wait to be part of this group. I had not been on a ship since I finished flight school in 1969. When this opportunity came up, I began to lobby Major Ike and the XO to go to the ship. The XO was also the Landing Signal Officer (LSO). I had been training with him on forward site work called Confined Area Landings (CAL). They both told me I would need 100 flight hours before I could go to the ship. After appropriate whining and groveling, I snagged a couple of extra cross-country flights, logging 100½ flight hours in the Harrier. I was going to the ship!

Field Carrier Landing Practice (FCLP) began mid-March 1974. The flights were flown at Beaufort. FCLPs consist of launching from a simulated carrier deck painted on a portion of the runway. After takeoff, you turned the aircraft downwind and flew a normal landing pattern to a hover over a specific position and then performed a Vertical Landing (VL). This involves precision flying as you are guided by a landing lens and voice commands from the LSO. The Navy has LSOs too but landing on an aircraft carrier utilizing a hook and a wire to stop is a lot different from landing a Harrier on a small deck ship, such as the USS Guam. We didn't need a Navy-qualified LSO, just a Marine LSO, qualified as a Landing Site Supervisor (LSS). The XO was well qualified, and he worked some of us up to eventually become Harrier-qualified LSO/LSS for both shipboard and CAL site work.

For FCLPs, the LSO parked in a pickup truck alongside the runway. The LSO would stand outside the truck using an FM radio to talk you through the approach. You worked hard to get it right. The LSO could identify your flight tendencies and help you correct an issue, almost before you realized you were having one. Flying the FCLP pattern was a great way to learn how to handle the Harrier in the landing pattern around the ship. The pattern was flown both day and night. At Beaufort, the night pattern was the darkest landing pattern I had ever experienced. When we completed the FCLP portion of the syllabus, we were ready to go to the USS Guam for carrier qualification.

Like many things in life, a glitch arose concerning our deployment to the USS Guam. Before we could go onboard the ship, we were required to attend the Navy Firefighting School in Jacksonville, FL. This was a hard requirement set by the Navy. As I remember, we had a special class set up just for us over the weekend due to the short time frame to deploy to the USS Guam. The training was very informative. It gave us a healthy respect for hazards of a fire onboard a ship. From the time the siren sounds, you put on your gear and man the fire hoses. Ultimately, putting the fire out required intense teamwork. In the event of a fire onboard, you could be working with sailors you did not recognize. This required everyone on board ship to know the procedures in order to fight the fire. Other than pilot water survival training, this was some of the best and most useful training I received in my career as a pilot.

While in Jacksonville, we rented a car and drove around some. The XO and a bunch of us wound up in some sleazy bar Saturday night and returned late to the hotel. We planned to drop off the car at the rental agency Sunday morning, get a ride to the base and board our plane back to Beaufort Sunday afternoon. Leaving the bar, we headed for the hotel when we discovered a serious problem. There was almost no gas in the car. The filling stations were all closed on Sunday due to the 1974 fuel embargo. We knew the car did not have enough gas to make it to the car rental office. Since all the filling stations were closed, there was no way to get gas. We put our heads together, as they say, and finally decided to call the base where we just completed firefighting training. They were using gas along with an additional additive to start the fires we put out during training. After some serious schmoozing, they agreed to give us enough gas to return the car to the rental agency. I am sure that favor cost us a case or two of beer.

The carrier qualification (CQ) process took three days. The first two days were for daylight qualifications. The flight deck was a busy place. It was organized chaos. There were sailors everywhere, in a variety of shirt colors, moving around the flight deck in a very coordinated manner. The Harrier was unusual for many reasons. Once on the deck, we could back the plane up using our braking stop setting. The first time I was asked to do that, I was backed onto an elevator. Eerie feeling. You felt you were backing the plane off the side of the ship.

The CQ period consisted of takeoffs and landings. We did that ten times to become daylight qualified. Each time we landed, we were directed to a spot by a "yellow shirt", the aircraft handler or taxi director. Flight deck handlers gave specific taxi instructions. They expected you to follow them, no questions asked! Once you taxied to the proper spot, the "blue shirts" hooked up the tie-down chains to secure the aircraft. The "purple shirts", the fuel people, pumped jet fuel to an exact amount required for the next evolution. They wrote the amount of fuel you should have on a board, which they showed you, so you could verify the amount in the plane. Plane captains, in brown shirts, checked your aircraft prior to takeoff. When you were ready for launch, the tie-down chains, were removed, the Navy launch officer gave you a launch signal depending on the pitch of the ship, and off you went in a running takeoff; no catapults.

The next day, March 31, we night qualified. It was a beautiful night, full moon, and so easy you had to wonder why people thought it was so difficult to land on a ship at night. All of us really enjoyed flying from the ship that night.

We were soon off to test the sonobouy theory. The question was simple: Could we get to the potential submarine contact quickly enough to make it worthwhile to utilize Harriers as submarine chasers while launching from a seagoing platform?

Flying off a ship is a wonderful experience, especially when you know you are only going to be there for a week or two. Our Navy counterparts were gracious hosts. We lucked out when the ship's captain told us we did not have to stand fire watches. We flew our sorties, watched movies and sometimes sneaked into the wardroom after hours to get a snack. There was usually a willing hand there to give us something to eat, should we want it.

As we began our first week of operations, a Soviet trawler arrived to follow and observe our flight launches and recoveries. Every once in a while, the trawler would get within 100 yards of the Guam. We launched and recovered Harriers each day with the trawler always in trail, at our six o'clock. One day, the captain of the ship asked the XO if we could hover, for a few seconds, over the trawler while it was steaming right under our flight path. I happened to be airborne, coming in for a landing. The XO told me to hover over the trawler in order to discourage it from trailing so close. I thought that would be great fun. According to the XO and other observers, the exhaust from the Harrier began to blow loose items off the top deck of the trawler. Sailors were holding on to the railings, and it was a good show for the Guam deck crew. I was having fun flying formation on the Guam as it was moving around 20 knots while remaining overhead the Russian trawler. So, I was quite surprised when, all of a sudden, the XO told me to climb immediately. I slammed the throttle full and climbed. It turned out the aircraft exhaust picked up a tarpaulin and was about to ingest it into the intake of my Harrier. That would have caused the plane to crash, not to mention an international incident. Once I climbed higher, the tarpaulin was forcefully blown back down on the deck. The trawler never came close to us again.

• • •

After the first week, we took the airplanes to NAS Norfolk for a few days. It took one day to get the feeling you were back on the ground instead of being at sea. There was not much to do except go to the PX and hit the O'Club for drinks and dinner. All of us were excited to return to the ship on April 17 to finish up the exercise. The ship and Harriers went on a twenty-four schedule.

Dale Heely, on a night flight, was launched with his outriggers still tied down. Here is Dale's story in his own words.

"From my logbooks, it looks like we were at sea during April of 1974. I am sure you remember our mission. On a dark stormy night, with a rough sea, we were in the middle of an exercise waiting for the fleet to pick up a sub contact. I think it was about midnight when it was my turn to relieve Mike Ryan and assume the alert status in the Harrier at the aft end of the flight deck. The aircraft was armed with sonobouys and chained down to the flight deck. It was a dark nasty night, and I only had about 15 minutes left until I would be relieved. I was not anxious to take off. Sure enough, about 10 minutes before I was to be relieved, the yellow light went off on the island. It was a rotating light and it meant to launch the Harrier. I saw the launch officer give me the signal to start the aircraft, and the crewman went under the aircraft to pull the ordnance pins and remove the tie-down chains. I was given the launch signal, and when I added power to the aircraft, it lurched to the right and I was pointed at the island at full power. Instantly, the aircraft lurched to the left and I found myself accelerating down the deck on centerline. I thought it could have been a cocked nose wheel and continued with the takeoff. I actually checked my end speed when I cleared the deck. That was the first time I remember doing that. I was given a heading and followed the normal procedure for getting in position to drop a "fence" of sonobouys in front of the sub so the ships could get an accurate fix on it. I was flying at 300 knots as briefed; even so the ship kept reminding me to stay below 300 knots. The operator said he would tell me why after I finished dropping the sonobouys.

When I was done, the operator told me that "They thought something fell off your aircraft on takeoff." I moved my left knee in the dark cockpit and saw two red lights on my outrigger landing gear [indicator]. I was so busy I still wasn't too concerned. I was given a vector to the ship, lowered my gear and came up alongside the portside. I saw the firefighting crewmen in their silver suits with hoses and a "Tilley" in position. (A Tilley is a crane to move things around on a ship). It was then that I got nervous. I translated over and made an uneventful landing. I had been launched with four chains on the aircraft. Fortunately, the sleeves over the outrigger oleo struts that had the tie-down rings on them broke in half closely enough to leave me pointed down the flight deck. If either one had held fast, I would have spun over the side of the ship. If I had tried to stop my takeoff, I probably would have slid off the bow in front of the ship. My helmet visor cover was cracked on the right side. The Guam's (LPH skipper thanked me for saving the operation. My group commander in Beaufort berated me for taking off without the deck crew showing me the chains.

That was not our procedure at the time. Evidently, the helo people had always done that. I hope it was then added to the Naval Aviation Training and Operations manual (NATOPS)! The chains and broken aircraft parts were blown over the side as far as I know."

• • •

Almost all the Marine captains were billeted in a single room. There were lots of bunk beds. Someone had smuggled some booze on board. It was not me. Previously, I had spent three weeks teaching defensive driving to sailors on the USS Lexington (CV-18) while waiting for flight school to start. When I met the captain of that ship, he told me in no uncertain terms that being a Marine, I might think it OK to bring some booze on board. He set me straight. It was not! As a newly minted 2nd Lieutenant, it was no problem for me to obey his order.

This was a different situation, and we partook of the booze to celebrate Heely's great feat of airmanship. Dale was not drinking. After a couple drinks, someone knocked on the door. One of us asked, "Who's there?" "This is the captain," came the reply. We didn't believe it was the captain, so we did not respond very quickly. The knock came again, a bit louder this time, same reply/response. Finally, Dale opened the door to meet the captain of the USS Guam, face-to-face. He had come to invite Dale to his stateroom to congratulate him on his airmanship. He could tell we had been drinking. They left together. Dale returned later in the night. The next morning, the XO told us to get rid of any alcohol we might have on board. "Yes Sir!", was our reply.

• • •

The first of the two times I scared myself in the Harrier happened a couple of days later. I had not flown at night in two weeks. I launched into a low ceiling and visibility situation with the ship in Emissions Controlled (EMCON). That meant stay off the radio. It was not quite like the difference between night and day; however, the lack of the full moon and clear sky we enjoyed when we had previously night qualified made this night recovery very different. Prior to this flight, I had landed at night on the Guam eight times, so I felt completely qualified. I just flew my sortie and returned to prepare to land on the ship.

Either I copied the ship's heading down wrong, or the TACAN had a 40-degree lock off, which happened on occasion, or the ship had changed heading. I came in for a straight-in approach and found the picture of the ship was much different than what I expected to see. Black was the word of the moment. The dark nights of FCLPs at Beaufort did help me prepare for this. I was about 150 feet above the water in the landing configuration, ready to land. The XO said he had me in sight and to continue. But I knew something was wrong. He could not have had me in sight. I then began to question my altitude. The Harrier did not yet have a radar altimeter installed in the plane. Concern for my altitude consumed a few precious seconds. I was on the heading I thought to be correct. But I finally realized the ship was steaming about 40 degrees starboard of that heading. My position, relative to the ship, was finally making sense. I was closing on the ship, probably 100 yards abeam, on the starboard side – the wrong side. I had to focus and utilize every skill I had been taught to get out of this predicament.

I was doing around 80 knots, slowing down. My first thought was to just turn the plane toward the ship. I knew that would end my flight a bit early and I would go swimming. I focused on flying to the ship and began to slowly translate left toward the aft end of the ship. The HUD was a great help throughout this maneuver. My scan was ship, HUD, ship, HUD, ship, HUD. It took me a long time to get behind the ship, with the landing aid in sight, then make an uneventful landing. The entire process seemed to me like a few seconds short of eternity. It probably took less than two minutes. I was one happy Harrier pilot to walk away from the plane that night.

(Above) (L to R) John Halloran, Wayne Peterson, me, Mike Ryan, Mickey Taylor, Marx Branum (in cockpit), Dale Heely, Larry Wahl, P.J. Lowery.

(Below) An AV-8 comes to a hover alongside LPH-9, USS Guam. The lead aircraft has already landed on the fantail.

We flew about every other day. It was truly an enjoyable experience for all of us. We never found the US submarine we were searching for day and night. Each evening at six o'clock, he would surface at our six o'clock position to rub it in, to let us know we did not find him.

I always wanted to go onboard a submarine. On my day off, I asked one of the Navy commanders on the Guam if I could do that. He made contact with the captain of the sub, and it was agreed the Guam helicopter would drop me down in a sling to the hatch on the sub. This was a dream come true. I watched many WW-II submarine movies and could not wait until I could go aboard one for an overnight. When the helo lifted off the Guam, the seas were a bit rough. We headed to the rendezvous point where the sub was to surface. The sub surfaced and I was let down toward the hatch. The sea was rough, and the wind was strong, and it started blowing me around. I had no control over it, just dangling about five feet above the hatch while carving about a five- to seven-foot diameter circle in the sky. While going in the circle, I was also spinning. This was like a ride in Disneyland. The hatch opened, as the helo let me down further. The sailor on the sub grabbed my feet but could not stabilize me long enough to get me into the hatch. We tried this maneuver a few times. I was pulled away from him each time. The sub captain gave the order to close the hatch. The helo lifted me into the cargo area for the return ride to the ship. I was exhausted. One of our troops was along for the ride and he told me I looked awfully pale. Am sure I did. The sub captain had no time to try it again. I was sad I missed my chance to get a ride in a sub.

We left the ship before the end of April. It was a wonderful learning experience for all of us, and we looked forward to returning to a ship again.

...

Once we returned to Beaufort, rumors began to circulate that the squadron was going to relocate to Cherry Point. That was awful news. LtCol Lewis finally told us it was going to happen. We would participate in Solid Shield 74, an annual peacetime military exercise. There would be a squadron change of command and we would be in Cherry Point upon completion of Solid Shield.

VMA-231 in Cherry Point was still training pilots to bring them up to the maximum that was in line with their authorized manpower numbers. At the same time, VMAT-203, the A-4 training squadron, picked up the task of training Harrier pilots, still without the two-seat Harrier, the TAV-8B. Those aircraft were to arrive later. In April we were doing normal flying and in May 1974 we were preparing to fly in Solid Shield 1974, which included operations from Beaufort, a couple of ships off the east coast, forward basing at Camp Lejeune and Cherry Point. VMA -513 was leaving with 14 aircraft for Iwakuni, Japan and also sending a six-plane boat detachment (DET) to the Mediterranean Sea on the USS Guam. The Harrier had expanded from one squadron in 1971 to four squadrons in mid- 1974. Although we did not realize it at the time, we were getting way ahead of ourselves.

We flew some cross-countries between commitments, from the completed Guam DET to Solid Shield. Mike Siepert and I flew together on a couple of these during this period. He had been an A-4 pilot in a squadron located at Beaufort, flying A-4M aircraft. Some A-4 pilots did not care for the Harrier. The A-4M they were flying was a fantastic plane. It carried more bombs than a Harrier and had better range and a history in the Marine Corps as the premier attack aircraft. There was good-natured, along with some not so good-natured, ribbing between the squadrons.

Mike and I were on a cross-country flight to refuel at NAS Memphis. We had not yet refueled when a couple of A-4 pilots showed up. They started giving us a hard time about the limitations of the Harrier regarding a vertical takeoff and the range after doing one. We decided to file a flight plan to Beaufort and told them we were going to do a vertical takeoff. They laughed at us and said no way you could do that. They watched us file the flight plan and refuel to vertical takeoff weight. We all taxied out together. Mike and I each did a VTO, joined up, heading toward Beaufort. The A-4's went somewhere else. I suspect they were disgusted we could go to Beaufort from Memphis. We changed the flight plan inflight and made it to NAS Meridian, MS, for fuel. We really could not make Beaufort after doing the VTO from Memphis. What they did not know would not hurt them.

• • •

60

By late March/early April, the second class was well past the "new guy" designation. We seamlessly integrated into the flight schedule. Major Ike had us flying in different events and locations. One favorite was Page Field, an abandoned WW-II airfield located at Parris Island. Page Field offered us an austere site to conduct flight ops very close to home. We worked at Landing Zone (LZ) Bluebird, Lyman Road (a highway on Camp Lejeune), and forward sites at Camp Lejeune in North Carolina in preparation for the upcoming Solid Shield exercise.

(Above) AV-8s operating at LZ Bluebird, Camp LeJeune, NC during Exercise Solid Shield.
(Below) Landing on 30 ft-wide Lyman Road at Camp LeJeune, NC

Harrier austere operations required fuel and maintenance troops to be available to launch and recover aircraft. The logistic footprint for forward site ops was relatively small, but it was not without a bit of effort to get it in place. A fuel bladder was placed near the landing pad to allow for refueling when the Harrier touched down. Fuel trucks were available for the short runway located at Page Field and LZ Bluebird. A forward site was made from interlocking metal sheets. It was 96 feet by 96 feet. Forward site operations were some of the more challenging and demanding flights in a Harrier. Finding a landing pad that size in the middle of a pine forest in North Carolina was a challenge. We worked on procedures to become proficient in carrying out this mission.

An AV-8 lands on a 96 ft x 96 ft pad at LZ Dove, Camp LeJeune, NC

The primary drawback to forward site operations was the limited amount of ordnance the plane could carry. We had to do a VL to land on the pad and could only use a VTO to depart. We did our best to prove and improve the concept of forward basing. The squadron decided to qualify all the new pilots, now no longer new, for forward site operations while we were flying from LZ Bluebird.

Capt. Rick Briggs was one of the "new class" scheduled to fly into a forward site with a lead pilot. That pilot had a priority meeting and was called away. Rick was assigned a different flight leader, Dale Heely. They quickly briefed, took off and headed toward the forward site. Forward site operations at Camp Lejeune can be difficult. The pilot is looking for an opening among acres of 50-75 feet tall pine trees. Somewhere among the trees is a 96 ft by 96 ft landing pad. Dale Heely completed his landings while Rick orbited overhead. Now, it was Rick's turn to land at the pad. On his first approach, while looking for the pad, Rick lost control of his Harrier and crashed. He was killed in the immediate vicinity of the pad. It appeared the STO stop was still set for a short takeoff and that had restricted the movement of the nozzles to the hover stop.

Approaching the LZ located among the 90 ft-high trees required concentration and the help of the Landing Site Supervisor to come in to a hover and vertical landing

Again, in Dale Heely's words: "The day after we came ashore with the aircraft to LZ Blue Bird, I was in the tent area and someone told me to get down to the flight line. Major Eikenbery had to go to a meeting, and they needed me to lead a section to do landings at a pad. I had never seen the pad. I don't think I had ever met Rick either. He was new to the squadron. Major Eik had already briefed Rick, so our briefing was short. My aircraft was light on fuel so, I told Rick to circle above and watch the evolution as I made some landings. We made separate takeoffs and the pad wasn't far away at all. I thought Rick was a bright-eyed, nice kid, and I liked him right away. He was a year or two behind me at the academy. I think he had flown A-4s before. We separated and I approached the pad from the south. It was tricky! The trees were about 75-feet tall and initially it was difficult to get centered over the pad. The guys in the jeep were a big help to get me centered over the pad at first. Once below the top of the trees, it was easier, and then the [reference] cones became visible. I made three or four landings, then headed out to sea to clear the area for Rick. I was flying off the beach between the Guam and the shore. After just a few minutes, I saw a black cloud back over in the woods. Initially, I thought it might be fake bombs going off. Then I had a sinking feeling right away and headed for LZ Bluebird. I was told he had over rotated and rolled over and crashed on the pad. He had ejected and his seat went into the trees, and he was found sitting up on the ground against a tree with his neck broken. Much later I heard the STO stop was at 55 degrees, and he could have been trying to hold the aircraft over the pad causing a stall. Worst of all, Rick only had five hours flight time the month before!!"

• • •

That really hit us hard in 542. The Harrier had been relatively accident-free until this time. There had been two mishaps previously involving the Harrier. The first one was at NAS Patuxent River during the Board of Inspection and Survey (BIS) trials about three months prior to the first flights in 513. We were told the test pilot waited too long to pull out of a dive bomb run and impacted the ground. He was killed. The second one happened at Beaufort, when a 513 pilot had a bird strike shortly after takeoff. He ejected safely.

It was certainly a sad day for all of 542. After Rick died, squadron life immediately slowed down. Mike Siepert knew Rick well from his A-4 days. Rick had not been in the squadron long enough for many of us to really get to know him.

This was the first fatality I had been around in four plus years of flying in the fleet. There had been one fatality during flight school and one in the F-4 training program when I was a student.

64

A fatal mishap requires a safety investigation to determine the cause. That took a few pilots off the flight schedule to conduct a thorough accident investigation. A few procedures were changed because of this mishap. It took some time after Rick's death for squadron operations to return to normal.

Unless it is obvious what happens in a crash, your first thought is to blame the pilot. When I first started flying the Harrier, if there would be a mishap, I wanted it to be the pilot's fault. I loved the Harrier and after flying it for a short while, I believed the Harrier would never let me down. It seemed to me that for a few years, the attitude throughout the Harrier community became, when a Harrier crashed, "It was most likely the pilot's fault!" The logic was simple. Who would want to fly a flawed airplane that could kill you? Since most of us truly loved flying the Harrier, we were usually unable to place blame on the aircraft, no matter how many were eventually lost. Finally, there is another excuse that trumps all others, "It's not going to happen to me! It always happens to the other guy." Unfortunately, the Harrier program later began to experience a significant mishap rate, and not all of them were pilot error.

• • •

The majority of the recent class were 542 squadron pilots, just like the rest of us, and we expected be together for a long time. This was the time to meet and make friends. Cross-country flights offered a chance to get more training, flight time and to establish camaraderie. Gathering at the O'Club after a day of flying was a great place to get to know one another and really debrief. In that era, many pilots tended to be drinkers. It just seemed to go with the job. And many of us loved drinking and the camaraderie and, perhaps on occasion, a bit too much.

The squadron was like any organization. You work with quite a few people and all were friendly. Sometimes you find a few like-minded people to become your close friends. In this class I found two. One was Mike Siepert, the other Joe Gallo. Mike was an Idaho native, tall, good looking, good athlete, natural pilot with a great sense of humor, and was a practical joker. He was three years younger than I, and a lot of fun to be around. Both our dads were WW-II Marines, starting Marine life in Guadalcanal. We had a lot in common.

65

Joe Gallo was a one-of-a-kind Marine. He was built like a fireplug. I do not remember him scoring all that high on the PFT, but I never saw him lose at arm wrestling. He was strong as the proverbial bull and, hands down, the best pistol shot in the squadron. He was a decorated Cobra helicopter pilot from his tour in Vietnam. His car, a yellow XKE Jaguar, would be in the parking lot first and oftentimes was the last one to leave. Joe was a go-to guy, and people of all ranks figured that out very early. On his off time, he would have a beer in his hand with a cigarette dangling from his mouth. He was one of a very few pilots who smoked. These two guys were honest, loyal and became two of my closest friends in life.

Capt. Mark O'Conner was a long-time bachelor, known for his ability to eat copious amounts of food. Mark was the definition of laid back. Bill Callahan had a lot of flight time in the A-4, was a very good pilot, and had a great sense of humor. I always thought of him as a jock. He worked out a lot and was physically active. Al James (Uncle Al) was a tall, good-looking Marine, sort of a poster Marine. He was quiet, but an outstanding pilot. Jim Eicher was our 1st lieutenant and a very competent pilot. Bill McDougal was a native South Carolinian and was the smoothest of us all. Bill was a good pilot and a great golfer. Win Rorabaugh had comedic talent that rivaled John Belushi. He was a good pilot and as I remember wasn't particularly into physical fitness. Mike Regan left the Marine Corps shortly after completing Harrier conversion.

...

A usual tour for a squadron pilot would be two to three years, then you were transferred. It was a rare occurrence for a group of pilots to stay together for a much longer period of time. In Vietnam, we had dribbled into a squadron on individual orders as replacement aircrew. It took a long time to get to know your fellow pilots well. I considered that to be a drawback. After my time in Dallas with the reserves, I believed leaving pilots in the same squadron for a longer period of time was in the best interest of squadron safety and performance. Now that I had new friends, I hoped we would be able to stay together for the long haul.

It is difficult to describe the amount of trust you place in a fellow pilot, be he your flight leader or your wingman. Saying one's life depends on the actions of the other may sound trite, but it is the gospel of high performance, military flying. Each pilot in the flight must be able to trust everyone else to fly as briefed or make adjustments as required. The more you fly together, the more comfortable you become with your fellow pilots. This applies to peacetime as well as wartime operations.

In the 10 months since I had joined 542, the squadron conducted two pilot FAM classes, deployed to Yuma, spent a lot of time operating from austere sites at Camp Lejeune and Parris Island, participated in multiple shipboard operations, had a Mess Night and become a very tight unit. One of the things I enjoyed the most was a lack of drama amongst the captains. I think any military pilot is extremely competitive in the air, but with the squadron environment that Col Lewis, Marx Branum and Major Ike created, the competition became, let us make 542 the best it could be, rather than a "Hey, look at me" attitude. I certainly felt when we finished our tour under Col Lewis that each of us had grown both as Marine aviators and officers.

• • •

Our Marine troops we had in Beaufort were a very mixed group. I spoke with Mike Ryan when I gathered input for this story. Mike was the legal officer. During his time in 542, there were 12 Marines who were absent in excess of 30 days, becoming deserters. We held 11 summary courts martial, and the CO held office hours, the CO's disciplinary authority, probably two times each week. The Marine Corps was populated with many great Marines who wanted to serve their country and do their best. They made the difference. But we also had Marines who were not happy being in the Marine Corps and were looking for a way out. Squadron life was not lacking in manpower challenges. We were essentially at the end of the Vietnam War era and moving quickly into the Cold War time frame.

• • •

As we prepared for the upcoming change of command, we were operating from four different locations. Under the CO's leadership, VMA-542 provided quality pilot training, mission capable aircrews, trained maintenance and support personnel, and produced many highly qualified and professional Marines. The CO's inclusion of families in squadron activities helped maintain high squadron morale. Looking ahead to the move to Cherry Point without Col Lewis made all of us wonder how it was going to work out.

When the squadron left Beaufort during May 1974 for Cherry Point, I had been in 542 for 10 months. The longest I had been in any other squadron was eight months, and that was in Vietnam. When we relocated to Cherry Point, I had accumulated 163 flight hours in the Harrier during those 10 months. I was very confident in my ability to fly the Harrier and very happy to have made some good friends. I was living the life the recruiting posters promised I would live after I received my wings and joined a Marine squadron. I loved it!

We were way too busy during this time and having too much fun to think about any self-reflection. While I feel sure I would not have admitted it then, now I believe at the end of my time in Beaufort I was probably an average officer and pilot, in a group of high achievers and performers. Having said that, it was a great place to be "average!"

PART 2 (1974-1976)

MCAS Cherry Point, NC

"If you want something really bad, sometimes that's what you get - something really bad!
Albert Doxey

Straight Up and Out of Control

1: Arrival
MCAS Cherry Point, NC

Cherry Point is a USMC airfield located in Havelock, NC in the eastern part of the state near the coast. The base is a huge complex that is home to 2nd Marine Air Wing Headquarters, Marine Air Groups, and many squadrons including helicopters. Additionally, the Naval Air Rework Facility (NARF) is located there, an industrial aircraft overhaul and repair plant that covers many acres and is a vital component for the support of fleet operations.

The change of command ceremony is a tradition in the US military services. It is truly a rite of passage for a Marine Corps squadron. In addition to facing a change of command the officers and men of VMA-542 were participating in exercise Solid Shield 74 and relocating the squadron from Beaufort to Cherry Point for a permanent change of duty station, all at the same time. We had aircraft operating out of four places concurrently, Beaufort, Cherry Point, LZ Bluebird, and afloat on two LPH ships.

For the 542 change of command, in May of 1974, it has been difficult to find anyone who remembers anything about it. The consensus among all of us is when we left Beaufort, LtCol Lewis was our CO, and when we landed at Cherry Point, LtCol W.G. Price was our CO. Research of records did not find the date or location for the change of command. I have to believe a change of command ceremony was held according to Marine Corps rules and traditions, but the pace of life at the time appears to have rendered it forgettable for many of us.

Unlike a squadron deployment to Yuma, this time we cleaned out the hangar. We took all our planes, aircraft gear, and maintenance equipment, parts, tools, and ground support equipment from Beaufort to Cherry Point. Our tech reps from various companies followed us as well.

We even took our families! Marines in those days did not put the same amount of emphasis on families as Marines do today. In 542, we were fortunate to have Col Lewis and his wife, Faye, involved with both the troops' and the officers' families. The squadron was in many ways one, big, happy Marine Corps family during the time Col Lewis was the CO, but now he was leaving the command. As a squadron we were doing well in all areas while operating in Beaufort.

Under even the most favorable of circumstances, relocating to Cherry Point would have been an immense undertaking requiring detailed planning and effort from many people both inside and outside the squadron. Looking back, we did not have or did not take the time required to ensure the move would be a well-executed event. I guess we could say we were either too busy to adequately prepare for the move or believed it to be somewhat like a squadron deployment. We were as unprepared as a unit could be to pull this move off without any glitches. In hindsight, unfortunately, much of that was on us.

Col Lewis had to leave early for a new assignment; the squadron move was scheduled by higher authority and was in direct conflict with commitments scheduled for the squadron by that same higher authority. This was one of the first times the tempo of ops degraded our ability to complete all our missions. For 542, this was the canary in the coal mine. We came out of this multitasking in a bit of trouble.

...

As we arrived at Cherry Point, all of us had met our new CO before, during or after, the now forgotten change of command ceremony. If you are a career Marine pilot, becoming a squadron CO is the pinnacle of your efforts as an aviator. And, if successful, it is probably the high point of many an officer's flying career, no matter how many promotions may follow. While you are the CO, it is the last opportunity you have to be up-close and personal on a daily basis with a large group of young pilots. You watch them fly, you get to know them, lead them, teach them, and watch them grow to become better Marine officers and pilots. They are your boys, and, in good squadrons, they will become lifetime friends!

There is always an element of the unknown in any squadron when a new CO arrives. If the incoming CO is well known in the community this tension can oftentimes be reduced, as many people would have had an opportunity to have previously served with the new skipper. The Harrier, being a new aircraft, did not have many senior officers familiar with the jet. A successful tour as a squadron commander is a step forward to becoming a full colonel. New COs join the squadron with ideas and plans to be the best they can be during the period of time they serve. Of course, most of the time that involves change from the old and familiar ways to new ways.

• • •

LtCol Price had been selected to become the next CO of VMA-542. As almost any LtCol would be, he was unknown in the Harrier community as he had just recently completed his first flights in the Harrier. (It should be noted that protocol permits a LtCol to be addressed as Colonel except in a formal environment and that will be the case for this narrative.) He had both a jet and helicopter background and should have been well prepared to fly the Harrier. He was not. He was just recently out of his FAM class in VMAT-203. It is fair to say that in those days many officers in positions of aviation leadership in the Marines thought the Harrier was "just another airplane" to fly. If you had the amount of previous flight experience Col Price had, it would be assumed by his peers he could get a few hops in the Harrier and press on like an old hand. That attitude would cost the Harrier program a few mishaps and fatalities in the coming years.

Though we do not remember the change of command, most of us do remember the first AOM shortly after Col Price took command. As confirmed by many, he began by telling us, as officers, that we had lots of room for improvement. He thought we were unprofessional. However, we would under his leadership become the number one squadron in the Marine Corps. He informed us that he was the best officer and pilot in 542, and he could do any of our jobs better than we could. Wow! Welcome aboard, Skipper.

For all of us, a cold breeze in the form of Col Price greeted our move north to Cherry Point from Beaufort. The change in squadron commander after the forgotten change of command was similar to attending an afternoon Fourth of July party with temps in the nineties and waking up the next morning with snow on the ground. It was an unbelievable feeling for us all.

• • •

Havelock was the town adjacent to Cherry Point; it looked like a rough place built one building at a time, as needed. Unlike Beaufort, nothing in the town of Havelock looked classically old, just old. Many of the stores looked as though there were wheels attached in anticipation that one day they might need to move on. A restaurant was placed here, a motel there, then other businesses added as the need increased. There were a couple of local restaurants, a few bars, a grocery store or two, and some fast-food eateries. If you wanted to replicate a military town from the forties, Havelock was an excellent example. The town was located about equidistant between New Bern on the Neuse River and Morehead City, an oceanside town that was near Atlantic Beach that was on the ocean.

The Naval Aviation Rework Facility (NARF) at Cherry Point was the largest civilian employer in the area. The NARF was slowly assuming responsibility for rework of many Harrier parts and modifications, as well as total aircraft rework when the planes reached certain flight time limitations. The NARF was rapidly increasing in importance as the Harrier program matured. It was soon to play a critical role in keeping Harriers in the sky.

• • •

Skipping the squadron issues for the moment, we all had family relocation concerns. Cherry Point was located on the south side of the Neuse River. The setting for the base was beautiful. The O'Club was located on a bluff overlooking the river. Senior officer housing was very nice and located near the O'Club and the golf course. Single family housing for captains were few in number. Some former Bachelor Officers' Quarters (BOQ) buildings located in general proximity to the senior officer housing were converted into apartments for company grade officers. The actual remaining BOQ had an informal bar on the second deck that was the perfect place to gather. It was called the *Dirty Shame*, or the *Shame* for short. There was also a very nice boat dock and marina, a pool and tennis courts not far from this area. This small cluster of housing and recreational amenities was nice.

Additional family housing for company grade officers was located close to the main gate. A few people moving with the squadron decided to make their homes in New Bern or Morehead City/Atlantic Beach. The majority of land around Havelock and Cherry Point was primarily timberland, with a few low-lying open fields, lots of water and a good bit of swamp.

Military housing in Beaufort had been nice; not elegant, but very livable. Cherry Point housing, except for senior officers, was for the most part substandard WWII housing. In some cases, a family with one child had to move into a six- or seven- hundred square foot house. Houses in Beaufort were about twice that size. My wife, Bonnie, and I managed to move into one of the converted BOQ apartment buildings. As one might easily imagine, there were many unhappy wives to deal with when married Marines of all ranks arrived at Cherry Point from Beaufort, sometimes bringing more furniture than their new quarters would accommodate.

Col Price had lived at Cherry Point for a number of years and had a nice home on base in the senior officer's area. Squadron family relocation issues did not impact him, or his family and they did not appear to be important to him.

To add to the housing issues, there was no formal plan from the air station to handle the influx of about 200 Marines from 542 and the housing office was hide-bound in inflexible rules and regulations. The turmoil may well have been our fault and could have been one of the unintended casualties of the ops tempo prior to the squadron movement. Finding fault was not important. Getting squadron personnel a place to live was the issue. The captains quickly turned to our three majors to help us out. We trusted them and knew they could get the skipper to help solve family housing issues for both officers and enlisted Marines. However, the majors were as befuddled as we were during the first few weeks at Cherry Point. Our new CO was no help at all in trying to iron out the housing situation. It became every man for himself. Many of us spent some of our first few weeks standing in line at the Cherry Point housing office for long hours until we were able to get our housing situations worked out. There should have been a much better way to make this happen.

2: Early Squadron Life

The flying was okay at first. But as the weeks passed, we had fewer aircraft ready for the daily flight schedule. Strung out as we had been prior to the move, we were well aware it was going to take some time to get back on our feet. Both Cherry Point Harrier squadrons were tasked to the limit to put the plane out there for military commitments, congressional visits and airshows. There were also increasing demands from the ground Marines we had been working with while in Beaufort. There was one advantage of being located at Cherry Point; we were closer to the 2nd Marine Division Marines located at Camp Lejeune, which entailed just a short flight from our base at the MCAS.

542 had always made our commitments and we were proud of that record. We continued to support all the exercises with our ground Marine counterparts, VIP tours and airshows. The attitude in the squadron when either the Air Wing or Group gave us another task was, "Sure, we can handle it. Bring it on." The squadron had always been a busy place since I arrived a year earlier. Now we found ourselves in an ongoing battle between the increasing operational commitments versus the maintenance department's ability to provide the number of aircraft required to meet the daily flight schedule.

We soon found out how much we regretted leaving Beaufort for Cherry Point. We had not been flying there many days before we were told the maneuvers 542 pilots executed at the landing pad in Beaufort would not be allowed here. Because of this attitude, mostly from senior officers who had never flown the Harrier, our individual V/STOL training lost a bit of flavor. To those unfamiliar with the Harrier, those unique maneuvers may have appeared frivolous or even a tad dangerous. The reality was that these maneuvers performed at our former home airfield allowed for an increase of V/STOL confidence and training. It mattered not to the powers to be at Cherry Point; this part of our flying was over.

...

77

Col Price continued having weekly AOMs to pass the word. These meetings covered a wide variety of topics. The CO, OPSO, AMO and the Administration Officer (AO) covered specific items needing attention in their areas. We would usually have discussions about Harrier maintenance, operations, and safety. During one of the early AOMs, the XO was explaining an issue concerning Harrier flight characteristics. Each of us paid attention to Major Branum because he was an outstanding pilot and was the most knowledgeable person in the squadron about the handling characteristics of the plane. We all benefited from his expertise during the Beaufort years. After a few minutes into the presentation the CO jumped up and told Marx to sit down. Then he told us the XO did not know what he was talking about. We were stunned! The XO was a test pilot and had been with the program for a long time. He was well schooled in all things Harrier and certainly a valuable resource. Plus, he had our respect because he had been there and done that. Col Price had not been there and had not done that. He did not yet have our respect as a Harrier pilot.

After that AOM, Col Price, still in the infancy of his tour, began to cause some of us to ask, "What have we gotten ourselves into?" People started asking questions about where this guy came from and where were we headed as a squadron. It did not take long for squadron morale to head south. The CO treated many of us like we were incompetent. He was visibly disappointed in anything the squadron accomplished. It began to seem like whatever we did was not good enough. It was impossible to make him proud of our efforts and therefore proud of his squadron.

Col Price also had an interesting way of pointing out any errors or failures he might think you committed. He would look you in the eye and wave his right index finger in your face and say these words, "Just one little fuck up, captain, just one little fuck up!" We got the message. While the skipper, he used this particular message many times. It became his trademark as far as many of the captains were concerned.

The bottom line was simple. This was the same squadron that was doing very well six weeks ago. With few exceptions, all the officers were the same people in the same jobs. The SNCO leadership in the maintenance department was intact. We may have lost some of our squadron spirit and momentum in the move, but that was to be expected. Leaving Beaufort was tough, and we had a rough introduction to Cherry Point, but we seemed to be going downhill fast and none of us liked it.

.

3: Aircraft Maintenance Issues

The CO's first concern each day was the number of aircraft that were available for the flight schedule. Our airplanes were in rough shape. We had flown them hard while completing the commitments prior to the change of command and the relocation to Cherry Point. We trucked one to Cherry Point and even left one plane in Beaufort with Joe Gallo, along with a small maintenance crew. They had to get it put together to safely fly it to Cherry Point. After a couple of months, 542 definitely entered tough times for maintaining aircraft to safely fly the ever-more-aggressive flight schedule.

The Harrier program started with VMA-513 in May 1971. They had excellent training and instructors, but most importantly they had flight time. 513 picked 10 pilots from other aircraft communities and added them to the squadron. Some of the pilots already there and conducting instruction in 513 had flown the Harrier early on as test pilots. In 1972, VMA-542 stood up and took some of the 513 pilots to be a core group of pilots and instructors. The last 542 pilot training class was completed in the spring of 1974 and was very similar to the training 513 pilots received. Six of the core officers and pilots for VMA-231 trained with me in the August 1973 FAM class. They began to train their own squadron pilots, in house, at Cherry Point and were finished in late 1974. While all this was going on, VMAT-203, the A-4 training squadron, began to train Harrier pilots, absent a two-seat Harrier trainer. The experience and instructor base were slowly watered down a bit. The rapid expansion of Harrier squadrons was difficult to manage. In five very quick years there would be Harrier squadrons operating at Cherry Point, Iwakuni, Japan, and deployed aboard two aircraft carriers, the USS Roosevelt, and the USS Guam, in the Mediterranean Sea.

...

When 542 was still in Beaufort and before 513 left for Iwakuni, Japan, both squadrons began to suffer somewhat from a parts shortage, resulting in fewer aircraft available for flight. This was an obvious issue for all of us, but we did not take it as seriously as we should have. There

81

were rumors about major aircraft components being removed and sent to Iwakuni to have in place as spares prior to 513's arrival. The 513 officers and men did not make these logistic decisions, but they were the beneficiaries of them, while 542 and 231 suffered.

I reached out to Duke Savage, call sign Ruby, a retired Marine Colonel and a well-respected Harrier pilot and leader in the community to provide his take on the parts issues at that time. He was a member of my Harrier FAM class and a pilot well versed in all things Harrier. He offered these thoughts regarding Harrier maintenance issues for the entire program, not just a specific squadron. His assignments placed him in a great position to observe maintenance and supply issues at all levels. For the earlier Harrier program, Col Savage had the best view of the situation of any Harrier pilot. Here are his thoughts:

...

"My transition class at VMA-542 consisted of several experienced fixed-wing pilots, assigned to stand up VMA-231, the third Harrier squadron, being located at MCAS Cherry Point, NC. The following is a general recollection of my journey with the amazing USMC AV-8A Harrier from 1973 until the summer of 1977. I have chosen the 73-77 "bookends" because I believe these were the critical formative years for USMC tactical V/STOL operations. I will attempt to focus more on the logistic aspects of the Harrier program during this time period. Several colleagues have written about specific details of Harrier operations, but few have addressed the challenges of aircraft readiness.

Frankly, the early Harrier program was introduced with a paucity of replacement parts, the inability to repair systems and problems with offshore vendor dependence. Frequent concept analysis of mission ops was required for the demanded flying the Harrier was tasked to do at its top end limits to validate the V/STOL capabilities. This created an accelerated demand for replacement or repair of components, especially for the hard-working Rolls Royce F-402 Pegasus engine. The result of these factors proved the initial supply system set up between the Hawker Siddeley manufacturer and the Washington, D.C. based Naval Air System Command (NAVAIR) was no match for the "full speed ahead" operational tempo of three tactical squadrons, all of which were manned with pilots demonstrating the Marine "hell bent, can do" spirit.

The plan called for VMA-231 to receive several older Block-1, Harriers (the original jets) from VMA-513. The transfer of older Harriers from 513 to 231 was a protracted process during the fall of 1973. Routinely, 513 would notify 231 of an inbound Harrier from Beaufort arriving at Cherry Point for transfer from 513 to 231. The "slow drip" of aircraft being received, coupled with maintaining the well-used Block-1s, resulted in low availability and limited flight operations. From the 231 perspective, we were prioritized as third in line for logistics support due to higher command's ambitious operational demands on 513 and 542. During the fall of 1973, VMA-231 at Cherry Point had a very hard time maintaining mission capable aircraft. Cannibalism of parts from aircraft that were "hard down" became routine to keep other aircraft flying. This quickly created a situation of diminishing aircraft readiness. Also, I must note with candor, 231's maintenance department consisted of a "few good men" and "a few not so good men". Thanks for the few good Marines and a couple of British technical representatives that kept plugging away to achieve flyable machines.

Amazingly, during late 73 and early 74, VMA-231 conducted 96' x 96' confined area ops, road ops at Camp Lejeune, expeditionary airfield ops at LZ Bluebird, Marine Corps Auxiliary Landing Field (MCALF) ops at Bogue Field, and at numerous WWII inactive airfields. Included also were LPH shipboard quals, routine simulated CAS flights in support of The Basic School, Quantico, VA and numerous air show demonstrations. The good news of '74: By mid-spring, daily ops improved as brand spanking new Block-4 Harriers were delivered directly from Hawker-Siddeley, England. By mid-summer 1974, daily flight operations improved dramatically with the addition of the new Harriers. Concurrent with the receipt of the new Block-4 aircraft, readiness problems for 231's older Block-1 Harriers continued. Several non-flyable machines occupied the hangar and flight line. Additionally, higher authority directed intense cannibalism of major sub-assemblies in support of VMA-513's upcoming deployment. As a result, a request was made and approved to transfer seven non-flyable Block-1 aircraft to Fleet Storage Custody, pending further approval for transfer to NARF at Cherry Point. Sadly, at the time, it was doubtful these particular Harriers would ever fly again.

During my time in 231, the normal training syllabus routine continued plus a couple of pilot transition classes. We experienced challenging times with several accidents and two pilot fatalities. As stated earlier, my intention in writing this is a focus on the AV-8A early years' logistical process.

I received orders for transfer to NARF from VMA-231 after three years as the maintenance officer. NARF was later rebadged as a Naval Aviation Depot (NADEP). I filled a new billet titled AV-8 Harrier project officer. This billet was created because of an immediate need for a Harrier pilot to join NADEP to provide operational experience to the depot level maintainers. Shortly after NADEP orientation briefings and introductions to numerous department heads, supervisors, engineers, manufacturer representatives, artisans, component repair shops, engine overhaul shops, paint shops, scheduled depot level maintenance bays and finally flight test, I felt a sincere welcome to this magnificent facility and for the majority of the dedicated workforce.

Oddly, the missing link to all this excellent capability was the presence of an airframe repair jig, one that had been purchased from England by NAVAIR, in approximately 1972. I knew the jig would be a critical capability to repair several aircraft already awaiting crash damage recovery. Immediate support for installing the repair jig came from Major Frank Pieri at NAVAIR. Honestly, Frank's professional tenacity for meeting objectives was second to none. Harrier readiness owes an infinite thank-you to Frank. (Frank was a Marine fighter pilot and a damn fine LSO.)

Vividly recalling the days after arriving for my assignment, I walked out alone to the back side of NADEP, where the flight line apron contained an array of aircraft (F-4, H-46, C-130, OV-10, and AV-8As). Far over in a remote corner sat several Block 1 Harrier airframes, all drooped nose down, engineless, void of numerous components, most wrapped with tape here and there. Damn, what a sad and overwhelming sight. I remember this strange mind game as if these hulks wanted to say: "Ruby, what took you so long to get here?" In addition to these pitiful Block-1's, there were 21 Harriers at NADEP, several of which were awaiting damage repair and others undergoing scheduled depot level maintenance. I joked that I had the largest Harrier squadron in the Corps.

By late 1976, the repair jig was installed and ready to rock 'n roll. The repair jig was operated by two amazing and skilled artisans, both of whom were USMC metal smiths during WWII. They were the critical link to the successful repair of crash damaged Harriers. The jig was occupied with Harriers throughout my two years at NADEP. In July 1978, I departed NADEP for orders to U.S. Army Command and General Staff School, Ft. Leavenworth, Kansas. I bid farewell to an amazing group of "NADEPers" and associated professionals at NAVAIR, MCAIR, British Aerospace, Rolls Royce and so many more. Today, after more than 45 years, I continue to be blessed with amazing friendships among many in the aforementioned groups. In summary, during those two years at NADEP, my logbook depicts 185 test flights among 49 different AV-8 bureau numbers. All, except four AV-8s (delivered to McDonnell Douglas, St. Louis), were returned to the existing Harrier squadrons at Cherry Point and Yuma. Every Block 1 Harrier on that back fence in July 1976 was returned to operational flight except for BuNo 158370. Major Bill Spicer, who replaced me at NADEP owned the privilege of returning -370 to VMA-231. To this day, "Sugar" reminds me that he 'finished the job'."

···

Now that we have heard from Duke Savage, I will continue with the story. A Marine Corps squadron deployed out of the Continental United States (CONUS) had a higher priority for parts. Therefore, Cherry Point squadrons had a lower priority. We jokingly referred to 513 as the tip of the spear in 1974. As amazing as it might sound, a Harrier in Japan and a Harrier in North Carolina often had the same parts fail over a given period of time. If all three Harrier squadrons requisitioned the same part, the part first went to 513, either in Japan or to 513 DET-B aboard the USS Guam before coming to a Cherry Point squadron. Many supplies for 513, including high usage parts and consumables, had been sent in advance of their deployment to Japan. As it turned out, they had been supplied in much greater quantities than any of us realized at the time.

...

As we were leaving Beaufort, Major Palmer, the 542-maintenance officer, left the squadron. Capt. Jim Cranford (Snacks) became the AMO and I became the maintenance control officer. Snacks was a workaholic and he confirmed that fact by working day and night to get planes in the sky. Most of the time it was a losing battle.

I firmly believe a CO's job is to work with the AMO to understand issues impacting aircraft availability, then go after any support he could find to help get his squadron's aircraft up for flight. It seemed to us Col Price would not look outside the squadron for help. In hindsight, there might not have been much help out there, but certainly the squadron would have had a better idea of what was happening regarding Harrier parts had he analyzed the situation better. We believed he would not ask for help from the air group or wing primarily because it would make him look bad. His favorite fix was to yell at Cranford and others, time and time again. Finally, the CO put the maintenance department on a seven-days-a-week work schedule in an attempt to improve aircraft availability. Fortunately, our senior SNCOs were usually able to schedule our Marines some days off, but I can say most of us were in there every day of the week at least for a few hours.

Due to the increasing lack of parts, cannibalization of other aircraft became our internal supply system. We would routinely have aircraft down in excess of 50 days. If an aircraft was not flyable for 60 days, then it had to be reported to higher headquarters as a Special Interest Aircraft (SPINTAC). Col Price wanted none of that. A SPINTAC aircraft looked bad for the squadron. So, after using a hangar queen (what a long-term down aircraft was called) for parts, we worked many hours to try to get the aircraft flying prior to it becoming a SPINTAC. It was a crazy way to operate.

Because of demands to produce flight time with fewer parts, cannibalizing ultimately became rampant in 542. That was essentially because the Harrier supply system for any unique electronic, engine or airframe part was not available in the normal supply system and thus could not be delivered in a timely manner. The man-hours required to remove a part from a hangar queen to install it on a flyable aircraft were tough enough. Then we had to reinstall the new part when it was delivered to replace the original part we had removed from the hangar queen. In many instances, this same part was also on order for another aircraft with a better chance to get in the air, so the part was not always installed on the hangar queen. This more than doubled the maintenance workload. There was also a fairly high chance of damaging a part during the process. Everyone knew this was a very difficult method to operate a squadron maintenance department, but without an adequate and timely parts supply we were forced to live with it. Despite the long hours and hard work, we had many Harriers become Special Interest Aircraft.

Straight Up and Out of Control

4: Getting Settled and Flying

The SNCOs in Beaufort we knew and trusted to keep things going became disgruntled due to the difficult working conditions and long hours. Snacks, Joe Gallo, Pat Owen and the rest of us in maintenance could offer them no good answers. We did not know when we arrived at Cherry Point that the maintenance department would work most every day during Col Price's tour, except Christmas Day.

The squadron was in an older hangar at Cherry Point and was the same hangar I had been in years ago during my F-4 training flights. We were next door to VMA-231, the third Harrier squadron. Our flight lines were adjacent to each other. We had very little interface with other squadrons. I thought squadrons were like county governments. The air group was like the state government. Air groups could have four or more squadrons. However, it was easy to spend so much time in your own squadron you might not know who was in the squadron next door. All of us were too busy working on our own squadron's issues to spend much time with our neighboring pilots. Of course, there were some exceptions to that, old friends being one. It seemed to me at the time we did not know the 231 pilots very well. Even at the *Shame* Friday night happy hour, we mostly tended to stick together as squadrons.

• • •

The ready room is the center of life in a squadron and we finally had a real ready room at Cherry Point, complete with old, yet serviceable chairs that looked like they came from an aircraft carrier. Squadron flight ops were controlled from there. You could tell a good squadron from the atmosphere in the ready room. Pilots and ground officers would be coming in and out all day long. It was a good place to hear a funny story, someone talking about their last flight, witness a good bit of humor or some good-natured harassment. The coffee pot was always brewing almost drinkable coffee, and there was always an Acey Deucey board (backgammon) waiting for players. A welcoming ready room is where you can take the measure of the morale of a squadron.

Unfortunately, the 542 ready room environment became morgue-like. It was no longer a welcoming place to visit, drink coffee and shoot the breeze. The CO would patrol the ready room like a fighter pilot searching for bandits. He was looking for any officer who might not be "doing his work." Therefore, you came into the ready room, briefed your mission, received your aircraft assignment and usually left as soon as possible.

One day the CO put up two signs with about eight-inch-high letters in the ready room. One stated "**Every Sortie Professionally Executed**!" The other one read, "**Excellence is Our Standard**!" It did not take long to realize these signs were put there for the benefit of the many visitors coming to see a Harrier squadron in action. Col Price never met a senior officer he would not invite to the squadron spaces to have a captain show off the aircraft or let the visitor observe how wonderful life was in 542. The skipper was a very good politician.

• • •

Harriers were always a big hit at an airshow. During the early years we all had an opportunity to fly them. After those first weeks of getting adjusted, I had a chance to fly my first airshow. It was assumed when you finished checking out in the Harrier and had a few more hours in the plane, you could fly an airshow. This mindset cost the Harrier program an aircraft or two. That changed for the better much later when airshow pilots were designated by the OPSO, checked out and signed off by the CO.

I suspect most of us remember the first airshow we flew. My first one was exceptional. Al James and I were sent to fly the Chicago Air and Water Show in August 1974. The Harrier had been there the previous year and they loved it.

Al was my wingman and announcer. He was a good-looking guy, a good pilot and a serious but fun person to spend time with. His plane went down for a mechanical problem, so I took off by myself mid-morning. Al was to join me later. I departed Cherry Point headed to Meigs Field, an airport along the southwest side of Lake Michigan, very close to downtown Chicago. It looked somewhat like a stationary aircraft carrier due to the proximity of the water. I performed a vertical landing as requested by the tower. There was a small crowd gathered on the visiting aircraft line where I was being directed to park.

I taxied into my parking spot and shut down the Harrier. As I opened the canopy, a work platform appeared on the right side of the airplane. Up the stairs came the most beautiful woman I had ever seen. She smiled, told me we were going live on a program watched by two million people called Chicago Today, or something similar. I was just starting to unstrap myself from the plane when she asked me my name and where I was from. I could not talk. I tried to answer her, but no words came out. What a time to have vocal cord failure. I tried twice more to no avail. Then I just laughed and she laughed. Finally, she asked, "Can we try this again?" On the fourth try, I finally gave her my name and hometown of Bowling Green, KY.

The cameraman was also on the work stand so she wanted him to get a shot of me getting out of the plane. My habit pattern had been broken when I started looking at her and she started speaking to me. I removed all the seat and parachute fittings and was ready to stand up. However, as I put my hands on the canopy bow, and pulled myself up I was unceremoniously jerked back down in the seat. I had neglected to unhook the oxygen hose from the side panel.

Eventually, I extricated myself from the plane, climbed down and gave her, along with the two million people she claimed were watching on TV, the standard brief about the Harrier. It was fun. After the broadcast was over, the two of us were talking about the plane when an older gentleman came to get me. I waved goodbye to the TV anchor and headed off with the gentleman. He seemed to be in a big hurry as he explained my duties for the day. In the afternoon, I was to be one of the judges for the Air and Water show beauty pageant. Later that evening, I was to be the guest of Mayor Daley, the first one, at a large dinner to celebrate the airshow.

The older gentleman, probably in his late 40s, was actually a Navy Reserve captain assigned to be our escort for the weekend. He asked me if I brought a suit or coat and tie. Of course, I did not. He gave me $200 and took me to Marshall Fields to get outfitted. Then we went to the Holiday Inn Hotel on Lake Shore Drive to get checked in. After that we headed to the beauty pageant. On the way there, he told me to hug the contestants and speak with them, ask questions, etc., BUT, he told me in no uncertain terms, to not hug or kiss the five or six women at the end of the line. I did not understand the reason, but it did not matter. When we arrived, there were about 10 to 12 girls vying for the title of Miss Chicago Air and Water. These were high school age girls. I did as instructed, hugged the girls and asked them a few questions. I got through them quickly. At the end of the line were women who looked like models. I just said hi to the women. All the time wondering what was going on!!!!

While we were standing there after walking the line, the announcer said the Golden Knights parachuters were just leaving their plane overhead, and we began to watch them head toward the ground. They were landing in an area adjacent to where we were standing. It was a great show, always exciting to watch. This same team had been to Chicago for the last three years. The team had made many good friends, and this was to be the last time this particular team performed in Chicago. It was a love fest when they hit the ground. There were hugs and handshakes all around. After a bit they were directed to meet the beauty pageant contestants and troop the line. They were my fellow judges. When they reached the women on the end of the line there were hugs and kisses galore. My Navy captain escort pulled me aside to whisper these women were transvestites. The airshow hosts were playing a joke on the Golden Knights on their last performance in Chicago. I thought, man, now that was rough! He saved me.

Al joined us at the hotel, and we made it to the dinner. I had written a few notes on the back of an envelope at the Holiday Inn. At dinner, I was seated two seats to the left of his honor. My talk about the plane, the Marine Corps and Chicago hospitality seemed well received. I really doubt anyone paid any attention to what I had to say. The Golden Knights were in the audience and I had trouble not laughing when I looked their way.

After dinner, Al and I went to a comedy club and stayed for a bit. We left the show late to return to the hotel. The Harrier was scheduled to fly at 3:00, so we left the hotel after lunch. The crowd was so large we could not get the car out of the parking garage. It was almost time to panic. With the assistance of Chicago's finest, we made it to Meigs Field on time.

The weather consisted of a low broken-cloud deck around 3500 feet and the Thunderbirds cancelled their show. Because of the weather forecast, the crowd numbered only about 250,000 out of an expected one million people. But as all Harrier pilots know, the show must go on and can go on because we do low altitude, high speed passes, hovers, left and right translations and steep climbs. While in the hover, we also perform a bow to the crowd. After completing my airshow maneuvers when I did my bow, since I was over the water, a rainbow-like spray came up around the entire aircraft. The Navy captain later told me, "It was a thing of beauty." I finished the show, headed back to Meigs Field, flying over the Playboy yacht, and landed. I was wiped out. The Sunday show was cancelled due to weather. Al and I headed home with my first airshow under my belt. It was an experience I will never forget.

5: Hard Times

Marine Attack squadrons are designed to provide CAS to Marines on the ground. To do the job correctly, squadrons train pilots and maintainers to become skilled in all matters of flying and maintaining the aircraft. Harrier squadrons were unique. We operated from short, isolated runways, forward site pads, roads and small deck ships. Harrier V/STOL allowed attack aircraft remote basing flexibility to speed up support for the Marines on the ground. The three Harrier squadrons, 513, 542 and 231 worked very hard to validate this concept during the early years.

Like all Marine organizations, the Harrier community had learned how to do more with less. There is an old saying in the Corps, "We have done so much with so little for so long, that we can do anything with nothing." We learned to cover our missions the best way possible. While we were learning a lot about the Harrier maintenance issues, our British and US tech reps helped teach us and helped us find parts or introduce random fixes to keep our planes in the air. The idea of including our tech reps in our social gatherings began in Beaufort and continued in Cherry Point. The camaraderie between pilots and reps continued to help us out in many ways. The troops enjoyed the same relationship with the reps, and that helped maintenance Marines smooth out many an issue with officers in maintenance throughout the years. Des Grout remained the senior rep from the UK. He was always a gentleman's gentleman, the perfect liaison and tech rep. These guys spent many long hours on the phone to England getting answers for our many questions.

...

Since the majority of the pilots had been in 542 approaching a year or more, we had become good friends. Like any group of people, some became closer than others. There were probably a few, loose social groups formed in the squadron. These were based on personalities, closeness of families and other interests, i.e., boating, fishing, golf, physical fitness, etc. Partying and drinking also brought a group of pilots together. I belonged to that group. On any given day or night, we would have others join the drinking and partying group at the bar if only for a night or two.

Early on, my close friends included Bob Snyder, Mike Siepert, Bill McDougal, Joe Gallo, Winnie Rorabaugh, Buc Taber, Bill Callahan, Mike Ryan and Ted Herman. I quickly added another close friend, as we were very fortunate to have Capt. Pat Owen join the squadron. Major G.O. Jensen also joined us from VMA-231. Pat possessed a great personality, was a good pilot from the start and a hard worker. Both he and Joe Gallo were decorated Cobra pilots from the same squadron in Vietnam. As a group, we loved to fly, and we liked to party. Work hard and play hard was our mantra, and we did both. To set the record straight, I will say, at times, we were over the top in each category. We lost Snyds, one of our leaders, to another squadron when we arrived at Cherry Point. He and Mike Ryan were assigned to different units, but still flew with us on occasion.

Capt. Joe Gallo getting ready to launch from LZ Bluebird at Camp LeJeune, NC

While we were trying to get our feet on the ground at Cherry Point, our sister squadron, VMA-231 had challenges of their own. They conducted three in-house pilot training classes to build the squadron to full strength. 231 had Squadron Leader Hoof Proudfoot, a British Royal Air Force exchange officer serving with the Marines. Hoof was well experienced in the Harrier and had quite a reputation as both an aviator and officer. He was good at the bar and a real jokester. He fit right in and was well respected by all the Cherry Point squadrons.

Due to a mechanical failure, VMA-231 lost a pilot in October 1974. At this point in time both 542 and 231 had experienced a fatal mishap during the squadron buildup. VMA-513, now in Iwakuni, and the 513 DET-B aboard ship, had not yet experienced a fatal mishap, but lost two aircraft, one to a bird strike and one aircraft during an airshow. Both pilots were fine.

In early 1975, there were now three, 20-plane squadrons. 513 was operating 20 Harriers in Japan. Two other full-up "gun" squadrons and a growing training squadron were based at Cherry Point. We were rapidly outflying the logistical system's ability to manufacture or repair certain components essential for readiness.

Straight Up and Out of Control

6: Everyday Flying

The flying, when we did fly, was still beyond wonderful and was challenging and rewarding. Once you figured the Harrier out, it was an easy aircraft to fly. You just could not get complacent or do something stupid as I had done and would do again, one more time. You had to push yourself to improve on every flight. Flying the Harrier, the more you challenged yourself to get better, the better you got. All of us wanted to fly every day. On every flight, you could see the improvement!

...

Mike Siepert, one of my favorite lifelong friends, was an A-4 pilot when he joined the squadron in Beaufort. He is one of the best natural pilots I ever flew with in the Marines. There is a difference. Some guys just naturally have a feel for it, and others, myself included, required actual flight experience to become good pilots.

Mike needed an Air Combat Tactics (ACT) check flight. I was designated to give him that flight. I knew how competitive Mike was, and I also knew he was going to work hard to kick my ass on this flight. Mike and I briefed, then manned up for the flight. The weather was somewhat cloudy, but good enough for us to complete the sortie. I won't say he totally kicked my rear, but he was more than I needed to handle that day. He got the best of me. As we were joining up after the last engagement, I maneuvered my Harrier about 2,000 feet behind Mike, placed his Harrier in my gun sight and asked him to start a left turn. I turned on the gun camera then rolled my plane hard right and left while filming the rendezvous from behind. Then I asked Mike to come back hard to the right while I kept his plane in my gun sight, recording his aircraft, as I kept flying around him in the 6 o'clock position. I finally moved up from behind him to take the flight lead back to base.

Mike arrived in the ready room before I did and was waiting for me to arrive. "Mammal, how did you think the flight went?" I asked. He was beaming. He said, "It went very well!" I replied, "I tracked you with the gun camera for almost two minutes." "Bullshit," came his quick reply. I said, "Mike, I have it on gun camera film." I tossed the film case to Mike, and he reviewed it. He walked out of the ready room about to explode. When I filmed him in the rendezvous, my thought was that he would easily recognize my lame attempt to show I shot him, call me on it and everyone in the ready room would laugh about it. Obviously, that did not happen.

Mike's a smart guy. Early the next morning he had to fly a plane to Bogue Field for a static display. It was a Saturday. While he was waiting for the people to arrive to receive a brief about the plane he was thinking about the flight. It finally dawned on him what I had done. We had a squadron party that night, and during that party my life was in the balance. I thought he was going to kill me. But it was a giant step forward to becoming lifelong friends. He still remembers it and won't let me forget it.

. . .

It is easy to remember the good times and fun events in 542, because we made them happen. But on the maintenance floor and in the ready room, things never really took off. It was a hard work routine day after day. The officers seemed to accept their fate and deal with it as best they could. One pilot took almost 60 days leave in that year, rather than stay around the squadron. Others found a way to get transferred to a different unit for part of the year. The rest of us did what Marines do best: get together, drink, complain and go back to work the next day.

This was 1974 and '75, the start of the post-Vietnam era. All the Marines in our squadron were not perfect Marines. We still had a few bad actors. In 1975, the commandant, Gen Louis Wilson, made it easier for Marines desiring a general discharge to receive one. This was the beginning of the diligent effort to recruit people into the Marine Corps who both wanted to be there and met new standards of performance prior to becoming Marine recruits. Marine Corps recruiters worked diligently to find these people.

. . .

Col Price had an MG; it was a beautiful car, and he was very proud of it. One day someone threw paint remover on the hood of the car, destroying a large portion of the paint job. The CO was convinced he knew who was guilty. He charged the Marine, and I was assigned the summary court martial. Military discipline is a useful tool provided to commanders. Properly utilized, it is a tremendous asset to keep people in line. But if abused, it can really cause morale problems.

I set the trial for 8 a.m. on a Wednesday morning. I had it on good faith this particular Marine didn't do this. The senior SNCOs in the maintenance department made a point to tell me we had the wrong Marine, but no one offered up another name. Talk is cheap and with the conditions in the squadron, it was difficult to know if what I was hearing was, in fact, true.

At 8 o'clock, the Marine showed up. He brought a civilian attorney with him, one who had been a former military attorney. That totally threw me for a loop. The attorney objected to everything that was said in the first few minutes. It became obvious he wanted me to make a procedural mistake large enough to have an adverse decision overturned on appeal.

After his second objection, I continued. He immediately objected again. I recessed the court to go search for some answers. I was a bit intimidated. The attorney knew his way around the Summary Court Martial procedures. I had only presided over one of these three years earlier in Dallas.

Mammal was now the legal officer, so I went to his office to look some things up. I returned and reconvened the court. I no sooner opened my mouth than the attorney objected. Once again, I recessed the proceeding. This time I looked my information up then spent about 20 minutes shooting the breeze with Mammal. I figured the attorney did not want to spend the entire day with his client sitting in the 542 hangar. The longer I took to get back after each objection, the longer he was going to remain at Cherry Point.

After another objection and 20-minute recess, he finally had enough and asked for a conference without his client in the room. I told him I could not in good conscience rule on an objection until I reviewed the applicable reference. However, it did come up that this proceeding would go a bit quicker if he reduced the number of objections.

According to all the information I could gather, this Marine did not damage the CO's car. He had an alibi from a Senior Staff Sergeant and his answers to the many questions did not place him at the scene of the crime at the right time. This incident happened on day crew. This Marine was on night crew. The CO's car was not in the parking lot when the Marine was working, and he left before Col Price arrived at the squadron. No one could even place him in civilian clothes at the scene of the crime with the car in the CO's parking space. This Marine had received "office hours" from the CO some time earlier. This is the lowest form of military discipline. That appeared to be the reason the skipper thought him guilty, a bit of payback for a lost stripe. I found him not guilty. The actual culprit was never identified.

If memory serves me correctly, it was soon after the court martial that the signs in the ready room had some overnight changes. "Every Sortie Professionally Executed" became **Every Other Sortie Professionally Executed**! With a two-letter change, "Excellence is our Standard", became **Excellance is Our Standerd**! All this helped to enrage the CO. But by this time, in the collective opinion of all the officers, most of his wounds were self-inflicted.

7: Business as Usual

The CO continued to sign us up for any exercise, airshow or flight opportunity to showcase the Harrier. Major Eik worked hard to get us normal squadron training in order to meet the ever-increasing list of commitments. We manned the few airplanes we could get up for flight and flew them hard. We spent a lot of time at LZ Bluebird at Camp Lejeune. It was a lot of fun to move there for an operation to work with the grunts (ground-based Marines) and get away from the chaos and frustrations we were experiencing at Cherry Point. We would take four to six airplanes to spend a few days flying from the airfield and the forward site. We lived in tents and reveled in living the life of a grunt except when we were flying. We had a lot of fun.

On one of these deployments, the CO was manning the five-minute hot pad alert. He was strapped in the plane waiting for launch instructions from the duty officer. When he received his mission briefing, I was standing next to his plane, speaking with him. I had my flight gear on and was waiting to climb into the adjacent plane to assume the five-minute alert status once the CO took off on his mission. The ODO called him on the FM radio to give the skipper his sortie brief. About the same time this was going on, a CH-46 helicopter landed in an open field adjacent to the airstrip.

After the helo landed, four colonels jumped out and headed toward our planes. I walked partway there to meet them. They asked, "Where's your CO? Where's Col Price?" I told them he was in the cockpit, ready to launch any moment. One of them said they were friends of his and they were excited to see him fly. They waved to Col Price. He smiled and waved back. The colonels moved back out of the way to watch the CO crank up and take off on his sortie while I headed toward my aircraft to climb in to assume the five-minute alert status.

The Harrier was designed to ground loiter, which means the aircraft has been preflighted, is sitting at the ready, all systems go for an immediate start and launch when the alert was sounded. To receive any flight brief or instructions, the Harrier pilot must have access to a radio. The Harrier had two radios; one was a UHF band which was used for normal airborne ops and the other an FM band to be used for communication with ground FAC's or with ground support personnel. To get power to these radios, there was a position on one of the two battery switches, labeled, "Cab Rank" (the British term for "alert"). The battery switch was placed in the aft position to power the radios, but not much else. To start the plane, both battery switches had to be moved forward for full DC aircraft power. Many of us had tried to start the plane with one battery switch in the cab rank position. That switch configuration would not supply enough power for the plane to start. After you tried with no success, you just reset the switches, started the plane and continued on. It was no big deal!

Col Price was waving and grinning at his colonel friends after he received his flight brief. Then he slammed his canopy closed, gave the turn-up signal to the plane captain and nothing happened. I knew he had left the one battery switch in the cab rank position. He had broken his habit pattern when his friends arrived. Happens to all pilots every once in a while.

He saw me walking to my aircraft and began yelling for me to come over to the plane as he began to climb out of the cockpit. Once on the ground, he started to tear into me about the quality of maintenance, etc. When he slowed down, I tried to tell him about the cab rank issue. He assured me the battery switch position was not the problem.

His words to me were these, "Climb up there and fix this airplane." He walked over to speak with his friends.

I did as I was told. I strapped in; after all, we did have a sortie to fly. I did a quick cockpit check. Gave the plane captain the start signal and the engine began to whine. I got my brief then launched on the skipper's 20-minute sortie knowing full well what awaited me upon my return.

The CO met me when I shut down. He asked me what I did to get the plane to start. I told him the same thing I told him while he was getting out of the plane. He did not have the battery switch in the correct position. He called me a liar. He implied I did some magic fix to make him look bad in front of his friends. I so wanted to tell him he had done that all by himself. He carried on for a bit longer and finally ran out of words. I just nodded my head, said, "Yes, sir," and walked away. I do not think he ever believed what I told him about the battery switch position.

...

One Friday, Pat Owen, Al James, one other pilot and I had the usual Friday afternoon cross-country flights planned. Until this time, we were only allowed to fly to seven bases. About 1 o'clock or so this particular Friday afternoon, the word came down from the air group you could go to any US Marine, Navy or Air Force base in the USA. The sky was the limit. The four of us immediately rethought our trip. We first flew to Selfridge AFB in Detroit to spend the night. The next morning, we did a low-level navigation flight to Wurtsmith AFB in Michigan. This was new territory for all of us and it was beautiful. When we checked in with the control tower, they asked what type of aircraft we were flying. We told them. They were unfamiliar with the Harrier, and we loved it. The Harrier had not been seen outside of a few Navy and Marine Corps bases. We asked for permission to show what the Harrier could do. We did a four-plane mini airshow at Wurtsmith. We had a blast. We refueled the planes and answered a lot of questions.

Eventually, the base commander, an AF general, came to visit with us. He missed our airshow and wondered if we might be able to come back the next day. We politely told him our story about being on the loose and did not want to return to the same base this weekend. Then he asked if he could get our names so he could send a nice letter to our CO, telling him how much the base enjoyed our show. We read the tea leaves and agreed to return for a demo and fuel the next day, provided no letter would go forward. A bargain was struck.

Leaving Wurtsmith, we proceeded north to Sault Ste Marie, MI, landing at Kincheloe AFB Saturday night. We went into Canada for a beer and headed back to the base. Sunday, we did our show at Wurtsmith. It was well received, and the general did not send a letter to the skipper. We then flew to Griffiths AFB near Rome, NY for fuel and returned to Cherry Point. It was wonderful to finally be off the cross-country leash.

Some of our best flying happened on cross-country flights. Once away from Cherry Point, we could schedule low-level flight routes or go to higher altitude areas where we could fly ACM. If the weather was good and the planes stayed up, we could fly up to three sorties per day. Then there was the opportunity to debrief the day's flights at the bar. It was a perfect way to get away from the squadron.

On one cross-country, Mammal and I headed to Randolph AFB in San Antonio, TX. We filed for a couple of low-level flights and landed at Barksdale AFB in Shreveport, LA late Friday afternoon. We noticed the entire transit aircraft ramp was packed. After we shut down our planes, a couple of Marine A-4 captains walked over to let us know they were ahead of us in the wait for a fuel truck. They told us our delay would be at least two hours. They were also quick to tell us Harrier pilots had no priority for fuel at Barksdale AFB. Occasionally, the Harrier received special consideration, and yet there was still a bit of animosity among other communities. I am also sure we did our best to aggravate those situations any time we were able.

All Air Force bases, like Barksdale, had a Supervisor of Flying (SOF) on duty for the day. It was usually a full colonel aviator. After the confrontation with the two captains, I told Mammal to stay with the aircraft and I would see what could be done. I found the SOF in his car and asked to speak with him. He explained the fuel wait would be at least two hours. When he realized we were in the Harriers, he asked, "You guys have a priority mission?" I answered, "Sir, see that big, tall, good looking fellow over there by the airplanes?" He nodded his head yes. I continued, "Well, we live at Cherry Point, NC. He is a bachelor, and I am trying to get him to Randolph tonight so he can get loaded and get laid." He smiled and said, "That is the only honest answer I have heard today. Are you self-start?" I answered. "Yes, sir." "Then tell your wingman to stay by the planes, you go file a flight plan, I'll send the fuel truck over. Tell him I hope he's successful." My reply was short. "Yes, sir!"

I walked over to Mike, to quietly tell him the story, and announced, loudly, to no one in particular, "I'm going to base ops to find something to eat." I went to the ops building, filed a flight plan and walked back to our planes. The fuel truck was finishing fueling my Harrier. The two A-4 pilots had been getting food. When they came out of the operations building, they saw the fuel truck fueling our planes. They were livid.

They were headed to Randolph as well. We climbed in our planes, started 'em up, taxied to the runway, and flew to Randolph AFB.

We had a big night at Randolph, but I can't speak to Mike's success. We did do a bit of drinking and had a fun time. The next morning found us eating breakfast at Randolph base operations for a flight to Bergstrom AFB. We briefed three air-to-air missions and had a good go at each other. Mike came up on the radio and said he was sick and had thrown up. I laughed but didn't take it very seriously. I thought all pilots burped sometimes and he had a mask. How bad could it be? We landed at Bergstrom AFB and taxied to the visiting flight line. While inbound, ground control asked if a VIP might look at our airplane. I parked, and said, "Sure thing, check out dash two." The work stand was placed next to his plane and the VIP climbed up, and looked at Mike, quickly telling him, "Thank you," and climbed down. Once again, my days were numbered, but it was another time we both will never forget.

· · ·

The social scene at Cherry Point was much different than it had been in Beaufort. For one thing, families were much more spread out. There was a cluster of us on base, a few lived in New Bern and the rest toward the coast. Nods and Mammal had a bachelor pad on Bogue Sound. They agreed to have a squadron pig-picking down there one Saturday. All the pilots, with wives and girlfriends, descended on the place in the afternoon. There was some serious drinking going on. Mike and Nods started cooking the pig around four in the morning, christening the event with a beer. Everyone was having a great time. It was one of the few times wives and girlfriends had joined husbands for a squadron function since we had arrived at Cherry Point.

As the afternoon moved on, Mike cranked up Nods' large Harley Davidson motorcycle, offering rides to all takers. Joni Branum was the first rider up. Mike took her out to the main road and went on a tear, going well past 100 mph. He returned and we convinced Pat Price to climb on. She had a great ride. She came back thrilled. Finally, Nita James, not to be left behind, got the third ride.

Later in the evening, Ted Herman and Snyds started hawking a three-man lift, taking bets that Snyds could lift three people off the ground. Des Grout, our tech rep and one of the wives were enthusiastic challengers, not believing the it was possible. While looking for a third "victim", Col Price taunted Ted's ability to get the lift going. Ted told him that if he would be the third man, we would give him the nod before we dumped beer on the challengers. With a knowing smile Col Price sat in the middle and locked arms. On the count of one everyone dumped their drinks on him. He was livid and sputtering but could say nothing. Everyone pretended what a good sport he was and hid their joy at the little moment of revenge.

That party was one of the most memorable events of the year. We all left there, knowing we had seen a different side of the Price family.

· · ·

We continued to operate from Bogue Field, along the Intracoastal Waterway, and our favorite, LZ Bluebird. Bogue Field had fuel and a permanent runway. Bluebird had a fuel truck and the forward site pad located nearby. This is the pad where Rick Briggs crashed in June 1974. We went to LZ Bluebird quite often. Every once in a while, I would remember that accident.

We kept working on our mission to launch as quickly as possible when called upon by Marine ground forces to go to a target to drop a practice bomb. Time to target was very important. We worked hard to reduce that number. The grunts would place a request for an airstrike up the line from their FAC to the Direct Air Support Center (DASC). The DASC would task VMA-542 to fly a specific sortie and we would respond. Marines have aircraft for one primary purpose. That is to provide CAS to the grunts.

All the antics Marine pilots get themselves into during the course of a squadron tour are secondary to the mission of CAS. When you sit in a cockpit, on alert, waiting to receive the next mission, is when you, as a pilot, truly appreciate why you are there. That Marine on the ground could be your brother, a friend from high school or a Marine who went through basic school with you. The Marine air/ground team concept is awesome and continues today.

As we only took a few airplanes on these deployments, the balance of the squadron remained at Cherry Point. That was when the search for parts and cannibalization was at its most critical time.

Things in the squadron continued to become a bit bizarre at times. Some of the original 542 captains were reassigned to different duties. Mike Ryan left right away to become the group legal officer after we arrived. Snyds went to another squadron when we arrived. Dale Heely and Ted Herman left to join a 513 Det A that was put together to handle airshows and other tasks. When they departed, we had about six or seven captains at one point in the squadron. The CO decided a captain would have to remain overnight when we were the Squadron Duty Officer (SDO). In Beaufort, since we lived about 10 minutes from the squadron, we went home for the night, and were on call. Many of us lived on base, even closer to the squadron in Cherry Point. This new rule had us staying in the squadron five or six nights a month. It made no sense to us. When you had the duty, you would put in 36 continuous hours at the squadron.

· · ·

The Marine Corps birthday was next on the squadron agenda. Col Price called me into his office and offered me a seat. He was so nice I wondered what was up. I was nervous. He asked me to go with Major Sabow to represent the squadron on a local TV show to discuss the Marine Corps birthday and the Harrier. I was stunned. We had a fun talk, laughed a lot and I agreed to do my best. I was sad when I left his office. If the skipper had shown that side of his personality, we would have had a much better squadron and accomplished what he wanted without so much angst. Sabs and I had a fun time doing the interview and the skipper was very happy about it.

We attended the officers' birthday ball ceremonies as a squadron and moved on for another year, slowly working our way towards the 200th USMC birthday ball in 1975.

About two weeks later, on Thanksgiving Day 1974, the airfield was closed. We were working the usual day shift in maintenance. We had a plane ready to fly, but it required hover checks to be ready for the flight schedule. That required three press- ups (vertical take-offs to a steady hover). That was a fairly simple thing to do. Col Price came by the squadron and told me to launch the test hop. We knew the field was closed for the Thanksgiving holiday. I loved to fly and we would have another aircraft ready for the Monday flight schedule; the CO said, "go." So off I went.

I had just finished the last press-up when a Marine Corps sedan pulled up alongside the aircraft. A LtCol about 6'4" in his uniform of the day climbed out of the car and gave me a signal to shut down the Harrier. I did. He then told me to climb out and get on the ground. I did. He was the base operations officer who had more than a few choice words for me. He started calling me some names, asking me a lot of questions, and indicated I might be too stupid to be a pilot since I was flying when the airfield was closed, and the crash crew was not available. He asked, "Who told you, you could fly today?" I answered. "My skipper." "Who's that?" I told him, "Col Price." He shook his head from side to side and became very nice to me. He gave me a ride to the hangar in his car. When I was out of the car, he told me, "Go home and enjoy Thanksgiving dinner." I think we both knew that was not going to happen. We towed the Harrier back to the hangar and kept working, but we did have another jet ready for the Monday flight schedule. At one time I had a picture of 542 maintenance troops working or deployed every holiday that year. We did not work Christmas Day.

...

A couple of weeks before Christmas, four of us wound up in New Orleans. Snacks and I with two others landed at NAS Belle Chase. We had some airplane issues. We contacted base to discuss our plan to get them repaired before we could return home. The plan was to send home the one good airplane on Saturday morning. Snacks, a Louisiana native, spoke the language needed to convince the reserves from the Belle Chase maintenance department to give us help.

Friday night we went to Pat O'Brien's and had photos taken of the four of us. We had another one taken of the three of us, and one more of the two of us. Our plan was to mail these photos to the squadron one at a time. First there were four, then three, then two, and finally all of us would get home. We wrote, "Merry Christmas, wish you were here," on the photos. We thought this would be great fun. The mail idea was good, but it was too slow. We decided the first pilot leaving New Orleans would take the picture of the three remaining pilots the following morning. When he returned to Cherry Point, he would put the photo on the ready room bulletin board.

The calls from the squadron came quickly. We explained we had the other plane repaired late Saturday to return Sunday. The second pilot left Sunday afternoon. Snacks and I were still trying to get our planes worked on. Both our planes had been checked out and were flyable, but they had issues. Snacks' aircraft had a temperature controller issue. It went intermittently full cold at altitude. My plane had communication and navigation issues, but I could fly wingman on him and make it back.

The CO called and ordered us to one-leg it to Cherry Point on Sunday night. We could not make it all the way in one flight due to fuel. Distance, night, and weather were all against us. We told the skipper we could leave Monday morning and two-leg it to Cherry Point. He gave us a direct order to one-leg it to Cherry Point. We filed our flight plan at NAS Belle Chase and annotated it to the effect that we could not make this flight in one leg, but were given a direct order to do so by Col W.G. Price, the VMA-542 CO. The base operations duty officer reluctantly signed off the flight plan after making sure we knew what we were doing. We launched into the night, working hard to figure out if we could stretch the fuel to make it to Cherry Point. Fortunately for all three of us, Snacks' temp controller went full cold. That was all the reason we needed to save face for all concerned. We landed at an Air Force base on the route to Cherry Point, spent the night and made it to Cherry Point Monday morning. A crisis avoided.

I had never before given much thought about the use of, "This is a direct order." All of a sudden, I wondered what would happen if a person refused to carry it out? I had never heard anyone use the term "direct order" during my career. Maybe that worked good in a movie, but what it really says to me is, as a senior officer, I cannot handle the situation. It is definitely the last bullet in your leadership weapon. I remembered that for my entire career and never gave one. There are probably exceptions to my thoughts about this, but I never found one.

We kept flying through the end of December on a reduced schedule as many Marines went home on leave to visit family and friends. We split the squadron in half to keep all shops covered in the event we were given any tasks from on high. By January, the squadron maintenance department was back to full strength.

8: A Flying Lesson

In February 1975, VMA-231 lost another pilot. Capt. Rock Davis, a member of my class in Beaufort, crashed doing a VTO. The mishap investigation determined he possibly had some control issues, and the Harriers were grounded pending the determination of the problem. When the aircraft were grounded, the XO had been flying a Harrier to McDonnell Douglas in St. Louis. He left his aircraft at Scott AFB in IL located a few miles east of the Mississippi River.

When the Harriers were returned to flight status, about two-and-a-half weeks later, I was sent to Scott AFB along with a sergeant from the hydraulic shop to check out the aircraft hydraulic system because of the recent accident. The Harrier hydraulic system checked out fine on the ground that afternoon. We spent the night at Scott and headed to the station operations building in the morning to file a local flight plan to check out the controls and the hydraulic system while airborne. Upon successful completion of the flight check I would return the plane to Cherry Point. This seemed like a simple enough assignment until I managed to inject enough terror into this local flight for it to become the second, and last time, I scared myself in the Harrier.

When we arrived at base ops, I ran into USAF Gen Chappie James. I had seen Gen James two times before. I do not remember the location of the first time, but I met him again when he was a general. I was at base operations, NAS Pensacola, FL, his hometown. He was in a USAF aircraft. I was flying an F-8 Crusader. He walked over to the plane and I introduced myself to him. He claimed he remembered me (he must have been a good politician) and asked if he could climb in the cockpit. He did and I gave him a brief about the Crusader.

It was two years later that I saw him again, this time at Scott AFB as I was preparing my Harrier for the test flight to check out the hydraulics system. During that time, he had become the first African American four-star general. He was in charge of the Military Airlift Command. He saw me, I introduced myself and he said, "I remember you, you let me climb in your F-8 Crusader in Pensacola. What are you doing here?" I explained the situation to him. I let him know I was preparing to fly a local test flight and would be returning to Scott to land. He checked the Harrier out and told me he was going to be on the golf course but would return to watch me land. He asked me if I could do a little air show upon my return. "Yes, sir." I answered.

The temperature was slightly below freezing with no wind. The plane was light loaded with fuel for the test flight, and it blasted out of there like a rocket. I completed the test flight and was headed back to Scott thinking of a maneuver that the general would enjoy. My good friend, Ted Herman, recently told me he had performed a maneuver that John Farley, the premier Harrier test pilot, had flown in airshows. It involved turning the Harrier in a series of circles while decelerating from 90 knots to the hover. I watched John Farley do it on film many times and it looked awesome. I also thought this maneuver was well past my ability (I was right), but I thought, heck, if Herman could do it, so could I.

Returning from the test portion of the flight, I hit the overhead break around 450 knots with a half-baked plan in mind. I completed all my checks and was beginning to decel to the hover in the last 5,000 feet of runway. I planned on three flat, 360 degree turns/spins, starting around 60 knots. When I thought it was time for me to start the turns, I put in some left rudder – a bit too much left rudder -- I might add. The plane started rapidly turning left at an alarming rate. I immediately put in a bit of right rudder to counter the left turn and slow down the turn rate. Again, remembering the words of John Farley, if you held the angle of attack at zero you would not lose control of the Harrier in vertical flight. This was the second time in two years I had to that take advantage of the wisdom in that statement. I am not a great student, but for some reason I hung onto those words and they saved my life twice.

For a few seconds, I was spinning out of control down the runway. I maintained zero angle of attack and was able to complete two-and-one-half turns before flying a few feet past the end of the runway. Fortunately, I was also able to maintain my altitude of 50 to 60 feet during the entire maneuver. The control tower asked if I wanted to land opposite direction. I replied, "Sure." I cracked the nozzles and did a 60-knot slow landing.

I taxied to the visiting flight line and the sergeant brought a ladder to the plane. When I climbed out, he said, "Sir, that was something to see! Are you OK?" I answered, "Yes, I think so."

Gen James quickly pulled up in his golf cart. I saluted and he climbed out. He said something to the effect he had never before seen anything like that being done in a jet airplane. I agreed with him. Then he added, "It looked like you were a little out of control for a bit." I told him he was right. We saluted, then he put his hand out, we shook hands, he wished me the best and drove away. He probably figured I was not too long for this world. The flight to Cherry Point was fun with no issues.

I was happy to have survived that maneuver and could not wait to find my good friend Ted Herman when I returned to Cherry Point. When I tracked Ted down, he told me he had never done the maneuver at 90 kts; he slowed the aircraft to below 30 kts before turning and it continued to slow to a hover during the pirouettes. Oops!

That was the second and last time I scared myself flying the Harrier. A combination of flight experience and working hard to never put myself in a similar situation again kept me safer from that day forward. I am convinced some Harrier pilots died doing what I just survived. The maneuver did not cause them to crash. The culprit was not having thought through whatever maneuver they were going to perform. I was showing off and not paying attention to what flight parameters I was getting myself into while trying something I was not ready to do. A decel to a hover with a bow would have been a good airshow. For me, this was one heck of a lesson learned!

9: New Pilots

VMAT-203, the training squadron, was located at Cherry Point and had been the East Coast A-4 Skyhawk training squadron for many years. Now they were training Harrier pilots in addition to continuing the A-4 pilot training program. This dual tasking had to have placed a burden on both maintenance folks and instructor pilots in their squadron. Initially there is a significant difference in the training required to fly the two aircraft. At the time, all indications were that the current 203 CO did not particularly like the Harrier. Harrier instructors were doing their best to put out safe and well-trained Harrier pilots during this time frame. Col Price was one of the early Harrier pilot graduates from 203.

I did my best to avoid 203. I could think of nothing worse than being a flight instructor in any aircraft. You just never knew when a visit there might turn into a set of orders to join the instructor ranks. So, I really knew little about the workings of the Harrier training squadron and was happy to be in that position.

In February, we began to get some newly trained pilots from VMAT-203. Major Dave Corbett (Tuna), Major Bill Spicer (Sugar), and Navy LCDR Mike Scott (Scotty) joined the squadron and fit right in. They were all experienced pilots transitioning to the Harrier. They were the first of a group of pilots arriving the next few months, as the original 542 pilots and many maintainers were headed to Japan in the summer to replace 513 Marines rotating back to the CONUS. Later, Capt. Ed Jobin (Viking), a longtime A-4 pilot also came onboard. Ed was the poster Marine officer and a welcome addition to any squadron.

...

The Cherry Point Harrier squadrons were working hard to meet commitments and keep 'em flying. This was no longer just a 542 challenge. The shipboard DET had long ago joined 513 in Iwakuni, and as far as we knew were flying as much as they wanted. HQMC was determined to have the 513 deployment to Iwakuni showcase Harrier V/STOL capabilities to the WESTPAC world. Who knows, maybe

117

someone at the highest levels at HQMC, hoped 513 could get the Harrier some combat experience in Vietnam as the war was winding down. When you are a group of captains in the trenches, you can come up with a lot of theories about life. Fortunately, many of them were not true.

. . .

The squadron environment failed to thrive under the CO's leadership. We worked all the time. I had to take leave or vacation days to go to Raleigh with my wife for a weekend shopping trip. Raleigh was a couple of hours away. Getting all the families together as a group became a thing of the past. When we finished work, we either went home or to the bar to discuss squadron life. Bonnie and I had a nice apartment in the converted BOQs and had a pool table. We had quite a few people coming over for late nights around that pool table while we drank Miller Lite.

I believe during the first few months is when all the officers from the XO on down began to truly bond with each other. A few of us took the friendships we had nurtured from Beaufort and advanced them to the next level. During the second half of the CO's tour, without consciously thinking about it, we worked hard to make sure no one was in the skipper's cross hairs. We truly did have each other's backs. However, we missed one downside from too much work and too much time at the bar. Some of us were developing problems at home.

Capt. Cranford (Snacks) truly put in the long hours to get the planes up. He was a workaholic: an unappreciated workaholic. His mother was in the hospital in his hometown, Ruston, LA. He asked for leave to go visit her and was denied by the CO. His mother was in serious condition, and none of us could believe the CO refused him leave. Snacks had a couple of months left before he was going to be transferred to Iwakuni to join 513.

Snacks was a serious and quiet Marine, but he was always thinking. During May, on a Saturday morning, he came to the squadron to fly an unscheduled test flight. That was no big deal. Joe Gallo and I would be called in to do that as well. This time, Snacks' test flight was a bit different. He ultimately landed in Ruston, LA, at the civilian airport.

He was a very experienced airshow pilot, so he decided to put on a small airshow for his hometown crowd upon arrival. He visited his mother in the hospital, then returned to Cherry Point later that afternoon. No one was the wiser. Nobody in the squadron had any idea of his adventure. It was a smooth move!

Two days after the airshow, the local Ruston newspaper did a nice job of telling Capt. Cranford's story and placing some good photos in a newspaper article. Unbeknownst to most of us at the time, anywhere there was a newspaper article about Marines, the Marine Corps District Public Affairs Office (PAO) collected them and forwarded them to Headquarters Marine Corps PAO. As they say, what goes up must come down. The CO received a call from on high about Snacks' flight to his home to visit his mother and soon had a copy of the article. Col Price lost it! He started yelling for Cranford to come to his office. It was obvious Snacks was in big trouble, but at the time, none of us knew why. Once we found out what happened, Snacks' squadron stock value soared. We loved it but we all were worried about his career.

Because he was the AMO, Snacks was always in hot water with the CO. It was not long before the CO began to imply to the officers in maintenance that we could read about our performance during our time in the squadron. Because of the manner in which the statement was delivered, none of us believed that was going to be career enhancing. At that point, we formed the Captains' Protective Association (CPA).

The majors did their best to keep the squadron afloat. They were the sounding board for all our gripes, complaints, and suggestions. They listened and most of the time agreed with us, but they only had minimal impact on the CO. He pretty much ran the squadron on his own, ignoring any advice or counsel.

Snacks, Joe Gallo, Pat Owen, and I put in a lot of hours on the hangar deck. Snacks did not drink, but Joe and I, and occasionally Pat, would make up for his lack of alcohol use. Many days, Gallo and I would stay late in the afternoon, looking around the hangar for anything we could do to improve the day's efforts. Later, we would head to the *Shame* for a drink to brainstorm or search for inspiration to solve some of the problems. We solved a few, but more kept coming. In the process, Joe and I became really good friends.

...

Late May 1975, we were again committed to Solid Shield. This was called Solid Shield 75 and looked just like the last one. We spent time at LZ Bluebird in tents. We had a small DET in Bluebird. Buc Taber and a few of us, every now and then, slipped over to Courthouse Bay, an engineer battalion location a few miles down the road to get a shower and a beer. We lived in tents and like the previous times had a fun time. Our flying consisted of air to ground sorties, five- and 15-minute standbys and some carrier flights off the USS Guadalcanal and Guam. The squadron performed well during this exercise.

VMA-542 was tasked with an Inspector General's Inspection or IG as it is fondly called. This is make-or-break time for a squadron. The IG inspection covers every aspect of a Marine squadron. Administrative section has all personnel record books checked for updated information. The aviation and ground safety programs are reviewed, maintenance procedures are checked and there is also a PFT and numerous uniform inspections. Needless to say, Col Price wanted to get an outstanding grade for the inspection. We were all aware of his concerns. Once again, the entire squadron pitched in to pull together and pass the inspection.

I was in the group to stand the uniform inspection. My uniforms were in good shape as I did my best to live in a flight suit. I think Joe Gallo and I probably wore flight suits more than most. I believe I was in my blues for the inspection. There was a lot of preparation required to make sure rank insignia was properly attached and awards and wings placed exactly in accordance with the uniform manual. It was not too long before the inspector arrived that Nods, a lifelong bachelor at that point, showed up with his white dress uniform. He had pulled it out of a sea bag earlier that morning. After the initial round of chuckles from the rest of us, panic set in when we saw the crumpled uniform. If he caused us to flunk that part of the inspection, the squadron would be downgraded. With a little help from his friends, Nods put together his whites. We made sure everything was properly attached, but we all agreed these were dress yellows instead of dress whites. Each of us passed our inspection. When Nods went in to see the inspecting officer, we held our breath. When he came out we knew he passed! Then we helped him disappear so Col Price wouldn't see him. There were some very happy captains that morning.

10: First Yuma Deployment

The only big event 542 had missed during Col Price's time was a deployment to Yuma for a weapons DET. We finally had the opportunity to deploy to Yuma starting June 9, 1975. It had been many months since 542 first went to Yuma. Now all of us had a good bit of experience in the jet and we had a few newer pilots that we needed to bring up to speed. We looked forward to a couple of weeks of serious flying, camaraderie and fun.

Again, the Yuma deployment was primarily an opportunity to work on our air to ground ordnance delivery techniques and proficiency. During the first half of the deployment, we concentrated on bombing with practice ordnance. The last half we were able to drop live ordnance, shoot rockets and strafe. The deployment was also a good time to increase the utilization of our aircraft. Planes just seem to stay up longer for flight operations when on deployment. We continued to work hard to maximize the flight time we had in Yuma.

One addition to this year's deployment was a chance to fly against the Navy Reserve F-4 squadron from NAS Miramar, CA. They were the best Navy/Marine F-4 squadron around. My good friend from flight school, Steve Arps, later became a member of that squadron. The reserves were airline pilots for the most part, Vietnam era veterans with a lot of shipboard experience. I knew how well they could fly because of the time I previously flew with them in Dallas.

We flew our Harriers, fully combat loaded with guns, fuel tanks and bomb racks while in Yuma. In pilot terms our planes were dirty, we had lots of drag caused by external loads on the plane. The F-4s that came to town had slatted wings that increased their wing lift capability in slow flight and improved turning capabilities. In pilot terms they were a clean aircraft with minimal external drag. They also carried an ACMR pod on a rack underneath the wing.

The ACMR pod was a relatively new technology that was available in Yuma for our Harriers. Each plane carried a missile-shaped pod that continuously transmitted flight data to a control room during the flight. This data was projected on a screen and could be replayed after the flight for review by the pilots when they finished the sortie. This really helped training. Without the actual tracking tool available, many times it was the first person to the ready room or the bar who won the fight.

I was surprised to find my name on the schedule to fly the ACM sortie with the Miramar Squadron, VF-401. The XO would be my ACMR controller. To date, the Harriers had no problem fighting an F-4. We had some advantages, and to my knowledge a Harrier had never lost an ACM flight to a Phantom. I was eager and proud to be on my way to continue that tradition.

The Phantom from VF 401 Navy reserve squadron flew into Yuma from NAS Miramar and parked on the visiting flight line. After my tour in Dallas, I had the utmost respect for reserve pilots. Usually, they flew for an airline for a living and flew in the reserves because they loved military aviation. They were good pilots; many times they were much better than their active-duty counterparts. We met the aircrew, shook hands, and headed to base operations to brief the flight. The pilot was Commander Pete Pettigrew, a PSA airline pilot but, more importantly and unknown to me at the time, one of the best fighter pilots in the Navy. He had a MIG kill to his credit when he was in Vietnam and his backseat Radar Intercept Officer (RIO) during that mission was Lt William Driscoll. Driscoll had also flown with Duke Cunningham, who had become an ace during the war in Vietnam. I liked these guys from the start. Both were heavily involved with the Navy's Top Gun program. Commander Pettigrew casually asked me how many dissimilar engagements I had flown. I suspect he knew from the amount of time it took me to answer his question I only had flown a few. I was not exactly counting them on my fingers but figured maybe 10 or 15 in my entire career. He said he had flown over a thousand. At that point it still seemed like an even match to me!

The plan was for us to fly one flight, return to debrief while observing the ACMR data, refuel and go out again. We finished our brief, and we went off to fly. Our objective on the first flight was to engage at mid-altitude, around 20,000 feet, with a closure rate in excess of 1,000 knots and go from there. There were three of these setups with different entry altitudes planned for the first flight. I do not remember all the details. I was behind him twice for a few seconds but never was able to maneuver to be in a position to shoot. He was behind me three times and nailed me each time. The range and angle off for each sidewinder shot were perfect. The engagements lasted a little over two minutes. I had a lot of trouble keeping them in sight as they took me into the sun. I did have a large piece of 70-millimeter film that was placed over my visor. That allowed me to help keep the F-4 in sight as it went vertical. Even though I had my butt kicked, it was a quick flight, and I was excited to do it again.

On the way back to base, I did not feel too badly about what happened because I was totally outmatched. I could blame it on the external load the Harrier carried because that impacted my ability to zoom climb, but that was not the half of it. Those guys were just much better pilots than I was. I was looking forward to getting some instruction this next flight.

We landed and met the XO in the base ops cafeteria. We all grabbed a sandwich and headed to the ACMR building to debrief the flight. On the walk over, the XO told me he was taking my second sortie and I would be the monitor. He said he had never seen the Harrier lose so badly to anyone and he would take care of that situation. I had never seen Branum (Carrot) ever get mad, but I could tell he was angry with me and my performance during the flight.

Pettigrew was surprised at the change of pilots, but ever the gentleman he said nothing about it. He and the XO briefed their flight. The Harrier is best at lower altitudes, the F-4, not so much. When Pettigrew offered the XO a slow speed entry at about 12,000 feet on the first engagement, the XO was already counting coup! They briefed four engagements.

When the flight took off, I was securely stationed in the ACMR dome. A big part of me wanted to see Carrot get his ass kicked. I watched, fascinated in the dome. It seemed to be a short flight. Carrot never got behind the F-4. They shot him during two engagements in less than 360 degrees of turn. Two went slightly longer. They landed, came into the building, and stayed for a quick debrief. Once again Pettigrew's shots were textbook for range and angle off. They shook hands with us, thanked us for our flights, said goodbye and departed for Miramar having confirmed the Harrier was no threat to them.

The XO and I had been together almost two years and I believed we were good friends. We spent many hours on the runway waving pilots for the ship and forward site work. It was a slow, quiet walk back to the squadron. I could tell he had something on his mind, but I said nothing. As we passed by base ops, the XO asked, "Would you like a drink?" I answered, "Sure."

We put our flight gear on the floor next to our chairs, got our drinks and sat down at the table. It took him awhile, but Carrot apologized for his earlier comments. Essentially, he said, "I never had any idea where they were, or how they got there during the flight." As they did with me, they took him into the sun, and he had trouble following them. The slatted F-4 was a different airplane than the earlier model F-4s both of us had flown. They could turn very well. Since our Harriers were loaded with external racks and guns, our drag increased, and the plane's performance degraded. But the star of the show that day and many others was the Pettigrew/Driscoll aircrew. As Carrot said, "They were just a hell of a lot better pilots then we were!" Pete Pettigrew became a Navy Reserve admiral and might best be known as the consultant for the first Top Gun movie.

. . .

We went to town most nights and a lot of the time we went to Chretin's for nachos and margaritas. Some nights we would try to best the existing squadron record for eating nachos, but we were never close. We went to another nice restaurant called the Stag and Hound, which we affectionately referred to as the "Deer and Dog." Yuma was not really a military town. The Marine aviation presence was fairly small and the Army's Yuma proving ground was located a few miles from town.

There were also a few bars in Yuma. I believe every squadron coming to town checked the bars out. We seemed to like one with a band playing country music called Johnny's Other Place. A few of us would go there after we finished dinner and hang out for a while. One night the CO accompanied us. He had a couple of beers with a few of us and we all enjoyed his company. He did begin to pass out after a few drinks, and we got him out of there and headed back to the base. As the CO, he had a car, so we got a ride back to the base. Later, Mike Siepert took an unserviceable oxygen mask and fitted a beer in it to give to the skipper for those nights when he wanted to drink but was becoming a little sleepy. The Col actually found this to be a very funny gift. We enjoyed those few times with him.

One night, I had a call from the SDO about two in the morning. One of the troops in maintenance had called to report to the SDO he was in trouble. In those days, payphones were all we had to use. The Marine worked for me, so I got up to go get him. When I reached the squadron the SDO told me one heck of a story. The Marine was down on Fourth Avenue, the main street in Yuma, at a phone booth on the side of the road that crossed the bridge over the Colorado River into California. The story was that he was naked. He had been given a sheet to wrap himself in by a motel night clerk and a dime to call the base from a payphone. I grabbed the car keys from the SDO and headed to retrieve him.

The Marine had been to one of the bars in Yuma and had met two 'nice' girls. While there he drank a couple of beers with the girls. During discussions over the beers, the girls told him about their convertible. After drinking with him a bit longer, they invited the Marine to join them as they drove out of town for a couple of miles to drink more beer and play some strip poker in the desert at night. Being a gentleman and a good Marine, he jumped at the chance!

Each time an article of clothing was removed it was tossed into their car. They seemed to be losing at first, but then my Marine had a run of bad luck. Quickly, he was completely naked. They were all having a lot of fun when the girls told him they were going to walk to the car to get some more beer and bring his clothes back. Instead, they jumped into the car and took off, leaving him stranded. He walked into town and banged on the office door of the first motel he saw. Eventually someone answered. The night clerk did give him a sheet and a dime for the payphone so he could call the base.

Sometimes it's very difficult not to laugh at some of the things Marines get themselves into at any given time. Being his officer in charge, I had to work hard to maintain a strict demeanor as we headed back to the base. Once I let him out at the barracks, I just burst out laughing. I was sure he learned a couple of good lessons that night.

. . .

The squadron finally finished the deployment and some of us were thinking about the upcoming change of command. Col Price would be leaving soon and so would many of us. We left Yuma to return to Cherry Point. We came limping home because we had punished the planes, the pilots, and most importantly, the Marines working on the Harriers. We were all looking for some down time.

The CO was leaving in a little over a month. He had completed his Yuma DET, we passed the IG inspection, we flew our flight hour program, and we had no mishaps. We all thought his time as the CO to be a success. The last thing we expected him to tell us was that we were heading back to Yuma for another DET before he left the squadron. But we were!

11: Yuma Again

This was the second Yuma DET in over a month. Marx Branum and Major Eik were already on leave headed to Iwakuni. Sabow (Sabs) became the XO and Major Dave Corbett became the OPSO. Snacks was still the AMO back in Cherry Point, with Major Bill Spicer in the batter's box for the job. Sabow also had orders to Iwakuni. There were some great captains on board, and the squadron personality was rapidly changing.

The airplanes arrived and we began the well-known ritual of AOMs, checking into the BOQ and getting ready for flying. Mike Siepert, two other captains and I went to town to shoot some pool. We drank a few beers and realized a tad late we were going to be late for the AOM. Sabs was all over us. He wanted to know where we had been; so, we quickly came up with a story about finding a gold mine in the desert, close to town. We told him we decided we were going to go into the mine later in the week after we got some equipment. We had him so excited he wanted to be in on it. A couple of days later we had to tell him what really happened. It was a great laugh for us, and a big letdown for Sabs. I think even Col Price, still the skipper, realized this was his last trip. It was about to be all over for him. He decided to head out to town for a couple of nights of drinking with the boys. But each morning, when we arrived in the ready room, there would be a diagram of a government car with a seating chart drawn to seat five people, including the driver. This was after we put eight or so in it the previous night, including the CO. Col Price wanted to be one of the boys at night, but still be the tough, unreasonable, and unrelenting CO during the day.

A few of us decided to have one more big night with Col Price. We started out with dinner at the Deer and Dog. We had quite a few drinks and decided to go to San Luis, Mexico to continue the party. The skipper was all for it. He was excited to be with his boys. We only had two cars, so we loaded them up with no concern about the five-person limit and nothing was said. The CO was in the front seat of one of the cars driven by Bill Callahan. Off we went to Old Mexico.

We parked the cars on the US side and walked into town, which

129

consisted mostly of bars and a couple of sketchy restaurants that were open at night. We found our bar rather quickly and the skipper was in good form. Our party started drinking beer and the CO was getting a bit tired. Actually, he passed out. We found a young lady to come sit next to him and we put his arm around her and leaned him back, enough to look like he was having a wonderful time. Then we had a fellow take two Polaroid photos. Soon after the photo op we left the bar heading back to Yuma. We picked up a few troopers and gave them a ride back as well. Once again, the next morning, it was business as usual.

We all left for Cherry Point during the next couple of days. Once back at Cherry Point, Major Spicer moved into Snacks' office as the AMO. Major Sabow detached on leave for Iwakuni and Major Dave Corbett took his place. Navy LCDR Mike Scott became the ops officer. It was rapidly becoming a new squadron.

12: Change of Command

The change of command for 542 was held in August 1975. The skipper held his last AOM prior to detaching from the squadron. He gave a speech that would bring a tear to a glass eye. It was a wonderful speech, but it was hard to believe a word of it. It was all about the wonderful year we had working and flying together, the camaraderie, good times, being a band of brothers, blah, blah. These were things to which none of us could relate.

When he finished his talk, I asked if I could present him with a plaque the captains had prepared for him. He looked excited, sporting a big grin, and invited me forward. As the CPA rep I had been chosen to give Col Price the plaque. When we returned from Yuma, we had a nice plaque made for the skipper. The plaque, suitable for any "I Love Me" room, contained the Polaroid photo we took in Mexico and the following comment, engraved on a plate at the bottom, "Just one little Fuck Up Col, Just one little Fuck Up!"

Standing directly in front of the CO placed me in a vulnerable position. He looked at the plaque and was speechless for a moment. As he started to explode and say something all of us might regret, Snacks, sitting in the back of the ready room got his attention by holding up the other photo. Col Price left the ready room without speaking another word. Any captain in the squadron would have hung that plaque on their wall with pride. But we figured a senior officer on his way up might not like for the photo to be spread around. It never was and I suspect the plaque did not make it past the first trash bin. In the eyes of many of us, we were now as close to even with Col Price as we could ever get.

We were in formation listening to Col Price's change of command speech for the troops. It was the exact same one he gave to the officers in the ready room. We all thought that a bit odd. We had been through enough changes of command to know the outgoing CO has a special rapport with his officers. He usually has a different one with the troops and those sentiments were reflected in the change of command speeches.

Later that night there was a going away party for the skipper, and we all had a great time. He was in his social personality and was the life of the party. His wife Pat was gracious to all of us and she enjoyed many laughs. At one point, when Col Price was about to go on the attack, Pat said, "Will you sit down and be quiet!" For the rest of us, as they say, "You could hear our packs hit the ground!"

Looking back now, I find it easy to remember but difficult to appreciate how toxic the squadron environment had become over time. Given my job in maintenance and my personality, I was right in the middle of it and certainly a large contributor. Somewhere along the way, it had become the skipper versus the officers. We made every commitment, we flew our flight hour program, we passed the IG inspection and deployed to Yuma two times in eight weeks at the end of his tour, but it did not seem to be good enough for Col Price.

13: LtCol Price

It was the best of times and the worst of times working with Col Price. Looking back on the experience, he became more difficult to work with as the aircraft became more difficult to maintain and the daily flight schedule was no longer flyable as written. I firmly believed he thought that once he took charge of the squadron and put his name on the squadron sign in front of the hangar, more planes would magically be in an up status for flight. I think he felt, due to his leadership, he would set records as the CO of VMA-542. After a few frustrating weeks into his tour, that had not happened. He was at a loss to understand what was going wrong. He began to pout and blame everyone for the problems but would not listen to suggestions or potential solutions. The skipper ignored his majors when they tried to give him some thoughts about the squadron. In short, he knew where he wanted 542 to go, but he could not figure out a way to lead us there.

As the CO of VMA-542, he seemed to lack a basic understanding of how to work with people. We were the same group of Marines that had been doing very well in Beaufort. There were very few personnel changes during the move to Cherry Point. I spoke with the XO a few times about what was going on. He firmly believed the skipper took command of a very good squadron that only needed a few tweaks here and there to get it back up to speed and keep it going. Instead of tweaking the squadron, the CO made things much worse.

The skipper had one heck of a temper. He told us that early in his career he had some fuel splashed on his face when he was flying jets. The spill caused him to have some skin damage. When he got mad his face went from his normal reddish color to a whiter color. It was something to behold, as he got mad often. In my experience, an impatient pilot with a hot temper is one you want to avoid. They are, by nature, unpredictable. Col Price was that and much more. Many of us finally came to believe he was intimidated by having to fly the Harrier.

Further adding to the confusion, Col Price had a bipolar personality, obviously an observation, not a diagnosis. He could be charming, witty and the life of the party. He invited each bachelor officer or officer and their wife to his home for dinner and conversation. We enjoyed these visits and looked forward to them. Plus, he had a secret weapon in his arsenal. His wife, Pat, was truly a wonderful lady with a great sense of humor. The officers and wives enjoyed visiting with her. She knew him well, and I believe she knew what was in store for us and her family. All the 542 pilots wondered how they ever got together.

I truly enjoyed Col Price when he was not in the squadron area. He had a good career before taking over 542 and I am sure he had a good one after he left. He was a good family man. He was a Marine officer through and through and was an outstanding staff officer. He excelled in any social setting. He had a great sense of humor. I believe all of us enjoyed Col Price away from the squadron. I knew him well enough to know he wanted to be remembered as a good CO and respected as a pilot. He just did not know how to relax and let that happen. He rushed it and he would not let us help.

During his tour, he did his best to alienate and intimidate 18 to 20 officers. He stated more than a few times that he did not need any of us. After serving in a lot of squadrons since 542, I believe Col Price only survived his tour as the CO of 542 due to the respect and discipline all of us had for the Marine Corps way of life. He was the CO, and we did our best to comply with his directives, whether we liked it or not!

After discussing Col Price with Buc Taber, Buc added an element to the situation I had not previously explored. In many ways, the Marine Corps set Col Price up for a rough tour. Any career aviator would believe command of a Harrier squadron in the 1970s would be good for their career. When Col Price took over the squadron, we were in the middle of a total relocation from one base to another. We were beginning to really feel the effects of a fleet-wide parts shortage. Our tasks from higher headquarters were increasing with no let-up in sight of the shortage of parts. Col Price had minimal flight time in the Harrier. Certainly, he did not have enough experience in the Harrier to assume a flight leadership role as the CO of the squadron. That is a key element in the leadership role for a squadron commander. You do not need to be the best pilot in the squadron, but you need to be good enough to earn the respect of your officers. Those qualities, should a leader be deficient in them, would be more than enough to cause anyone major concerns.

The skipper had to believe he was not going to be able to achieve the goals he set for himself while CO of 542. When I look at it with this perspective, it is fair to say he was not given some of the tools required to experience a successful tour as a commanding officer of a Harrier squadron. That is the sad part about Col Price. His squadron did everything it needed to do and all that was asked of it. We were a very successful squadron when you look at the numbers. I just do not know if he ever really enjoyed his accomplishments.

Straight Up and Out of Control

14: The Next CO

Before Col Price left the squadron, I put in for more than 30 days leave, starting soon after the change of command. My wife and I had arranged to spend three weeks in Iran visiting her aunt and uncle, then to Egypt, Lebanon and Italy for an additional week or more. This would be the first time in a year that I would leave the squadron for more than three days for a personal trip.

I met the new CO, LtCol Jahn, just briefly after the change of command. Then I left to go on a much desired and needed leave.

...

When I returned from leave, a little over a month later, I finally received my orders to Iwakuni to join my buddies who were now in 513. Major Spicer (Sugar) was now the AMO in 542, and he was my replacement. I was tasked to show him around the squadron maintenance areas. The squadron was being populated with some pilots and troops being reassigned from 513 and new pilots from VMAT-203. They were all good, but I missed my friends that were now in Iwakuni and could not wait to join them. One Friday before leaving the squadron, I had a call from one of our pilots. He had blown two main tires on his Harrier in Dallas. The Harrier had tires that were not available at transient bases. We needed to get a couple of them to Dallas that afternoon so he could continue his flight. We used either the A-6 or the C-130 squadrons to help us if we needed to get a part, tire or maintenance people to a Harrier stranded on the road.

The duty officer would call the Group ops people with our request for assistance. They would ask the Wing if the Group, MAG-14, that owned the A-6s and C-130s could help us out. We were in luck that day because the A-6 squadron was launching a flight to Dallas and would be happy to take the tires. I helped to make arrangements, and we were a go. We just had to deliver the tires to the A-6 squadron.

I briefed my replacement, Sugar, a recently returned pilot from 513, about what I had done. He quickly walked away. I was soon called to the CO's office, this time standing tall in the same spot, but in front of a different CO. Col Jahn started in on me with both barrels. He asked me if I had worked with the group to find an aircraft to take the tires to Dallas. I answered, "Yes, sir." He told me I just embarrassed the squadron, and he would not have it. He quickly explained to me that my replacement, who knew much more about the Harrier than I would ever know, had just come in to tell him 513 put main mount tires in the Harrier hellhole (an accessory access hatch in the fuselage) in WESTPAC. When they needed to replace tires on the road, they carried them to the down aircraft themselves. The CO told me we would send one of our Harriers to take the tires to Dallas. He told me to stop the A-6 from taking the tires and reiterated that 542 would be capable of taking care of its own problems. All I could say was, "Yes, sir!" He was the new CO in town.

I cancelled the A-6 tire delivery flight as requested. Of course, I knew the two main tires would not fit into the Harrier hellhole. I knew that even one main tire would not fit into the hellhole. By the time I finished undoing the tire issue, it was late in the afternoon, and possessed with a short timer's attitude, I headed to the O'Club. It was not long after I arrived there that I had a call from Col Jahn. After the call was completed, I had an early morning appointment with him on Monday. Joe Gallo joined me at the O'Club, and we commiserated about life for a few hours. We seemed to understand each other when it came to aircraft maintenance. I knew I was really going to miss him when I departed for Iwakuni.

Monday came and we still had a Harrier in Dallas needing tires. The CO asked me if I knew the tires would not fit into the hellhole. I answered, "Yes, sir." Then he asked me, "Why didn't you speak up when I told you to cancel the A-6?" I replied, "Skipper, you told me the captain taking my place was far more experienced in the Harrier than I would ever be, and you told me I embarrassed the squadron. I thought since my replacement had all that experience, he might know something I didn't." I was dismissed from his office. Fortunately for me, I left the squadron a few days later.

Much later in life, I actually ran into Col Jahn when we were both retired. We went to lunch, and after a few pleasantries, he commented, "John, it's probably a good thing for you, that you left 542 when I became the CO." I smiled and said, "Oh, yes sir, it was. Iwakuni was a much better place for me to be!"

15: Departing Thoughts

As I left Cherry Point for Iwakuni I had some time to look back on my tour in 542. Frankly, I was unprepared to accept how much I learned about leadership from Col Price. I believe he was an "Old Corps" Marine, a leader doing as he had been trained. Some Marines, back in the day, would lead their troops using power, fear and intimidation. If I ever thought that tactic might work, he taught me it would not. Col Price showed all of us what happens when you stifle or waste talent of those in your organization. This tour confirmed my belief that a good leader must allow everyone's talent to flourish and grow together. The successful leader only reins it in when required.

Another thing I had to acknowledge was how I became caught up in the drama playing out in the squadron. The squadron environment became toxic over time, and I was a part of that. That was not only the skipper's fault. When he attacked, we engaged! I was probably nowhere near as wonderful as I thought I was during the past year. In today's vernacular, I, along with my close friends, had developed "an attitude."

Col Price wanted to be the CO of a Harrier squadron really badly, and in many ways that is just what he got, something really bad.

I learned nothing from my time with LtCol Jahn as the CO. It was a short tour. My head and heart were in Iwakuni a few weeks before my body caught up. Other than escaping death by being stupid, the best thing that happened to me during this past year was to continue to develop deep friendships with the 542 pilots.

My total flight time while in 542 at Cherry Point was 216 hours, averaging about 13 per month. That gave me a total of 379 Harrier flight hours in 25 months, barely enough to remain proficient.

Straight Up and Out of Control

PART 3 (1975-1976)

MCAS Iwakuni

In the 1970s, it seemed like every Marine squadron that crossed the International Date Line lost its mind. The one coming in felt obligated to outdo the one it replaced! Could we call it the Great Santini effect?
A retired Marine colonel!

1: Arrival
MCAS Iwakuni, Japan

I arrived at Iwakuni in late October 1975. I had been to Iwakuni once before, in August 1970, during the time I was flying my combat tour in Vietnam. I flew an F-4 to NAS Atsugi, Japan for rework. My RIO and I stopped on the way, at Iwakuni, to link up with two F-4 pilot roommates from flight training. I do not remember much about the base, but the surrounding countryside was beautiful. The base was on the water and the town was surrounded by small, steep hills. The Kintai bridge was built in 1673, spanning the Nishiki River in a series of five wooden arches. The bridge is located on the foot of Mt. Yokoyama, at the top of which lies Iwakuni Castle. It was a very picturesque setting. I remember enjoying the countryside from a bullet train I took from Iwakuni to Kyoto. Small homes with thatch roofs were scattered throughout the countryside. They were located close to small rice paddies providing an amazing contrast to the huge commercial farms in the US.

To say I was excited about finally getting to my new duty station at Iwakuni would be an understatement. My time in 542 was forgotten as soon as I headed out the main gate at Cherry Point. All my close friends, with the exception of Joe Gallo, were in Japan. The trip was long but much more comfortable than the flight I took to Vietnam five years earlier. I landed in Tokyo and caught the train to Iwakuni. My clothes weighed about 50 pounds, but my flight gear weighed much more. Most of us carried our flight gear with us on the trip. The rumor going around at the time was to bring your own flight gear. If you shipped it by government means, it could take up to six weeks to arrive. That is a lifetime for a pilot to be without his flight gear.

It was old home week when I arrived. I was back in familiar territory among my closest friends whom I had enjoyed for the past couple of years. When you arrive in a new Air Group to be assigned to a squadron, there is no guarantee you will actually be assigned to the squadron. There are many jobs at the group level requiring a pilot. It is always a bit tense to check into the group. You kept your fingers crossed hoping the group admin officer sends you down to the squadron for assignment. He did!

It was Friday afternoon when I arrived. I found my room, stashed my personal gear and hauled my flight gear to the squadron to begin the check-in procedures. I saw Major Sabow, Major Eik and then the XO, Marx Branum. Check-in was that simple. They were happy to see me, and I was happy to see them. The CO was LtCol Gustafson. I did not meet him during the day. Col Gustafson was an impressive Marine. His reputation was well known in the Marine aircraft attack community. During my earlier visit with the XO, he had told me serving under Col Gus, as he referred to him, was very refreshing after what we had experienced in Cherry Point.

We all went to happy hour and that turned into a huge night. Later, the XO decided I should come over to his hooch, and he would introduce me to Col Gustafson. Mike Siepert came along with us and I went to meet my new CO. We were in the CO's hooch talking about 513, and how he was glad I was there, how happy I was to be there, the usual stuff. Marx Branum, who in our experience really was not much of a drinker, hit the bottle that he brought from his room and quickly had a buzz on. He went from zero to 100 in record time. I did not notice if Col Gus had been drinking, but Mike and I had more than a few beers at the O'Club before we arrived at the CO's hooch. Sometime during this friendly welcome aboard visit, the subject of wrestling came up. There was the XO, a good size guy; Mike, who was a good size guy and athletic; Col Gus, who was about my height but appeared to be much stronger; and then there was me. All of a sudden, the four of us were in a wrestling match. We needed a ring. It was not tag team, but every man for "his" self, as we say in Kentucky. It seemed I spent the majority of the time on the ground with at least three people trying to remove a different appendage from my body. I was taking the brunt of all this fun, athletic activity. Col Gus put me in a headlock, and I could not breathe. I could not get out of it, tried to give up to get out of it, but nobody was seeing my white flag. I was close to passing out. Finally, Mike pulled Col Gus off me and the match ended.

We literally went as close to the corners of the CO's room as space would allow. Col Gus sat on his bed and I was sitting on a chair diagonal from him, trying to breathe. Mike and the XO were sitting in opposite corners of the room. I guess they were debriefing the match. I could not catch my breath, and my throat was killing me each time I tried to swallow. I could not talk, but I could think. I grew up in Kentucky, and the more I thought about what just happened, the more I began to think there is nobody going to do that to me. I thought about it for a few seconds then leaped up from my seat, got a couple of good steps and drove into the CO's chest with my right shoulder. Then I began throwing punches. Mike and the XO quickly pulled me off, but I had enough of a head start to get my point across. That move truly ended the match.

We left the CO's hooch, and I headed to my room with Mike. I suspected I was out of the squadron, but at that point, did not much care. Saturday morning, I found Marx to ask him how much trouble I was in. He said he did not know. I asked if I should go see Col Gus this morning and he said the skipper was on a cross-country flight. Marx also said Col Gus may have sustained a couple of cracked ribs.

I was pretty bummed after that night. Of course, my friends heard about the big match, so it was the topic of discussion when we met for a late breakfast. The next topic was what job I was going to be assigned to, out of the squadron, when Col Gus returned from his cross-country. I knew I was gone from the squadron after last night.

I had never been much of a fighter, just too small, too weak, and too slow. I, previously, had only fought a couple of times in high school, and had one large one at the Air Force O'Club in Yokota AFB in Japan on my previous visit in 1970. There, I was having a discussion with an Air Force LtCol, the CO of an F-4 squadron based at Yokota. He was making fun of Marine Phantoms in Vietnam. I reminded him that we were a combat crew and that he patrolled the skies of northern Japan in safety as a non-combatant. After a bit he thought that Ben, my RIO, and I ought to leave the O'Club and pushed me into the door that happened to be locked. I bounced back, turned, and with a very slow and wide roundhouse swing hit him just behind his left ear. He was knocked out and fell to the floor on his back. I wanted to apologize to him. I located a pitcher of water, put my foot on his chest and poured water on his face. There's more to the story, but that was the only big fight in my life, until the recent one with Col Gus!

I can say the hours waiting to hear my fate in 513 passed at glacial speed. Saturday afternoon I walked around the base trying to get into conversations with my buds, but my brain was thinking how badly I screwed up. Sunday was more of the same. The CO returned Sunday afternoon, but I did not see him. The XO told me to check in with Col Gus at 8 o'clock Monday morning. I was uncertain as to what to expect when I knocked on the door and was called into the office. After I reported in, Col Gus had me take a seat, looked over my records and said, "I'm glad to have you in the squadron, Captain." He assigned me to be the safety officer. This news was stunning. I thanked him and disappeared as quickly as possible from the area. I could not wait to tell my buds I was still in the squadron. I never heard another word about the incident from Col Gus.

After a sine wave of emotions, I was back where I started Friday afternoon. This was a complete reset. It was great to be "home" again. These guys were my family. I flew the next day and was right where I left off after leaving 542.

· · ·

I now joined Mike, Pat Owen, Ted Herman, Win Rorabaugh, Snyds, Buc, Snacks, Few, and my other friends. I met Capt. Ken Shrum there. He had been in 513 for a long time and decided to stay with us for another year. Ken was the first Marine pilot to get **1,000** flight hours in the Harrier. That was a feat. Ken and I became good friends. Then I met Capt. Bobby Light. Flash was his call sign. He was a Naval Academy grad but played it low key. He was a good West Virginia boy, and we became close friends and enjoyed spending time together. I also met 1stLt Skip Klinefelter. Skip was an anomaly because he was a Harrier pilot when only a 1stLt. There were not many in the program at that time. He was a bit older and started flying about the same time he received his first pair of cowboy boots, probably around 10 years old. Skip had much more total flight time than many of the captains. His commercial flight time translated well to the Harrier. He was brash, obnoxious, loyal, and seemed to be the perfect Marine lieutenant. So, the stage was set for a fun and rewarding year in WESTPAC. I could not wait to get started.

...

The MAG-12 group commander, Col Bob. Lewis (Snake), was leaving a few days after I arrived. He came to give us his departure talk. The word was he was not a fan of the Harrier. He said a few things in his goodbye speech, but the quote we all remember was, "You Harrier pilots are just a bunch of hard-dick prima donnas!" Since the original 513 pilots, except for Ken Shrum, had returned home and we had just joined the squadron, Col Lewis did not know anyone in the squadron very well. He had to have based this remark on our predecessors, who obviously gave us a tough act to follow. We could not help but take that as both a compliment and a standard we needed to live up to.

Col Lewis turned over MAG-12 to Col Leo LeBlanc. Col LeBlanc and Col Lewis brought their wives over to celebrate the change of command and the Marine Corps birthday ball. The ball is a great tradition for all Marines. After a few drinks and completion of the serious festivities, one of our captains decided to convince Col LeBlanc and his party that he could pull the tablecloth from under the plates and drinks and not spill one thing. He professed he did it all the time. All of us certainly encouraged him and told all who would listen he could do it, every time. The captain negotiated for a bit and then received permission from the colonel to pull the tablecloth. It was truly a sight to see. The drinks spilled, food, dishes and flatware flew everywhere. Col LeBlanc asked all of us who had done it, and we told him we did not know. He was new to the Air Group. He told us it happened so quickly he did not get a good look at the perpetrator. He promised us he would find the culprit before his tour was up. That was our first meeting with the new group CO.

We went back to our seats for the remainder of the festivities. I had been tossing ice cubes forward and was told by an older tech rep to stop. We were all fired up after the tablecloth trick and were having a great time being rowdy. I started tossing ice cubes and once again, I was told to stop. Once again, I continued. This time, the group XO, LtCol Jimmy Green, came back and asked me to come to his office in the morning, Sunday morning. I told him how late I would be staying up and begged off until Monday. He said, "OK, I'll see you Monday at

8 o'clock." What a dumb move on my part. I could have had it over in a few hours, but no, I had to prolong it until Monday. Whatever debauchery I planned for Sunday with my buddies did not happen. My mind was not up for it.

Monday morning, I checked into the group adjutant's office for my appointment. Col Green called me to his office. I stood at attention and awaited my fate. He said a few things, then came around in front of the desk, looked me in the eye and said the following words. "Captain Capito, remember this; I won't always be your group XO." He gave me a hug and said, "Now get the hell out of here." All that was said with a smile on his face. I never forgot that moment.

In about 20 days I had put my career in harm's way more times than I had in my entire eight years in the Marine Corps. I knew this behavior had to change, and it did, somewhat.

POSTSCRIPT: Some 13 years later, I was the MAG-12 XO and had been promoted to LtCol, I was sitting in the same office, behind the same desk and probably the same chair. It also happened that I was the acting Group commander. There was a 1stLt from one of our squadrons who had gotten himself in a lot of trouble at the O'Club the night before. He challenged the base CO about something and said a few words that landed him in serious trouble. His detachment Officer In Charge (OIC) called me to say they were leaving for a commitment the following morning and wanted to know what I was going to do to his lieutenant. Later that morning, the base CO called me to ensure I understood the seriousness of the issue at hand. "Yes, sir!" was my answer to him; I had known him well from my F-4 days and was not a fan of his.

The lieutenant arrived, I called him in, kept him at attention, lectured him for a bit, walked around my desk, looked him in the eye and said, "Lieutenant, remember this, I won't always be your group XO." I gave him a hug and said, "Now get the hell out of here." What goes around can come around. I loved it!

. . .

All the time we were flying cross-countries we were busy during the week going to the target ranges in Japan at Mt. Fuji, South Korea, Okinawa and the Philippines. The XO was able to get some of us to conduct shipboard work with LPDs, which were small ships with very small wooden landing decks normally used for helicopter landings. We were also able to get flight time in WESTPAC. We were getting almost twice the monthly flight time here as we were getting at Cherry Point. Finally, we were the tip of the spear!

Capt. Bobby Light greeted by BGen K. Smith USMC after landing at a new forward site in Korea.

2: Squadron Life

Col Gus was a tremendous CO. He gave us guidance in the highest tradition of the Corps, set the pace, and we tried to keep him in sight so as to follow his lead. Most of the day-to-day operational decisions were made by the majors in the squadron and Snacks was the AMO. We were essentially right back where we had been prior to Cherry Point. Squadron morale quickly climbed back to the Beaufort levels. We brought over the senior SNCOs and many troops from Cherry Point. They were happy, the troops were very busy, but they enjoyed the nomadic life of 513 in the Far East. Life was good again.

The flying in Japan was off the charts. Soon after I arrived, we were dropping bombs on target ranges in South Korea. We were in Okinawa working with ground Marines. We flew near Mount Fuji to work with other ground Marines. We went to NAS Cubi Point in the Philippines for air-to-air work and ordnance sorties. We conducted shipboard ops. I flew 80 hours during the first three months. This was what a Harrier squadron with an adequate supply of parts, combined with great leadership from the top down, was capable of doing.

We took cross-country flights to Korea, Okinawa, other bases in Japan, the Philippines, and even transited through Taiwan on occasion. It was a Far East tour.

Normal flying from Iwakuni could be challenging. While we were on a local flight the weather could go to landing minimums in a short period of time. While flying in the area, we flew a good bit of actual instrument time. There was a lot of water between Iwakuni and anywhere else we went. We were flying a single-engine plane, but we had supreme confidence in the Harrier's Rolls Royce Pegasus engine.

Some of our tech reps accompanied us to Iwakuni. Dave Clegg came with us; Duncan Hastie, our Smiths Industries rep, too. We met some new ones, and they were all good. We first met one of our favorite reps, Frank Armanno, in Iwakuni. He was the McDonnell Douglas rep assigned to the Harrier and was there with the original 513 pilots and troops. Frank was one of those people who could make things happen in the maintenance department. He could find parts where there were

153

none and offer training when needed. We leaned on him hard for many aircraft issues. He was a man about town and was able to procure a Harrier model for $40. A few of us purchased one for our "I love me desks." Frank found a home with us.

Since we were going to be there for a year, four of us decided to buy a car. In Japan, when you bought a car as cheap as we were looking to purchase, the requirement to buy government insurance cost more than the car. The Japanese manufactured autos were very small but, when required, we could fit the four of us in it. It ran fine until we gave it a Harrier camouflage paint job. After we did that, it had problems all the time. We used it around the base, took a couple road trips in Japan, once going to Sasebo, and took it by ferry to Okinawa for a long deployment.

Ted, Pat Owen, and a few of the others began to ride bikes in Iwakuni. The indigenous populace was very respectful to a person on a bike. The mamasans (older women in a position of authority in Japan or East Asia) would be on the road riding a bike so fully loaded with groceries and staples that they had trouble seeing the road. No one would ever hit or ever bother one of these ladies. As bike riders we were afforded the same respect.

From my perspective, the months were passing quickly. I was having the time of my life flying, hanging out and enjoying life. I loved flying the Harrier and I loved my buddies. It was the most rewarding time of my life.

I started a "Super Giant Club" in the squadron. We had one in Dallas. It was crazy at the time but so much fun. Eight of us finished the initiation. The criteria were simple: work and fly each day, close the club each night and do this from Friday through Sunday night the following week. We mostly ate free food at the club. The good part about it all was that the heavies (the upper echelons of rank), pretty much ignored us and left us alone.

3: NAS Cubi Point

NAS Cubi Point was the air station co-located with the Naval Base at Subic Bay in the Philippines. It was known for its shenanigans by the officers and enlisted men alike from throughout the services during the Vietnam conflict. We certainly attempted to uphold, or outdo, any of their previous misdeeds. We spent a few months there and thoroughly enjoyed ourselves. The base was renovating the runway and half of it was closed for repair. The Navy wanted to operate any aircraft that were able to on the other usable end of the runway. They invited us to come down during the repair cycle. Once the work on half the runway was completed, we switched ends, remaining there until the work on the entire runway was completed.

The entire area was a tropical paradise. There were small hills covered by jungle for the most part that almost surrounded one of the most beautiful bays in the world. Not far away were large rice and sugar plantations. The area has a lot of history. Discovered by Ferdinand Magellan in 1521, the Philippines were claimed as a colony for the Spanish empire and were occupied by them until the Spanish American War in 1898. The US opened the base in 1901 and lost it to the Japanese in 1942. We regained the base in 1944, and later it was the primary naval base and airfield supporting the Vietnam War. Cubi was only a few miles from Clark AFB, a very large USAF facility, and reasonably close to Manila.

From time to time, while we were there, an aircraft carrier pulled into port. It is a wonderful, majestic sight to watch a carrier coming into the pier alongside the runway. There were many sailors on the deck, in formation, wearing white uniforms, waiting for their moment to visit Olongapo City, the town located right outside the base. Olongapo was the closest place people in the 1970s could find to replicate Dodge City of the 1870s. There were bars, houses of ill repute, honky-tonks, and many people waiting to relieve sailors and Marines of their money.

The first time I went to Cubi Point was 1970. I went there from Vietnam with three F-4 squadron mates and a helo pilot to attend jungle survival training. We had to check out Olongapo City. We were briefed to all stay together and take small amounts of money into town. Four of us from our squadron stayed together and enjoyed the sights, drinking famous San Miguel beer. Our helo pilot friend decided to go to town on his own. He was a former college wrestler and explained to us that no scrawny Filipino could take him on. He told us not to worry because he could take care of himself. So, we did not!

The four of us finished our tour of the town and returned to base early evening, awaiting the start of the jungle survival training. The next morning when we went to class, the helo pilot was not there. He arrived in class about two hours late. We could not wait to hear his story at the next break. It turns out, he could take on one Filipino, but five or more with switchblades were a bit much for him. He returned to base without any clothes or ID card. It took him lots of time to establish his identity with the Marines guarding the gate. Olongapo City could be one rough town.

It seemed as though not much had changed since I was there the first time. Trapper told me about a wonderful place to go when I arrived. When he was there with 513, while I was still at Cherry Point, he sent me a letter asking me to send him all the Mario Lanza cassette tapes I had or could find. Trapper and I were big fans of Mario. It turns out, a fellow by the name of Ernie Gaines, who owned and operated Gaines Beach across Subic Bay from Cubi Pt., was also a Mario Lanza fan. The most reliable rumor about Ernie was that he retired from the Navy after WW-II and remained in the Philippines. He built boats for many years, but that venture was ultimately closed in favor of providing a clean, private beach for sailors and Marines stationed at Cubi or Subic Bay. He hosted many events when the ships made port visits during the Vietnam War.

To get to Gaines Beach, you rode in a single person banca boat. These boats had one outrigger with an engine mid-ship turning a long shaft powering the prop. When more than one person was going at the same time there were races to get to Gaines Beach. Once there, you could spend quality time on the beach and stay the night if you wanted. There was plenty of food to eat and lots to drink. It was a fun place to visit, and we did often.

We were there one day when Ernie's wife told us about a carrier coming into port. It was unscheduled because it had an elevator damaged in rough seas. That movement was considered secret information on base but Ernie's girls knew all about it. When it docked, we were there when Ernie put more than $15,000 in his pocket from the ship's special service division to fund the party. And what a party it was!

Col Gus, the XO and Major Eik did not accompany us on most of our adventures. Major Sabow, Stranger, would come along with us providing some field grade leadership. Our group became tighter and tighter during our months in Cubi. We had no contact with the squadrons at Cherry Point. This was a time when it felt like we were the only Harrier squadron in the world.

• • •

The squadron was flying ordnance sorties almost every day that we were in Cubi Point. We went to Wild Horse Creek target area to drop live ordnance. This was an unmanned target. That meant there were no safety officers or FACs on site. We would make a clearing pass over the area to make sure there were no obstructions, animals, or people, then we would begin our bombing runs. If we had both bombs and rockets, we usually fired the rockets first, then dropped the bombs. There was a group of Filipino men who would run out and mark the bombs for salvage each time we dropped. Then they would disappear somewhere and wait for us to drop another bomb and then they would mark it. These guys had it figured out. Selling metal from the bombs supplemented their income. This salvage operation had been in business for many years.

One early afternoon, it was very hot, humidity was off the charts, and I was checking on some airplanes on the flight line as the safety officer. Major Sabow came running up to me and said something to the effect, "Caps, we killed two people at Wild Horse Creek, you're going out there in the helo to see what's going on." I stammered a bit, said, "Yes, sir" and walked over to the helo for the ride to the village. I was in my flight suit and had no clue what to expect. The ride was very short, so I had no time to even think about what I was getting into, and that was probably a blessing.

We landed in one of the most beautiful places I had ever been. It was a small primitive village on the beach overlooking the Pacific Ocean. The houses were small huts. There were no vehicles other than a few motorbikes. Tall trees shielded the village from the sun, rain, and the wind to some degree.

It was late afternoon when I climbed out of the helo. There were about 50 people gathered in a group: men, women, and kids, many crying. The helo was going to take off, leaving me there alone. A friend of mine, Capt. Charlie Davis, was working with some Marine ground troops. When he saw the helo land, he brought them over to check it out. He helped convince the helo pilot to stick around for a bit.

When we looked toward the ocean, the sun was setting. The shape of the sun as it was beginning to rest on the horizon resembled a mantle clock. The color was almost red. This was, to this day, the most beautiful sunset I have ever seen. The setting, coupled with the reason I was there, was completely surreal to me.

The mission I was given was way past my pay grade. The plan was for me to get the closest relatives of the two men back to Cubi on the helo. A young man who spoke English came up to me. It turned out both men were married with kids, and their widows were looking at me like I was their killer. Initially, it was a bit unnerving.

I told the translator how sorry I was and asked him what happened. He told me, "Normally you pilots shoot all the rockets, then drop bombs. Today, the flight shot some rockets, then dropped bombs, then finished firing rockets on the last run. Those rockets killed the two men." The translator told me they thought the flight was finished with rockets after the first pass. I negotiated with him to get the wives on the helo to take them back to Cubi Point to work with the base legal officer. The translator, with the two new widows and I, took off for the short helo ride to the base. I saluted goodbye to Charlie Davis as thanks for his help keeping the helo on the ground.

After a few minutes in the helo, the translator told me what the women wanted. They wanted to go the PX and would like to be paid $50 each for their husbands. I told the translator I could promise nothing. They would need to work it out with the base legal officer. The helo landed on the flight line. I took my charges and escorted them to meet the base legal officer, along with additional officers whom I did not know. I said goodbye to the ladies again, telling them over and over how sorry I was for their loss.

A couple of days later, I heard they each signed a release, had a fun time in the PX, and spent their $50 there. I did not confirm this story but had no reason to believe it was not true.

This experience was an insight to a life unknown to me. Two or three of us would spend $50 on food and beer at the Cubi Point Officer's Club, thinking nothing about it. It was hard for me to believe the U.S. Government would pay these two women 50 bucks apiece for their lost husbands, let them spend it in the PX, then call it even. That experience is another one I will never forget.

I think the US abused the Filipino people. You got a haircut in Japan, probably cost $2.00. You get one in the Philippines, $.75. We paid them nothing to work on the base; even back then I felt this was The Ugly American story in real life.

• • •

The Cubi Point bar was a favorite of naval aviators for many years. There was a tremendous amount of history associated with the club. The Filipino people were creative people. Sometime during the Vietnam War, squadrons returning from the line, flying into North Vietnam, would stay there until the ship was ready to return to the waters off the coast of North Vietnam. Most of the squadrons had commemorative plaques made with the names of the pilots engraved on them and left them in the club for future pilots to see. There were a few Filipino stores that made these plaques. Their handmade work was nothing short of art on many occasions.

The first plaques were reasonably simple: the squadron name and the squadron mascot colorfully placed along with the names of officers and the dates of the tour. As the war began to drag on, the plaques were often joined by almost full-size versions of the squadron mascot or some other item saying, "We were here." The original 513 pilots had a plaque made and so did we. All the other Harrier squadrons who made it to the P.I. had one made as well. Many people donated helmets and other flight gear to decorate the club. There definitely was a bigger and better plaque competition going on between squadrons.

Downstairs there was a simulated aircraft carrier deck and a cockpit mock-up on a sled that was launched by air pressure toward the swimming pool. You rode in the cockpit and tried to catch a wire before it went in to the pool. The more drinks you had, the harder it was to stay dry. Later that was removed and the pool was filled in; too many intrepid pilots had injured themselves trying to prove their prowess.

Fortunately, the Cubi O'Club has been rebuilt at the Naval Aviation Museum in Pensacola, FL complete with the original plaques and other donated gear. It is a museum within a museum.

• • •

While we were in Cubi, we FAM'ed Colonel LeBlanc in the Harrier. He was a good pilot and a great guy. We enjoyed flying with him and he enjoyed spending time with us. He had just been selected for brigadier general. He was the first general officer many of us ever knew. I'm not sure he ever found out the name of the captain who pulled the tablecloth off the table, but after spending time with us flying the Harrier, I'm pretty sure he didn't care.

Col LeBlanc was scheduled to take a Harrier back to Iwakuni and Ken Shrum was selected to be his wingman. The Colonel was the flight leader. After takeoff, Ken was checking with him while climbing to altitude to confirm his wing fuel tank transfer. After leveling off at altitude there was not much radio chatter. Ken told us he began to realize two things were going on. First, the navigation was not tracking correctly, and second, there were altitude deviations much larger than normal. He said initially he was somewhat reluctant to address these items with Col LeBlanc, now a brigadier general selectee. He finally made a call on FM asking what radial (heading) the colonel showed them to be on with the idea of saying perhaps there were some differences in the planes that needed to be resolved.

Ken was alarmed at Col LeBlanc's response. His speech was very slurred, and he did not answer the inquiry. Ken immediately moved to close formation and asked him to verify he was on 100 percent oxygen and also confirm his oxygen warning light was not on. The colonel looked down and Ken assumed he was checking the system, but he did not answer. Then Ken took the flight lead and was waving and pointing downward to descend. Col LeBlanc looked over, nodded, and Ken initiated a very rapid descent, which was both a good and bad idea. They needed to get down fast, but the colonel was not following very well in formation. Ken had to level off several times to keep him with the flight and had to do a circle to rejoin at the bottom. At 10,000 feet, Col LeBlanc revived and communicated he had oxygen, but the regulator was not working. This was later verified. He did not seem fully alert, so Ken did some really fast fuel/time/distance calculations to see where they could go. The winds favored going to Kadena versus turning back, so they pressed on, ended up with enough fuel, obviously declared a medical emergency and landed straight in. Col LeBlanc went to the hospital and the doc wanted to keep him overnight. Ken told us Col LeBlanc did not look so good, and he thought it was a pretty close call. They went to Iwakuni the next day and everything worked out well.

. . .

We often used Clark AFB as our turnaround base. We could increase the number of sorties we could fly and reduce the maintenance load by landing at Clark after one flight, refuel, and then get a second one out. We flew many low-level navigation flights and air-to-air sorties while living in Cubi.

One afternoon, Skip and Buc were sent to Clark AFB to do an airshow. As Skip tells it, when they landed it was hotter than hell! Knowing they had to do an airshow, they decided to remove the explosive devices from the hard points on the wing pylons. They were used to jettison the fuel tanks in an emergency. Then they manually released the empty 300 gallon drops from one aircraft for the airshow. The AF had told Buc they had no one available on that short notice who was capable of doing the drop tank removal, so they just did it themselves!

The AF ramp officer got to them just as they were setting the second drop in the grass by the ramp. He was beside himself. It was no big deal to Buc and Skip, and Harrier pilots had done this before for various reasons. Skip said they had the ramp officer "mostly" calmed down until Buc handed him the explosive cartridges and asked if he could have them secured until they needed them when the tanks were put back on the plane. It was almost too much for the ramp officer to handle.

They arrived early, as Marines have tendencies to do, and since it was so hot and humid, they stripped down to their blue T-shirts, flight boots, red nylon running shorts and sunglasses and sat under the wing of an A/C to wait until the start of the airshow in a couple hours. Soon after they disrobed, a couple of Hueys (UH-1) swooped in and landed. Skip said they thought it was no big deal until a squad of Filipino guards jumped out of the first Huey armed to the gills with automatic weapons, magazines inserted, looking very, very, serious and deployed into a classic defensive perimeter. As the second Huey touched down, the base CO, an AF full bird, went directly to the chopper to offer his assistance to the deplaning passengers. Buc and Skip then proceeded to put their covers (hats in the Marines are called covers) on because they had no idea who it was or why those people were being treated like royalty.

The entourage came directly their way led by a very well kempt black-haired lady accompanied by her bevy of gorgeous young Filipinas. Still not yet sure of the identity of the visitor who wanted to see the Harriers, meet the Marines who were flying them, Skip and Buc were standing at attention awaiting some explanation. The lady got to Skip first, standing at attention in his PT uniform. When she approached Skip, she put out her right hand, and he had no idea what she wanted him to do! So just like in the movies, our boy Skip took her hand in his right hand, leaned forward, and kissed the top of her hand. She never even flinched, she just said, "Oh, how continental" as he released her hand and went back to the position of attention. She then walked over to Buc who was also standing tall in front of his plane, shook his hand, and then the entourage returned to the chopper and departed. They soon found out the lady they just met was none other than Imelda Marcos!

A couple weeks after we returned to Iwakuni I received a letter from the Cubi Point Naval Air Station safety officer. This sort of correspondence usually filtered down from the wing to the group, then the squadron. This was sent directly to the CO of VMA-513. Col Gus sent it to me to answer, since I was the squadron safety officer. So, I did. The safety officer referenced the Harrier division (three plane) take off from Cubi a couple weeks past. He was jogging at the time. He thought the takeoff was a dangerous maneuver that only the Blue Angels should be allowed to perform. He asked the CO to have the 513 Safety Officer brief the pilots about these maneuvers and then assure him they would not happen again at Cubi Point.

Essentially, in the first paragraph, I told the Cubi Point safety officer that what he described was a maneuver we practiced on occasion but realized some people did not think that squadrons should do this type of formation takeoff. And as the safety officer, I would brief the pilots not to perform a division takeoff at Cubi Point. In the next paragraph, I assured him the pilots in the flight were briefed about their behavior and disciplined accordingly. In the last paragraph, I asked him how did it look? And, I signed it, Captain John Capito, Dash Three on the takeoff? VMA-513 Aviation Safety Officer. I was grounded for a week after sending the letter; well deserved, I might add!

There were a couple of places to visit in the P.I. Some had a chance to visit Corregidor, and a Rest and Recuperation (R&R) base or two. Manila was not far, and I suspect most of us made it there once or twice. The Cubi tour was very beneficial to our training and readiness.

4: Kadena Air Force Base

We went on our first deployment to Kadena Air Force Base to work with the Marines in the northern training area. The Marine Corps had a helicopter base at Futenma, but jets were not allowed to land there. Deploying squadrons shared space with the US Air Force at Kadena AFB. It was a huge base and had been used for support missions during the Vietnam War and for a while B-52s flew out of there. It was many times larger than Iwakuni. The Air Force operated the SR-71 Habu reconnaissance plane from Kadena as well. The Habu trumped the Harrier with aviation aficionados. In 1975-76, the American military presence in Okinawa was in a drawdown period. During the war, there were many airmen and sailors stationed there with their families. The DOD operated many schools on the numerous bases located around the island. Even as it was being slowly reduced in size, the large civilian population on the island made you think you were back in the US.

The first time we checked in to Kadena, we wasted no time in letting everyone know we had arrived. The XO told us to throw a party and invite everyone we could find. We did. We held the party on a hill close to our BOQ. Food and entertainment were first class. This is the first time I realized that Bobby Light (Flash), was a connoisseur of fine, or not so fine, wines. Siepert (Mammal) and another captain entertained us with a couple of skits. Siepert was the hunter and the other captain was the buffalo. Mike would stalk the buffalo until he was able to get a shot. The buffalo would die in agony to a great deal of sympathy from a bunch of slightly inebriated Marines and guests. Then Mike became a deep-sea fisherman. He hooked his fish and they engaged in an epic battle to bring the fish on board the boat to the cheers and applause of the adoring crowd. Sounds crazy as I write it, but it was a great time watching this play out.

We flew a lot in Kadena. On a cross-country flight from Kadena to Cubi Pt., Mike, Skip, and I headed to Ching Chuan Kang, (CCK), a Republic of China Air Force Base in Taiwan. This occurred in mid July 1976. The entire world had just celebrated the 200th anniversary of the USA. We headed to CCK unaware that a small tiff had developed between Taiwan and the US. We had a normal takeoff and climb to altitude. At altitude, Skip realized his drop tanks wouldn't transfer fuel, and he began to worry about having enough fuel for the flight. Mike and I had completed transferring our tanks, but even without the external fuel, we had fuel for our scheduled cross-country flight. Skip climbed to a higher altitude and pulled away from us. Mike and I kept him in sight and caught up with him for the landing. We all landed safely at CCK, expecting to gas up and press on to Cubi Point.

CCK had a huge concrete ramp and parking area. It was constructed of many acres of concrete. Once on the ground, we noticed a Navy A-7 parked by itself on the ramp. When we came to a stop and climbed out of our planes, we were met by a Taiwanese general. He refused to allow us fuel. The three of us discussed this among ourselves for a while. We had to have fuel to continue and were rather uncertain of our next move. We met with the general's aide, who spoke perfect English. He explained that there was a situation between our government and theirs, and our aircraft would be held on the ground, not allowed to leave, just like the Navy A-7 sitting on the ramp. We countered that there were no Notices to Airmen (NOTAMS) stating we could not get fuel, or that our aircraft would be impounded upon landing. If there had been, we would not have landed there. The aide and general discussed this situation for some time and the aide returned. The general gave us the fuel and once we were refueled, he allowed us 10 minutes to be off the air base. It was close to becoming an ugly situation. We did not want our names and pictures in the paper for starting a confrontation with Taiwan, but we were not happy.

This was a ticklish situation. We could not file a flight plan due to time constraints. The general and his staff remained close by, keeping an eye on us during the entire refueling operation. When refueling was completed, the three of us climbed in, started up, and instead of taxiing all the way to the runway, we performed short takeoffs from the large ramp. I know we were blowing anything on the ramp to the rear toward the general and his staff. Thinking we might have left on a bad note, we flew probably 50 miles from CCK between 100 and 200 feet, staying below their radar. We thought they might launch fighters after us. They didn't. I guess we were not worth the hassle, and it was good riddance to let us leave. We popped to altitude and filed our flight plan in the air to Cubi Pt. and landed there.

We were really a tight group of pilots. Some of the captains brought their wives over to spend some time in Kadena, or the P.I., or Iwakuni. Four or five of us were sitting around waiting for the Air Force bus to take us from the billeting area to the hangar. One of the captains was asked how much longer his wife was going to be there. He held up his right hand, spread it out and said, "Five more days, fuckers. Count 'em. Five more days." That became a line that has survived though the years.

5: Change of Command

Snyds and I arrived in Iwakuni about two months after the majority of the squadron was already in place. In early summer, 513 had a change of command. Col Gus was headed to the states and we hated to see him go. He was a good man and he quickly earned our respect as a pilot and leader. The time I spent with him was a learning experience for sure. The XO and Major Eik departed for the States earlier than the rest of us. Sabs became the XO.

LtCol Bob Reed became our new CO. He had been the CO of VMA-231 a couple of years earlier. It was certainly unusual for someone to have command of two different Harrier squadrons back then. I do not think many of us knew much about Col Reed, but it did not take long to get to know him. I think most COs of that era and maybe even in today's squadrons tend to lean toward micromanagement. Col Reed was anything but that. He was a little misleading in one area. He probably crowded the weight limits for a Marine, but when he put on his PT gear, watch out, he was a runner.

Snacks, the Maintenance Officer, was leaving the squadron and we had no majors to take that job. I asked Sabs to put in a good word for me. He must have done so because Col Reed called me to his office to ask if I wanted to be the AMO. I jumped at the chance. What a gift for me. Our availability was starting to decline. Once again, parts were becoming an issue.

My first day on the job is still fresh in my memory. The skipper wanted to fly to Cubi on his first cross-country. He launched and was on his way. Life was good. About two hours later, I had a call from Kadena that his plane was hard down. He did not make it to Cubi.

I was happy to join the ranks of captains who had become Harrier squadron Aviation Maintenance Officers: Duke Savage, Jim Hajduk, Jerry Fitzgerald, Larry Roberson, and Joe Gallo, Jim Barksdale, Terry Mattke, Jon Dempsey, and I am sure there are others I missed.

Col Reed followed the same leadership principles as the reserves I was with in Dallas. He gave general guidance, asked if you had any questions, and then said to come back if you had any problems. He let you do your job without looking over your shoulder or calling every few minutes to ask questions. It was fun to keep him informed about the maintenance department. The troops loved him, and he was on the hangar deck often. He knew their names and talked with them in a style all his own. With Col Gus gone we were fortunate to have Col Reed take over the command.

· · ·

When Major Sabow became the XO, I had to ask Col Reed for my first request for assistance. The XO was calling me five to 10 times a day to ask questions. Col Reed shut him down. One time I started to ask Sabs why he avoided the AMO job the entire time he was in the Harrier program. But I did not. Maintenance is a fluid operation, and he never had any interest in getting involved with it. In the Harrier community there might have been some career risk for a major who performed poorly. Not so much for a captain. He was not happy that I invoked Col Reed to cut off his phone calls. Will Rogers has always been my hero. Like Will, I never met a person I did not like, but sometimes I had to meet a person more than once. Sabs was sort of like that. I really liked Sabs; I think we were good friends. He was very competent, professional, and fun to be around. The new XO could be full of himself on occasion, and those were the times he was most vulnerable to good-natured harassment from the captains.

We were flying in Kadena on a short-term DET there. I was flying a test flight for engine performance and completed that portion of the flight. There was lots of gas left over, so I checked in with the duty officer asking if anyone was airborne. The SDO told me Siepert was also airborne. We joined up and did some ACM and landed together. The XO was waiting for me when I came back to the ready room. He approached me to say he was going to pull my maintenance check pilot designation because I flew the plane for reasons other than the check. I told him I finished the "engine check" portion of the flight and just burned up the gas with Mike. He was hot about it and I eased away from the ready room. Nothing happened.

Later in the week, Sabs was on a test flight and I was in the ready room. He finished the check flight portion of his flight and found

Callahan (Few) airborne. They also flew some ACM. I was waiting for Sabs when he landed. I told him, "Sir, I'm going to have to speak with the CO about revoking your check flight designation because you were flying ACM on a test flight." It was a gotcha moment and we both laughed about it. He was a good XO for 513 and held the job for quite a while.

6: VMA-231, VMA-542 and VMAT-203

While we were having this wonderful time in WESTPAC, we essentially forgot about the rest of the Harrier program. We did not care a whole lot about them because we were too busy locked up in our own Far East world. We were the **tip of the spear!** In those days civilian communication was difficult and expensive, so unless you had a very good reason you did not make many calls home. Letters were the primary means of finding out what was going on with the family and other Harrier squadrons. The military phone lines were essentially off limits to check in to say hi to someone in the CONUS. We had not interacted to a great degree with 231 or 203 while in 542 at Cherry Point. Little by little, the longer our tight group stayed together, the more we became isolated from the rest of the Harrier community.

One thing was true, the more we flew the better we became. There was no doubt in our minds that we were the best trained Harrier pilots and therefore the best Harrier squadron in the Marine Corps. This isolation from the East Coast squadrons most likely helped breed institutional solipsism (the theory that the self is all that can be known to exist.). We knew we were the best and did not care much about the rest.

However, while we were in Japan the east coast Harrier squadrons were just as busy as we were and as well were flying the same challenging sorties as we did. We just did not have any visibility on what they were doing.

From January to June 1976, 231 deployed to Roosevelt Roads, located in Puerto Rico (PR) for a two-week weapons DET. Then there was a sidewinder missile exercise. Next, they spent three weeks in Yuma, and some members of the squadron flew a trans-Caribbean flight. They also found time to perform numerous airshows and static displays. During the same period, 542 returned and became a formidable unit about six months after the change of command. Major Spicer was able to get all of 542's 20 Harriers in the air at one time around the end of January. They had a three-week Yuma DET, spent time in Camp Drum, NY, had two DETs to Twentynine Palms, CA and participated in Solid Shield as well as multiple small DETs up and down the East Coast.

...

VMA-231 began workups in June 1976 for a cruise on the USS Franklin D. Roosevelt (FDR, CV-42)). 231 lost one AV-8 during the workup for the carrier deployment due to engine failure, but the pilot safely ejected and was fine. Their workups were completed in early September and they arrived onboard the ship later in the month. The cruise lasted until April 1977. During that tour, they cross-decked from the Roosevelt to the Guam for a real-world contingency in Africa. They were constantly demonstrating shipboard capabilities of the Harrier.

We did not quite understand how VMA-231's shipboard deployment would impact us in the Far East. With 231 now aboard a ship, our spear tip turned into a pitchfork with two tines. 513 no longer enjoyed the highest priority for parts as the only squadron deployed from CONUS. 231, now on the ship FDR, became equal to, if not a higher priority for parts than we were. They still called Cherry Point home, close to the NARF, and I suspected they enjoyed some hometown support while 513 was out of sight and out of mind.

VMA-542 had a good run going. They now had good aircraft availability and a strong lineup of pilots. They had one airplane crash during a rehearsal for the air wing change of command. The pilot ejected, but the aircraft was returned to flight status. A month later there was a second mishap. The pilot was okay, but the plane suffered strike damage. The last half of 1976, they performed 18 air shows. The squadron had Harriers at Twentynine Palms for two, one-week deployments. 542 continued to train Harrier pilots and completed shipboard work with the USS Trenton and the USS Guam.

...

VMAT-203 became a Harrier training squadron in June 1976. The squadron now had three TAV-8As and an unknown number of AV-8As. They no longer trained A-4 aircrew. 203 was tasked to complete 40 pilots a year to send to the three gun squadrons. Also beginning in 1976, VMAT-203 was able to provide the fleet with a 60 percent combat qualified contingent of Harrier pilots. Prior to this, the gun squadrons had to bring the newly arrived pilots to this percentage of combat qualification before moving on to advanced sorties. Receiving a pilot this far into the training cycle was a huge improvement over what had been accomplished in the recent past and made the life in the gun squadrons more efficient in getting new pilots fully combat qualified.

While our east coast brethren were doing well, 513 was starting to experience aircraft availability pains. Four full-up and hard charging Harrier squadrons still continued to tax the supply system, the manufacturers and vendors. The community looked good to the world, but there were many supply and support issues waiting to take their toll.

7: Summertime

Once you got to know Sabow, he was a delightful person to be around. Mike and I often followed Sabs and Few on cross-country flights, landing at the same base on numerous occasions. On the first flight they left Iwakuni a few minutes prior to our departure. We were all headed to Kunsan AFB in South Korea. After refueling we were all going to Kadena for the night. The weather in Kunsan was awful. Mike and I utilized a section formation approach for landing, taking separation when the runway was finally in sight. It worked well, but the rain, ceiling and visibility were marginal for landing and we were most likely below landing minimums. Mike and I landed with no issues, then proceeded to base ops to file a flight plan. After that was completed, we walked to the cafeteria to grab something to eat. Stranger and Few were already there and finished eating a few minutes before we arrived. On the way out of the cafeteria, Sabs stopped at our table to tell us in no uncertain terms not to perform a section takeoff because of the bad weather. We nodded our heads in agreement, and after he left the cafeteria, we briefed the section takeoff. The weather we had flown through was solid overcast with clouds in excess of 35,000 feet. Without a radar if you did an individual takeoff and could not keep sight of the flight leader due to weather, there was no way to join up the flight once you left the runway. Mike and I briefed the weather, the flight, then ate and headed to the flight line.

After completing the preflight, we climbed into our planes. Few and Stranger had already started their planes and we watched them taxi into position on the runway, awaiting their takeoff clearance. While we were taxing to the runway, we watched Few launch and Sabow followed after a short interval. Mike and I were then cleared into position and hold, waiting for our takeoff clearance, when we heard Sabow frantically calling Few on the FM radio and receiving no reply. The calls were coming more quickly and sounding desperate. We did not know it at the time, but Few lost all electrical power, except for the standby battery, immediately after takeoff. His primary instrumentation consisted of a wet compass, an antiquated standby gyro, the Vertical Speed Indicator (VSI), airspeed and altimeter. Kadena was a long way from Kunsan flying completely in the weather.

(L to R) Bill (Few) Callahan, Jim (Stranger) Sabow, and me

Mike and I did the section takeoff with no problem and stayed in formation for the remainder of the flight. During our climb to altitude, we were in the weather flying trail behind Sabow, all of us heading toward Kadena. We did not break out of the weather when we reached our cruise altitude, and we did not have Stranger in sight either. There was no word about Few from anyone. He had not been picked up on any radar we contacted, and he never answered a radio call. The three of us brainstormed the situation over FM radio, and finally decided to just get to Kadena as soon as possible. We also agreed to join up as a three-plane as soon as we were able to make contact with each other.

178

Mike and I broke out of the weather about 50 miles from Kadena and were vectored to Sabow so we could join on him. We were in contact with approach control as we closed in on Kadena. The weather at Kadena was forecast to be 1,500 hundred feet broken, with 10 miles visibility.

Kadena approach told us they picked up an unidentified aircraft on radar. They gave us a vector to check out the aircraft. It was Few. We were ecstatic. Our flight joined him as a four-plane and hit the break at Kadena for landing. In my personal flying experience, the manner in which Few conducted his flight was the best instrument, navigation and piloting I ever knew about, or experienced, while flying in the Marines. We were all very happy to see him.

   The AV-8A had a propensity to lose electrical power when on the ground in heavy rain. The water drained into the fuselage and shorted out the transformer rectifier unit. This had happened before to other people. There was a fix in the system to take care of it, and it was later installed in our aircraft, but in the interim, we often would use a hair drier to blow it dry.

· · ·

   On another cross-country weekend Snyds, Buc and I were in a three-plane flight out of Cubi Pt. to Iwakuni. We decided to refuel at the Taipei International Airport in Taiwan because none of us had landed there before. The weather was forecast to be a broken cloud deck about 800-1200 feet. The visibility was very hazy, not great, but it was doable. The landing aid was not at the airfield, so we flew over the top of the landing aid to shoot our instrument approach on a back azimuth (an angular measurement) toward the runway. We began to separate the flight as we approached the runway. The approach end of the runway was not visible on our first pass, but we could see the ground intermittently, from about 1,000 feet. Snyds flew to what he believed to be the end of the runway, then turned for a left downwind, Buc followed Snyds and I followed him. The three planes were about 1,000 feet apart feet in trail. Each of us was looking down to our left, trying to find the runway, when I happened to look straight ahead to see we were bore-sighted on the golden roof of the Grand Hotel. We were headed directly for it at a comparable altitude. I urgently called over the radio, "Pull up, Pull up, it's the Grand Hotel." Just as I called that, Snyds reacted with a modified wingover as he saw a piece of the runway passing beneath us. Buc followed him and I followed Buc. We literally fell out of the sky in a most unusual formation and landed. After landing, we were unable to get out of our aircraft for a few minutes, as armed soldiers inspected our planes prior to letting us get out.

The Grand Hotel was commissioned and built by Madam Chiang Kai-shek in the 1950s. At one time it was one of the top 10 hotels in the world. We joked about what would have happened to us had we hit the hotel. It would not have been pretty for us.

Our landings must have been quite a sight. Snyds went to Taipei some months later, and the ground crew told him a story of Marine airplanes falling from the sky. They were delighted to find out they were speaking to one of the pilots.

. . .

Winnie Rorabaugh and I were at Clark AFB headed to Iwakuni on a Sunday afternoon. The night before, we had spoken with a Marine F-4 and A-6 crew at the O'Club bar. They gave us a lot of grief about the range of the Harrier. It could not go far and could not carry much. It was more of the same stuff we had heard for the past three years. Winnie and I talked it over and we made a little bet with them. The first aircraft to land at Iwakuni would get free drinks from the losers. These guys were laughing at their good fortune.

Many of the ideas regarding the range of a Harrier were not grounded in fact. We were carrying two, 300-gallon fuel tanks. It always seemed these tanks became your aerodynamic friends at altitude when the fuel was depleted. We routinely cruised at 40,000 feet when the tanks were empty of fuel. We knew the F-4 could fly much faster than we would be able to go, but they had to stop and refuel at Kadena AFB. That could cause them a serious delay. The A-6 could go the distance without refueling, but their cruise airspeed would be much slower than ours.

Winnie and I decided that if we had 2,200 pounds of fuel overhead Kadena at 40,000 feet or higher, we would press on to Iwakuni. The weather was forecast to be Clear and Visibility Unrestricted (CAVU). In those days, we had a circular slide rule type computer to determine flight information. We had our speed figured, the distance to Iwakuni and fuel burn. We updated this every few minutes after we departed Clark AFB. Once I thought I might actually overheat my computer through friction. We arrived overhead Kadena with 2,000 pounds, slightly below our bingo fuel. A quick FM radio transmission confirmed we were going for it. We landed in Iwakuni with "lights," meaning we had less than 1,500 pounds of fuel. We actually had about 800 pounds. That was plenty given the weather. We drank a few, courtesy of the Phantom and Intruder aircrews.

. . .

There were many bases to visit in the Far East. One of them was Misawa AFB in Japan. It was located in a beautiful part of the island of Honshu and was the northern most air base in Japan where we could land. One Friday, I was there by myself. At the O'Club, the US base commander asked if I could fly an airshow the next afternoon. The base was having an open house. An air base open house in Japan is something to behold. There are many thousands of Japanese eagerly awaiting the chance to visit the base, explore and look at the planes. I called back to Iwakuni for direction. They called the Group, who told me to call 1st MAW. I wound up speaking to a colonel in operations. He told me I could fly all the airshows I wanted up there, but I could not land at Misawa after the airshow. He knew the fuel required to perform an airshow does not leave very much left over for a long-distance flight after completing the performance. The nearest US air bases were close to Tokyo, a long way from Misawa. It was his way of saying you can do it, but you really cannot. I was grinning from ear to ear when he told me that. I thanked him and hung up.

. . .

My good friend Dave Deats, one of the earlier 513 pilots, told me about a year earlier of a Japan Defense Force air base at Hachinoe, a small town a few miles from Misawa. I contacted the Misawa CO to explain my situation. He called his Japanese counterpart, and in a few minutes had clearance for me to land at Hachinoe after the airshow. I could refuel there for the flight to Iwakuni. I flew the airshow, in front of a large crowd, then departed and landed in Hachinoe, refueled and was on my way home. A few days later, the airshow was printed up in the newspaper, and the colonel from the 1st MAW contacted me at the squadron. He started to chew on me about disregarding his order. After he ran out of words, I told him, "Sir, I followed your orders." He cut me off to say. "There's no way you could fly a Harrier to Yokota to land after performing that airshow, Captain!" I agreed, and said, "You're correct, Colonel. I landed at Hachinoe, a JASDF base near Misawa." The conversation came to an abrupt halt and he hung up the phone. I felt a bit like Snacks in this situation, caught by a newspaper story, but this Colonel did not write my fitness report.

• • •

One unusual event occurred during August. The Panmunjom axe murder of two US military officers brought 513 to an alert status. During that time, we picked up the maintenance pace and operations went to work overtime to make sure we were both ready and able to join in any military action. We stayed on alert for about a week and then the situation was resolved. I knew we were ready to go but suspected no one was unhappy to have avoided any hostilities. We did have a few pilots who had not yet been in combat, so they might have missed this opportunity more than others of us.

8: Korea Deployments

There were three deployments to Korea while we were in Iwakuni. One was in Kwang Ju, one in Taegu and one in Pohang. I did not go on any of these deployments with the squadron; however, I did go on the Pohang deployment as a ground FAC.

The Kwang Ju deployment had rave reviews because the South Korean Air Force flew the North American F-86 aircraft, essentially the ones very similar to those flown in the Korean War that were so successful in downing MIG-15s. I heard many stories of people being up for an early brief and watching F-86s taking off at sunrise. One afternoon while the Kwang Ju deployment was wrapping up, I was the squadron duty Officer and received a phone call from a Kwang Ju U.S. Air Force police sergeant. After I answered the call, it went something like this, "Sir, this is Air Force Sergeant Smith, is there a Major James Sabow attached to your command?" I replied, "Yes there is. What's the issue?" I could hear Sabs shouting in the background, asking to speak with me. The sergeant put Sabs on the phone. He had been closely checked for contraband and was not too happy about it. He was the DET OIC as I remember it. The air police were squeezing toothpaste out of his tube searching for any illegal substances. This put Sabow over the top. I asked Sabs to put the sergeant back on the phone. I spent a few minutes speaking with him about Major Sabow and the fact that he would not be bringing contraband to Japan. It all ended up with a million laughs when the squadron returned to Iwakuni. Sabow took a lot of ribbing about the incident.

● ● ●

The Pohang deployment was interesting. I was a last minute "volunteer" for the ground FAC position. There was no time to check out the field gear Marines refer to as 782-gear. I had a couple of pair of utilities (camouflage uniform) and my flight boots, and that was it. I was missing things like a pack, a shelter half, a field jacket, and a cartridge belt with assorted gear attached to it. I had more equipment when I was a kid playing with my dad's WW-II gear than I had when we lifted off the ship in a Huey helicopter headed to the field.

183

Fortunately, I had a corporal radioman assigned to me who stood about six-two. We met and I explained my situation to him. It was not long before I looked like GI Joe from the toy store. I had everything. It cost a couple of bottles of very good Bourbon, but worth every penny of it when the rain hit and I was nice and dry under a brand-new Marine poncho.

The time I spent with my fellow ground Marines lasted a few days. I caught a ride to the airfield knowing I could not fly a Harrier back to Iwakuni, as I had no flight gear. I was there just looking to catch a ride home with the squadron. Not much time passed before the XO called me to his office. It seems we had a problem with one of our troops, and the XO handed it over to me to sort out. I met with the Marine that was involved in order to get the facts of the case. It seems our young Marine, after a few drinks, fell in love with a young Korean lady walking down the street to her home. He followed her to her door. Actually, he followed her through her door, made out of glass, and then met her husband and kids inside the home. The Korean police were called, and the Marine was apprehended and was definitely in a lot of trouble.

Since the DET was leaving that very afternoon, we scheduled a morning meeting with the Korean elders in the area of the village. I was the Marine rep and brought along the offender. There were four people in attendance, not counting my Marine who probably thought he was going to skinned alive or eaten by the natives, or something like that. One spoke perfect English, and all the other fellows looked like they were from some central casting, wearing traditional clothing. I felt honored to be in their presence but was sorry it was under these circumstances. I knew one thing would be required to mitigate this situation. That would be money. I scrounged up 500 bucks before I arrived for the meeting. Things did not move quickly. There was much discussion about the gravity of the crime. Each of the elders lectured us about our behavior as Marines and the need to respect the country of Korea as well as the Korean people. Eventually it came up that there would need to be a pecuniary price to pay for this Marine's transgression. There was the broken door, but of much more importance was the dishonor of the family. My Marine could also possibly go to a Korean jail. We were on the ropes for a long time, a couple hours, before I could ask what might be done to make amends for these offenses? After much discussion I offered $500, figuring that was a fair price to pay and thinking that trying to get out on the cheap might keep us there much longer.

The elders conferred for a few minutes and agreed the payment was sufficient to repair the door and restore the family's honor. I gave the Marine a sufficiently hard Marine-like look of admonishment and was thinking we were free to leave. Trying to be polite, I waited for someone to adjourn the meeting. Suddenly there appeared on the table a gallon jug of dirty water full of soil, roots and floating things that were totally unidentifiable. The English speaker told me since this meeting went so well, we should seal the deal by drinking this mixture. I was second in line. It was awful, but I smiled, nodded, and took a drink each time it came around to me. I suspect it was considered a polite thing to do after a situation such as this, but I was not going to fold in front of the Koreans or my Marine.

When we finally adjourned after draining the jar, there were a few roots and leaves remaining to refill the jar for another appropriate time. I told the Marine if he were smart, he would maintain his good behavior for the rest of his tour. He repaid the money out of his paycheck and all was well with the world.

One other Korean story of note happened to Mike Ryan (Rook). Mike was another poster Marine. The Harrier program had quite few, but he was certainly the correct choice for this next assignment. Mike flew a Harrier to the USAF Airbase at Osan. He was scheduled to meet the president of South Korea, Mr. Park Chung-hee. Mike met the president, who was heavily guarded during his tour of the plane. Mike returned after the president departed. He told us the guards for the president reminded him of the character Odd Job in the James Bond movie, Goldfinger.

9: Joe Gallo's Arrival

I should call this the arrival of the Det "B" pilots, but I had also been looking forward to Joe's arrival. A few of us were very good friends and Gallo was a card-carrying member of the group. He was well liked by everyone in our squadron and every other place he had been in the Marines. Joe and I had a few things in common. We loved to work in maintenance, we loved to fly (but so did everyone else) and we liked to have a drink now and then.

There were some gigantic nights at the Iwakuni O'Club. Booze and pilots can be inseparable on occasion. One night, Gallo was in the club drinking and smoking a cigarette when Mike Ryan, a serious arm wrestler, challenged Joe to a contest. As I remember, the match between the two of them had been a goal of Mike's for many weeks. Joe had always deferred, but tonight, he said yes. This event drew quite a crowd. We all knew how good Mike was at arm wrestling but had no idea about Joe. I do not know if anyone wagered on the outcome, but we were all excited to witness the occasion. Surrounded by smoke from Joe's cigarette that he had placed in an ashtray, we watched the first go. If you looked down at the floor or adjusted your place around the table, you missed it. Joe quickly won the first match. The second one, though, had a very quiet group of squadron pilots as an audience. It took a bit longer, but Joe prevailed. It was quite a display of arm wrestling.

• • •

The city of Iwakuni had open sewers, called benjo ditches, with bridges to cross them. After you got used to the smell, it was no big deal. One night, Siepert (Mammal), well-lubricated, left the club headed for the BOQ on his bicycle and was faced with a serious dilemma. He saw three bridges ahead. He chose the wrong one. He took a lot of flak that night and the next day because he had landed in the benjo ditch.

Major Eik had a good, meaning 'bad'. bike wreck on his way home from the O'Club and my crash was coming. Joe and I, along with a few

187

others, had been in the club for some time when the two of us decided to head to the BOQ. We also decided to race home on our bikes. I developed a significant lead when I made a rookie biker's mistake. I turned around to spot Joe and soon after hit the curb. I did not complete my left turn. Joe caught up with me and we determined that my bike was crash-damaged, thus no longer rideable. We started walking home together when he noticed blood flowing from my head to my flight suit. I made it to the BOQ and surveyed the body damage. My mother was a nurse, and we did not go to doctors unless we were close to death. I walked into the shower and ran water on my head for a few minutes, then wrapped the wound with a T-shirt until I could get a real bandage the next day at sick bay. The next morning when I opened my BOQ room door, what was remaining of my bike was parked in the hall directly in front of my door. It had been completely dismantled. The spokes were removed from the rims, any attached parts were removed, disconnected, and laid out on the hall floor. I knew it was Gallo's handiwork because it was so detailed, but he never 'fessed up. My head wound healed rapidly, and all was well.

The last large night we had at the O'Club found us ready to celebrate our upcoming return to CONUS. Ted Herman and I were partners in a jousting battle in the club. He hoisted me on his shoulders, and we took on our opponents. Ted was a gymnast and had a lot of balance. He was a good person to partner with in these battles. We took on a few challengers and were doing well until I slipped from his back and landed on my head on the O'Club floor. As luck would have it, neither the floor nor I suffered any damage. We continued to enjoy ourselves that night at the club. Prior to our departure, we paid the club a few hundred dollars for damages. It was all in good fun.

10: The TRANSPAC

Just before the Trans-Pacific (TRANSPAC) flight, (which is a movement of aircraft across the Pacific, and during recent years, either from the US to Japan, or Japan to the US.) to return to CONUS, we were getting ready for the main body of the squadron to head to Australia for some work with our Marines and Aussies. I hoped to make this deployment as I had already missed the three deployments to Korea.

Around the same time, a TRANSPAC rumor began to circulate around the squadron when we found out we were going to take some of our planes to CONUS. This would be the first attempt at flying the Harriers across the Pacific rather than sending them in transport aircraft or by ship! As the AMO, I was tapped to go to Yuma for a meeting to determine the best way to get our Harriers back to Yuma. The first Harriers to be delivered to the Corps at Beaufort, SC had been floated over on a ship from England. Of course, the squadron pilots, always wanting flight time and more adventure, thought TRANSPAC, what else and why not!? We were excited about the idea of flying our planes across the Pacific to the US. I was not scheduled to participate in the squadron deployment to Australia because of my upcoming trip to Yuma. I was briefed by 1st MAW Commanding General (CG), Major General (MajGen) Kohler, not to bring up the subject of TRANSPAC. He said I was not to even mention the word. I answered, "Yes, sir. I understand."   When I arrived in Yuma and went to the meeting, I was the only rep from the 1st MAW. I was the only Harrier pilot in the room, and all the other attendees were LtCols or colonels. There were supply reps from HQMC and FMFPAC, but none from 1st MAW. A colonel from HQMC chaired the meeting.

We sat down, and the first question asked of me by the colonel in charge of the meeting, was, "Captain, can you TRANSPAC the Harriers to Yuma?" As brazen as I could be at times, I had to tread lightly answering that question. I was really excited about the possibility of a TRANSPAC but adhered to the guidance from MajGen Kohler. Technically, I did not bring it up. I decided to play it straight. I answered the question this way, "Sir, I have been instructed not to bring up the subject of a TRANSPAC by the CG."

The colonel said, "We don't care about that. I asked you if it could be done?" My answer, brimming with enthusiasm, was, "Yes, sir!!!"

We began discussing the planning for the TRANSPAC. There were many supply, logistical and support issues to deal with in a short period of time. The meeting lasted one and a half days. I was told to plan on coming to FMFPAC in Honolulu in a week or so to complete the planning process.

I got on the second nonstop flight of a Boeing 747 SP from Los Angeles to Tokyo the next day. I started working on the issues I thought would come up to bring seven aircraft back to Yuma. The first and foremost issue on my mind was how to brief MajGen Kohler about the meeting.

First, I briefed Col Reed that we were going to TRANSPAC. He was getting ready to leave for Australia, but like all of us he was excited to be the first group of pilots to TRANSPAC the Harriers.

The meeting with the CG and his staff went well. Unknown to me, they had been told it was going to happen, so support it. They also knew it was not my idea, so I was off the hook.

One morning before I left for Hawaii for my meeting, I was rather rudely awakened by a phone call around 4 a.m. from none other than LtCol Frank Pieri. He introduced himself, and asked, "Are you Captain Capito, the 513 AMO?" I answered, "Yes, sir." He asked me about a part we had on order that was grounding four aircraft. I told him I thought that we had ordered four. The order had been for four, but I did not have the exact number at the moment. "I was asleep when you called.," I said. He replied, "Get out of bed, get down to the hangar, find out how many are on order, and call me back." I copied his phone number, and again, I replied, "Yes, sir." I got up and went to the hangar to check. Our records showed that four cockpit temp controllers, the parts we needed, were on order. I called Col Pieri back to tell him we did have four controllers on order. He told me, "You only have two on order. Two have just been cancelled. Reorder them again, right now." Again, I replied, "Yes, sir." He hung up. My first day of conversation with Col Pieri consisted mostly of "yes, sirs."

My first contact with Col Frank Pieri offered me no clue that one day this would be the man that I, along with many others, believed saved the AV-8A Harrier program. He worked magic at his level to find and arrange for misplaced Harrier parts to be returned to the supply system. He expedited repairs for AV-8A Harrier electronic parts for the next few years. He then was instrumental in the successful introduction, from a logistical perspective, of the AV-8B Harrier II to fleet squadrons. He worked in NAVAIRSYSCOM, a command located in Crystal City, VA. To this captain Harrier pilot in Iwakuni, that command was about as foreign to me as astrophysics. That morning I had no idea what he did or who he was in my chain of command. But I did what he asked and very quickly found out who he was!

. . .

A TRANSPAC is a movement of aircraft across the Pacific, and during recent years, either from the US to Japan, or Japan to the US. Going east, the route is normally from Iwakuni to Guam for an overnight. The next stop is Wake Island for a couple of days to ensure that the aircraft are airworthy for further flight on the next long leg. From Wake, the next stop is MCAS Kaneohe, Hawaii. Once there, you stay overnight for crew rest and to service the airplanes for the next leg to NAS Alameda in Oakland, CA. Our final flight was to MCAS Yuma.

Aerial refueling from KC-130 tankers was a requirement for the TRANSPAC and each division of three or four Harriers was led by a C-9 Pathfinder. An advance maintenance party flew a day ahead of the Harriers, two flights of four KC-130s refueled the Harriers on each leg, and a trail maintenance party followed after the departure from each stop. It was a complex operation.

The squadron had arrived in Australia when I headed off to Hawaii. I checked into the military hotel on Waikiki beach. Nice place. I was to meet with TRANSPAC planners, one of whom I had met in the Yuma meeting. We found each other in the hotel then headed to FMFPAC headquarters. There I met two LtCols. I do not remember one of their names, but I do remember the other one. His name was LtCol Ray Bright. His call sign was "Not So." He told me he was a Naval

Academy grad, graduating in the lower regions of his class, thus his call sign.

We worked on the TRANSPAC fuel requirements, flight planning, number of troops required, parts and supply concerns, billeting issues and on and on. "Not So" Bright was anything but. It took me about five minutes to realize he was on top of it all. If I just listened, answered questions, and made my concerns known, this was going to be a piece of cake. He knew more about what was required for a successful TRANSPAC than any Marine around. We finished the first day way ahead of schedule.

After the day's work, he and his pal hauled me off on a tour of Waikiki nightlife. Every bar we went in, the hostess or bartender knew these two guys by name, poured their drinks before they ordered and talked to them for a bit before we could even sit down. This being the first stop, I thought it was pretty cool. When it happened again at the next bar, I realized I was with a couple of pros. The same thing happened all three nights I was there. After we finished work, we went to new places each night and the story was the same. On one occasion, I thought we were reliving a bar scene from the movie "From Here to Eternity."

When the conference was finished, I had a couple of legal pads full of information, as well as the confidence to know the planned TRANSPAC was going to work out fine.

• • •

Back in Iwakuni, we were still flying our commitments, but also planning a return to Yuma with seven of our 13 airplanes. We had expected to be returning with eight aircraft, but one of the newly arrived pilots ran one out of gas attempting a landing. The plane did not burn but was certified, after an inspection, to be a strike damage aircraft due to structural problems. This was a bit of a setback, but when given lemons, it is best to make lemonade. I worked with Col Reed to see if we could ask the CG to allow us to part out the plane. CG 1st MAW had the authority to strike the aircraft and allow us to part it out. All parts would, of course be inspected, and those in need of repair would, in fact, be repaired.

Col Reed sent me to Okinawa for a meeting with the CG and his maintenance and supply staff. The meeting started slowly, like why are we all here? The general finally asked, "What do you want, Captain?" I replied, "I'd like to part out the recently crashed Harrier. It's a strike aircraft but didn't burn, so there are many parts we can use." He looked at me and replied, almost verbatim, "What else were you going to do with it? Fly it?" I quickly answered, "No, sir. It's my understanding you have the authority to release the plane, and I'm asking for your permission to use it for spare parts."

The CG looked at the two colonels and said, "Take care of the paperwork." He looked back at me and asked, "Anything else?" "No, sir!" was my quick reply. I then walked out of the meeting with the wing supply colonel to discuss the paperwork required to make this happen. He departed and the wing maintenance colonel discussed the testing and certification of the parts being removed from the crashed Harrier. After we finished, I was on my way home to Iwakuni.

I was getting too many CG briefing opportunities for my liking. Throughout my career, I always believed the fewer officers I knew above the rank of LtCol, the better off I would be.

VMA-513 maintainers, working through the night, remove the wing to change the engine.

We worked hard to get the planes ready. Daily phone calls from Col Pieri were standard. He hustled parts and we were beginning to see a light at the end of the tunnel. The goal was twofold. First was to get the seven designated TRANSPAC aircraft ready for flight. The second was to leave Det "B" with six flyable Harriers when we left. Gallo was the Det "B" AMO, so I doubly wanted this to happen. We were all pulling together to make sure the remaining planes were in good shape. Since Gallo was the AMO, the DET could not have been in better hands. The squadron worked hard to get 100% availability before the main body left Iwakuni. Unfortunately, the DET availability went south soon after we departed.

One of the reasons for a reduction in the availability of parts for 513 was that VMA-231 was now onboard the USS Roosevelt in the Mediterranean Sea. At the time, this was a surprise to us, but they trumped our priority status for parts due to the contingency they were covering.

The tasks required for the TRANSPAC planes to be ready for extended flight required some long hours for the troops. We needed to have all the avionics gear working, the refueling probes and ferry tanks checked out and the engines and hydraulics systems ready to go. It was not business as usual for the maintenance department.

November 25, launch day for the first leg to Guam, finally arrived. We were well briefed, airplanes were in good shape and we were excited to be heading home, flying "first class." As the AMO, I was flying an aircraft that had been in a down status for a few weeks. When we were working to get it up for flight, we all had reservations about it coming together in time for the TRANSPAC. I flew a couple of check flights on it a few days prior to launch. It was up for the first flight and I flew all the way home without one gripe. It continued to fly for about two weeks after we landed in Yuma before it finally went down for maintenance.

The first leg of the TRANSPAC was from Iwakuni to Guam. The skipper, Col Reed, Snyds, Klinefelter and Al James were in the first flight. Stranger, Few, and I were in the second. The weather was good, we hit the tanker once on the way, and the three-and-a-half-hour flight was uneventful. All the planes were in good shape when we landed in

Guam.

The excitement of flying across the Pacific was still there as we manned up the following morning for the next leg from Guam to Wake Island. It was also about a three-and-a-half-hour flight. We air refueled, had good weather and all was well upon landing. We had two days there. Wake is important in Marine Corps history. When you land there, you can feel the sense of desperation the defenders must have felt during WWII as the Japanese attacked. There is not much there. Since Wake is a small but beautiful island and well used as a TRANSPAC base, there were lots of things for crews and maintainers to do. We took advantage of sunfish sailboats, snorkeled in the bay, had a few drinks at the bar and enjoyed the down time.

The Wake to Hawaii flight was close to five hours. We air refueled two times on the way with no issues. We spotted MCAS Kaneohe Bay, a long way out. Hawaii never looked so good, as five hours in the Harrier can be a bit cramped. We landed there on November 28.

We had one day in Hawaii and we made the most of it. The troops were ready to hit the town. There was sure to be some problems with them on liberty in Honolulu. I worked with the maintenance chief and left some money in my flight suit pocket to handle any unforeseen expenses, with the caveat I would be paid back in Yuma. Some money was borrowed and was returned soon after arriving in Yuma. The troops did have a big night, and two of them said they could never return because they had court dates they were not going to make. You learn not to ask questions when you do not want to hear the answers.

. . .

The "low key" officers and gentlemen headed to Waikiki Beach for a job, "almost well done," celebration. The choice for this celebration was the Top of The I restaurant in the Ilikai Hotel. The dinner was to be a "we love us" occasion prior to arriving in Yuma. We were very proud to be part of the first of many AV-8A TRANSPACs. Once seated, we began to drink a bit. Skip felt we needed some female companionship, so he found a couple of gals to join us. They were like fish out of the water and got no recognition. The celebratory atmosphere was all about Marines being Marines and telling each other how wonderful we were. We had mastered some sort of crazy sound, which we used on occasion. After our meal, we began to emit the sound, and it carried throughout the restaurant. We were warned about it a couple of times and just blew it off. Eventually, the restaurant staff told us the shore patrol was headed our way. We scoffed at that threat. Someone made a remark like, "There's no shore patrol sailor going to throw us out of here," followed quickly by our loud squadron noise. To say we were obnoxious would not adequately describe the situation. We finally had the good sense to move on to a new location. The bills were settled up and we began to walk down the stairs. On the way up were two, very large Navy shore patrol officers. We passed them on the stairs as we were going down. We acknowledged them and I am sure they recognized us as the source of the complaint. After we passed them, we headed back to the base to get ready for the next day.

...

The following morning, we gathered the troops and the pilots, and prepared for the five-plus hour flight to NAS Alameda, in Oakland, CA. We were briefed on the weather along the route. It was not wonderful, but Col Bright and the Navy TRANSPAC staff decided to launch.

This leg also required two air refuelings. The skipper's division took off first and then we launched, about 20 minutes later, with me in the second division of three planes. We were in the clear for a long part of the flight out of Hawaii. "Not So" was in one of the C-130 tankers and was able to keep an eye on us as we refueled. Since all aircraft were listening on a common frequency, we were aware of the skipper's flight's position. We were told the C-130s were entering a squall line, which is a large grouping of thunderstorms. They were going to look for better weather rather than abort the flight. The C-130 could not find better weather.

The Harrier does not have radar, but the C-130s had a rudimentary one. The first division used a combination of headings from the C-130s and a makeshift ADF (auto-direction finding) signal using our UHF radio to finally get a visual sighting of each other. The AV-8A Harrier is usually an easy aircraft to air refuel. As the skipper's flight split to refuel from the two 130s, the weather was awful with a lot of turbulence. As Snyds recalls, he and Shrum were trying to connect with

196

the basket. Snyds missed on his first try. When the two of them were in the basket, he said you could see the bottom of the 130 one second and the entire top of it a couple seconds later. It took longer than planned 100-mile track to receive enough fuel to top off all four aircraft.

The weather was the same when my division arrived at the tankers. Visibility was poor. Few and Sabs had their 130 and I had mine. I assume they had no trouble. I missed on my first attempt. Not So came up on the radio to give me a hard time as we had to get plugged in because we were a bit farther down range then we planned. He also told me I would have to personally brief the admiral if I screwed this up. I missed on the second attempt while he was talking to me. I backed out, took the proverbial deep breath and slid right in, one happy Harrier pilot. Not So came back up on the radio to give me an attaboy and started laughing about me being a rookie. Like the skipper's flight, I saw the top of the 130 then quickly I was looking up at the bottom. After we landed, while debriefing the flight, we all agreed it was the roughest air refueling any of us had ever experienced. We were much farther down range than we planned and our ability to return to Hawaii had been compromised. We could not have returned to Kaneohe without a tanker coming along with us.

The second refueling was a piece of cake, in good weather, and we were now headed to Alameda. The flight was a bit over five hours and we were all happy to be on the ground. We hit the O'Club in Alameda for a celebratory beer then hit the phones to let our families know we were back in the USA. We had an early night then off to our new home in Yuma the next morning.

The flight to Yuma was uneventful. When we arrived, Major Pete Wallis (Gator) had set up the hangar spaces for us. He was the OIC of an advance party, bringing people from the east coast Harrier squadrons to be assigned to 513. This was the second time I had been involved in the relocation of a squadron. So far, this one was much easier.

Reflections

VMA-513 cruise plaque on display in the Naval Aviation Museum,
NAS Pensacola, FL

We had a great time in WESTPAC. The squadron deployed to Korea, Australia, the Philippines, Okinawa, and flew all over the Far East. It is safe to say we were full of ourselves. However, during our time in Iwakuni, 513 had become isolated from the main Harrier operations base at Cherry Point by both distance and lack of curiosity. I believe, in our thinking, whatever they were doing could not possibly be as meaningful to the furthering of V/STOL operations as what we had been doing. We were wrong! At Cherry Point, all three Harrier squadrons were doing very well. The pilots flying with those squadrons would become the leadership of the Harrier community for many years to come. We were completely out of touch with the real Harrier world when we landed at MCAS Yuma.

Looking back on my time in Iwakuni, there are many things upon which to reflect. We had COs who let us thrive in our flying and job assignments. I will say they were very forgiving to tolerate our somewhat out of control behavior. Some of us consumed a lot of alcohol and spent some long nights in O'Clubs during our time in WESTPAC. I had a candid talk with Marx Branum later in life when we were both retired. The question came up about our best tour as a Harrier pilot. He told me his best tour was being the XO and flying with us in 542 and 513 from 1972-1976. He knew all of us could fly any mission assigned safely and competently. He also knew we could handle our job assignments and paperwork without oversight and could pass any inspection. He did say he had a lot of trouble understanding our behavior. We had a good laugh about his summation of the resumes of a few of the 542/513 captains. I think he nailed us.

I also had a chance to speak with Major Eik about his thoughts concerning his time in 542 and 513. He said it was second only to his time as the CO of his own squadron. He laughed about some of us burning the candle at both ends, but he echoed Marx Branum in saying he never worried about any of us in our jobs and flying.

There is really not much more to say about Major Eik and the XO. They were low-key people who enjoyed their jobs and were very good at them. I do not believe anyone who knew them would have a bad thing to say about either one. That statement cannot be said about everyone in the Harrier program. Major Eik and the XO were special to us, and we became good friends.

When I started flight school, Col Don Conroy, the Great Santini, was the CO of the Marine aviation detachment in Pensacola. When I was in the last few months of my Vietnam tour, I knew him when he was First Marine Air Wing G-1. By the time 513 finished our Iwakuni tour, gigantic characters like Col Conroy and other well- known hell raisers were slowly beginning to vacate the ranks of Marine aviators. Higher headquarters no longer seemed to appreciate individuals becoming colorful characters. Marines have always been proud to have larger than life characters around. We were proud to have a few in our numbers. To paraphrase the NFL saying going around at the time, "On any given day we could have a Great Santini show up at the squadron." Marines and certainly Marine pilots seem to be largely fueled by adrenalin. This was certainly the case for a few of us during our Iwakuni tour.

All the officers continued to become closer friends during our time in WESTPAC. The original 542 captains were now celebrating over three years that they had been together with in squadrons. We had flown enough with one another that we were able to brief a sortie in a few minutes, requiring only the specific details of the mission. In my group of friends, for the closest of us, our personal lives were common knowledge. Family issues, financial issues, and other things had all been discussed and dissected in WESTPAC, many times, over many beers.

Our confidence in the Harrier was sky high. We loved and respected our jump jet. We had been thoroughly tested flying the Harrier in the Pacific. On occasion, some of us had experienced mechanical problems or weather issues but we all matured and grew as pilots and officers. When we departed Iwakuni, we were very good at our jobs and we knew it. We also knew our troops were good and could produce when challenged. It was not always pretty, but we always finished the job.

In Beaufort, we had one mishap with a fatality, Capt. Briggs, a new pilot. During our time in Cherry Point we had been accident-free. In Iwakuni, with the exception of a flameout landing by a new pilot arriving with Det "B," we had been accident-free. We were confident both the fatal mishap and the flameout landing in Iwakuni were pilot error, so we had experienced no mechanical, material, or maintenance mishaps since we started flying together in 542. Back at Cherry Point, VMA-542 and VMA-231 had a few aircraft losses, including fatalities, during the time we were in Iwakuni. Looking back, as we were departing Iwakuni, I was proud of our maintenance department, our pilots, and the work we did. At the time, I never really thought about accidents or mishaps. I believed the squadron was performing to the best of our ability and our mishap record, though not perfect, confirmed it. In a bit of honest and reflective hindsight, I suspect the squadron also enjoyed a gigantic amount of luck along the way.

Things were on track for another good tour in Arizona. I was still living the Marine recruiting poster life I always wanted. I was the AMO of the squadron, a Harrier pilot with great friends, a few even much closer than my family. I was flying a wonderful aircraft and totally satisfied with my life as a Marine. I was still living out my idea that a tight group of pilots spending multiple years together would be the ideal squadron makeup and certainly the most combat ready group of pilots. Our squadron culture was still intact after our overseas tour.

My flight time in Iwakuni was 332 hours, averaging almost 24 hours per month.

PART 4 (1977-1979)

<u>MCAS Yuma</u>

**Some of us were talking about flying the Harrier.
The thought came up that you really can have too much of a good thing.
We laughed it off.**

1: MCAS Yuma
Getting Settled

Major Pete Wallis (Gator) was the OIC of the advance party to Yuma from Cherry Point. He brought six aircraft to Yuma in early November and brought close to 60 troops and eight pilots with the goal of getting the hangar ready for flight operations. The tasking began before the main body arrived. Almost as soon as the advance party was on the ground, Gator's pilots were flying at the Naval Air Weapons Station (NAWS) in China Lake located in the Chocolate Mountains of California. China Lake is located just a short flight from the MCAS at Yuma, AZ

Some of the pilots who arrived with Gator were Captains Chuck Reed, Dennis Greene, Alex Whitten, and Nelson Hall. The early pilot and maintenance personnel transfers from 513 in Iwakuni reported to the squadron in Yuma and by the first week of December, 513 was back together as a squadron (minus) with 13 aircraft. 513 Det B with six aircraft was still in Japan. In the weeks prior to Christmas, we were all new arrivals in Yuma, some having returned from Japan and the others who came from Cherry Point. There may have been a few small integration issues between the old hands coming from Iwakuni and the Marines who had recently transferred from the east coast, but we were too busy to let any drama build up in the squadron.

Gator made us feel right at home when we landed. I cannot say we learned anything new about moving the squadron from Iwakuni to Yuma because Gator and his crew had us set up very well when we arrived. We landed and taxied to our new hangar just like we were returning from a deployment. 513 left a lot of equipment in Iwakuni for Det "B" to utilize. That inventory of tools, parts, etc., would return to Yuma when Det "B" TRANSPAC'ed from Iwakuni in April 1977.

Many of the TRANSPAC pilots and troops took leave to move their families to Yuma. We returned to settle into housing. From the beginning of our relocation, our squadron life in Yuma was very similar to the Beaufort time period. We made friends quickly with the pilots

205

from Cherry Point. Gator brought a seasoned group of aviators with him to Yuma, so the squadron did not lose any capabilities through pilot transfers that were made prior to our return. We also had additional maintenance Marines to replace the ones we lost through transfers when we left Iwakuni.

Gator replaced me as the AMO, and I became the assistant AMO. Jim Sabow remained as the XO, and Major Rudi Maikis became the ops officer. Pat Owen, Ted Herman, Al James, Ken Shrum, Skip, Few, Buc, and Mammal all came to Yuma. Majors Eikenbery and Branum were transferred to schools during the move. Mike Ryan and Snyds went to different commands once we arrived in Yuma. All in all, the original 542 pilot group was still pretty much intact.

We arrived from the Far East facing issues we did not have to consider in Iwakuni. We had to relocate families to Yuma, many from Cherry Point. It was quite a change from our Iwakuni lifestyle. We had wives, kids and responsibilities for the first time in 12 or 13 months. Everyone had challenges of some sort to deal with due to the cross-country move. Many of us bought houses in Yuma from one real estate lady who got the bulk of our business. Bill Callahan, Denny Greene, and later, Joe Gallo had moved to within a short walking distance of one another, fairly near the airbase. The rest of the officers were scattered around town.

In addition to relocating, I was looking forward to seeing my son Mike, our first-born child. That presented a new family dynamic.

My previous experience in Yuma consisted of a cross-country flight before I left for Vietnam in 1970, a few visits when in Dallas, and three deployments with VMA-542. I knew nothing about the town other than Chretin's, the Stag and Hound and Johnny's Other Place. I saw most of that at night after we finished flying. Watching westerns while growing up, my mental image of Yuma consisted of a prison and a desert with the Colorado River running through town. In reality, Yuma had nice vegetation, many varieties of trees, had affordable housing and was much larger than Havelock in North Carolina. There were many acres of irrigated fields in the valley. Once we were settled in, Yuma turned out to be a very nice place to live.

Getting everyone moved into quarters seemed to be one of Col Reed's top priorities. Due to the advance party and the hospitality of the Air Station and the city of Yuma, this relocation went much smoother than the move to Cherry Point from Beaufort.

(L to R) Win Rorabaugh, Jim Sabow, Bill Callahan, Mike Siepert, and me on the ramp at MCAS Yuma after our return to CONUS

Straight Up and Out of Control

2: 1977

The squadron began flying a routine schedule and went back to a more normal operation. Many of our senior maintenance SNCOs returned with us, so they were able to keep the aircraft up and flying. However, now that we were stateside and no longer one of the two "pitchfork tines," we soon began to experience the now familiar lack of parts issues. Our tech reps, Frank Armanno, Dave Clegg, and others accompanied us to Yuma.

The squadrons at Cherry Point were doing well. VMA 231 was still operating from the USS Roosevelt and 542 was conducting pilot training and generating a lot of flight hours. Major Spicer was true to his word when he said he would improve aircraft availability. All of a sudden, 513 became the maintenance laggards and none of us liked that position. Now, even though we were stateside, we were still isolated from Cherry Point.

One thing the Iwakuni tour did for many of the 542 pilots was to complete our bonding process. We became friends in Beaufort. We melded together from the XO on down at Cherry Point, and a few of us became closer than brothers in Iwakuni. Our small group of pilots began our fourth year knowing we could count on being together in Yuma for two more years. Ken Shrum and Skip joined us in Japan, came to Yuma, and we were all one.

When we settled in after a short period of time, many of us continued our visits to the bar after work every day and the camaraderie never slowed down. We were reluctant to abandon our Iwakuni lifestyle. We quickly added a few newcomers to our crowd. Gator was Snyder-like in his ability to get things rolling. He had a large presence in the squadron.

Ken Brust was one fine person to know. He avoided the total craziness some of us continued to embrace, but he was there either in person or in spirit with a great sense of humor and common sense when needed. Denny Greene fit right in with us. We all liked country music and Denny introduced us to some Texas singers.

It was not long before our antics began to be tough on a few marriages. We had been away for over a year, and some pilots and troops were deployed for short times almost as soon as we arrived home. Most of the wives knew one another and the new wives coming in seemed to be right at home. They were carrying a lot of responsibility in the homes and raising kids. Some were very concerned about their husbands flying the Harrier, as well as being at the bar after work many nights of the week. We did not help ourselves out at all.

Although Det "B" lost an aircraft and pilot in bad weather shortly after we left Iwakuni, the 542/513 pilots still had not experienced the mishaps the east coast squadrons were dealing with in 1977. From the start of the Harrier program in 1971 until the end of 1976, 513 lost three aircraft with one fatality, which included the Det "B" mishap. VMA-231 lost four aircraft with three fatalities and 542 lost one airplane with one fatality.

Even with our lower aircraft availability in Yuma we remained certain we were the best-trained and most combat ready Harrier squadron in the Marines and were prepared to tackle any task. Tested against ourselves we knew we were the best! Our Iwakuni, Det "B" would arrive in a few months and we looked forward to becoming a whole squadron, once again.

• • •

In the maintenance department, my interaction with Col Pieri continued to grow. Col Pieri continued to be about all things Harrier. His gang at NavAirSysCom continued finding Harrier parts that had either been lost or misplaced in the Naval supply system for three years or longer. Many of those parts had been sent to WESTPAC in anticipation of the arrival of 513 but were lost in numerous supply warehouses. He started a program to keep track of all parts requiring off-site repair. He was full of energy, liked to drink and became a good friend to the entire Harrier community. Earlier in his career he had been an F-4 pilot. He would come to Yuma to visit us on occasion. We would go to the bar to bend his ear about our issues and whine about Cherry Point squadrons having easier access to the NARF. We believed this gave them a head start in the ongoing search for parts. He heard our cry and helped us out. Gator and I got to know Col Pieri well and he got to know us. It was a rewarding relationship in the ongoing quest for the parts required to fly our flight schedule.

Soon after we arrived, there was a lot of talk being generated in Washington, DC about a new Harrier, possibly called Harrier II or AV-8B. There was a bit of humor in calling it the AV-8B since there were AV-8Cs currently in the fleet. Apparently, the AV-8B was to be a variant of the AV-8A. We were told the next generation Harrier would be very similar to the AV-8A in design, but with much greater capabilities. These rumors were going around and all of us looked forward to getting a newer, more capable Harrier. On the other hand, as it was so far into the future, it had little meaning to us at the time. We just had to work with what we had available.

. . .

Col Reed was due to leave the squadron fairly soon after we arrived. He was the first Harrier pilot to have commanded two Harrier squadrons, and it was soon time for him to give 513 up. There was to be a change of command, and the rumor going around the squadron indicated that our new CO was to be Major Rich Hearney. Col Reed was a fine CO. He had the ability to let you do your job; if you needed help, ask him and he would find what you needed. I felt very fortunate he selected me to be his AMO in Iwakuni. I was both excited and a bit concerned to find out Major Hearney was coming to the squadron. Rich Hearney has always been my ideal of a Marine officer since I met him in flight school. He was an instructor when I was a student. In Vietnam I ran into him a couple times and ultimately worked for him a few months at 1st MAW, G-3. Soon we were both getting orders back to MARTD Dallas and I worked for him there.

On my return to the States from VietNam, I was planning to get married. I received my regular commission in Vietnam, courtesy of the Great Santini, Col Conroy, who was the 1st MAW G-1 (personnel and admin section). At this point in my life, I had two career goals. One was to get stationed in Texas and two, to fly the F-8 Crusader. When I got my wings, F-8s were no longer in the active Marine Corps air wings. However, they were in Dallas, TX and Atlanta, GA with the reserves. Having no interest in returning to an F-4 squadron, I applied to fill an active-duty position at NAS Dallas to fly the F-8. Major Hearney had previously flown the F-8 in Vietnam, and he applied for a different active-duty position at NAS Dallas to once again fly the F-8.

Hearney and I arrived at MARTD Dallas, about the same time. He was a tough boss. He was fair but worked very hard and expected others to do the same. While at Dallas I attempted to become a bit like Major Hearney in my Marine officer ways. It was not working for me. As a matter of fact, some of the reserve pilots who knew Hearney well told me if I did not stop trying to act like him, they were going to call me Little Richard. That was all it took for me to change my ways.

It was in Dallas where I began to learn how to be a Marine officer and a much better pilot. I did not attend the Marine Officer Basic School due to needs of the service. Marines needed pilots, quickly, so I did not have to go. I will always give the Dallas reservists credit for teaching me many of the leadership skills required to become a competent Marine officer. My goal if I were ever fortunate enough to have command of a squadron was to run it like it was a Marine reserve squadron.

Major Hearney and I spent slightly less than two years together in Dallas before he headed to England to learn to fly the Harrier. I left for Beaufort a few months later. We went to different assignments after becoming Harrier pilots. His arrival at 513 was the first time we were going to be in the same Harrier squadron.

I briefed my fellow captains that Major Hearney was fair, tough, and worked hard, a Marine's Marine. Compared to Col Reed, he was a bit of a micromanager, a popular term at the time, but I told them I knew he would be a good CO.

We said goodbye to Col Reed and his wonderful wife Gail as they moved down the street to the air group. We then welcomed Major Hearney (Horse) and his wife Maggie to the squadron. When it finally happened, I was excited to have him become the CO because I knew him and was comfortable working with him, but I did have concerns about how he would adjust to our way of life. I knew, as a squadron, we were probably going to experience a cultural sea change. Admittedly, as a group of pilots, we were a bit salty, cocky, and a tad arrogant. All the captains had about seven years in grade at the time, which for us seemed to be a long time. We were good and we knew it. I suspect we would have been a handful for any new squadron commander coming on board. Fortunately for us, Major Hearney seemed to fit in quite well into our way of life soon after he took command. He loved to fly, and we were trying our best to do a lot of it.

• • •

I had always been a Safety Officer or a maintenance guy. Being in operations always looked pretty simple to me. Schedule some events, then hit the pool, work out and live the good life. Actually, you can write a schedule or an op plan for anything you want, but without enough airplanes it won't happen. That is why I loved working in maintenance. No planes equal no flight schedule.

There was probably one issue affecting some 513 pilots. We were looking to raise the quality of our flight training. It is hard to believe you could get bored flying a jet fighter, but it can happen. I was the wingman on a two-plane F-4 flight in Vietnam with three other 1stLts (Marine F-4's were two-seater aircraft, a pilot and RIO, or radar intercept officer). We were heading west, flying below a 5,000-foot overcast to rendezvous with an airborne FAC (Forward Air Controller). Both F-4s were loaded with ordnance going 450 knots when the flight leader transmitted, "Isn't this some boring shit?" The other three of us keyed our mikes at the same time to transmit a few choice words to the flight lead. Boredom or complacency leads directly to mishaps.

I do not think we were anywhere near bored when we began operations in Yuma, but we had been at this for a long time and were looking at two more years of the same type of flying we had been doing the past four years. The best descriptor of our mental state might be we were just tired. We needed more challenging flight opportunities. I suspect Major Hearney might have picked up on some of those feelings we were experiencing after being around the squadron for a while.

From my perspective in the maintenance department, all of a sudden, the ops shop became a very busy place with very creative pilots who were still able to hit the pool and work on their tans. They started finding commitments that were a step above what we had been flying the past years. We began to maximize training ranges and opportunities that were right in our backyard. We were placing our names on lists of inter-service exercises and raising our game.

In April 1977 Det "B" returned from Iwakuni via TRANSPAC. They were welcomed to Yuma and we were glad to have them back with us. In particular, I, along with the rest of the squadron, was very happy to have Joe Gallo back in our orbit.

Gator sent planes to China Lake as soon as his advanced party's wheels touched down. Looking back, that deployment set the standard for the quality of operations we were beginning to experience. Internally, we accelerated the pace of the squadron and quickly became more focused and very busy. Pilots were either flying in a deployment or planning one. I remember being much more involved in the "ops" world as a maintenance guy than I had ever been before. There was a team effort being put together to take advantage of any training opportunity we could find.

The holy grail of the fighter and attack pilot world at that time was the Red Flag weapons training exercise at Nellis AFB near Las Vegas. This was a multi- service gathering of diverse aircraft and aircrews for intense training and tactical evaluation. All the pilots in 513 really wanted a squadron invitation to participate in this event. We received one for October 1977.

It was not all work and no play in 513. During 1977, Major Pete Wallis was getting married. We knew his bride, JoAnne, and her family. A small group consisting of Shrum, Siepert, Klinefelter, Denny Greene, Few and I were close friends of JoAnne's mother, Shirley, and her father, Frank. They owned a produce company in Yuma. It seemed they knew everyone in town.

Gator's wedding had been planned for some time. Many in the squadron wanted to give him an appropriate bachelor's night send-off. I was the best man. Gator lived with Shrum, but as a bachelor he also had a BOQ room. I inquired many times about Gator's uniform and was told, not to worry. So, I did not.

I, along with Shrum, Siepert, Denny Greene, Klinefelter, Gallo, Few, Owen, and a few others, constituted the bachelor party planning committee. We wanted this to be special. We started discussing our plans about six weeks ahead of the wedding date. Those sessions were held in a bar in Winterhaven. That was a short drive across the Colorado River, in California. We did not want word of our plan to leak. The meetings were once or twice a week, after work. This was to be a well-thought-out and planned operation, with all details being kept secret.

It took a few visits to the bar with lots of beer to devise the "foolproof" plan. It was a work of art. Something only the right group of Harrier pilots, with wild imaginations and unbridled by convention, could come up with for the big moment.

Gator was a drinker and Gator was a talker. He, like Snyds, could take over a room in a heartbeat. These two people never met a stranger. I can personally say the times spent with these two were some of the most fun times ever. Knowing Gator possessed these two traits, we moved forward with the bachelor party of the century, scheduled the night before his wedding.

Our plan was simple. We held the party at Shrum and Gator's house in town. We were going to get Gator loaded enough to pass out, then early in the morning put him on a train to Phoenix. In his shoe, we placed a one-dollar bill. On a normal day, Gator with a dollar bill could have figured a way to go from Yuma to New York City. He had that gift.

During our research we found there were two Hughes Airwest flights from Phoenix to Yuma in the morning or early afternoon of the wedding day. We had all the confidence in the world Gator would arrive at the Phoenix train station in the morning, figure out a way to get to the airport and come home in time for the wedding. No problem.

The plan was reviewed many times, from one end to the other. There were no holes. It was simply foolproof!

Our wives finally had an inkling of something going on, but we kept it secret from all those without a need to know.

The day for the bachelor party arrived. We had a full house of officers show up for the festivities. The CO avoided the affair. I think he might have smelled a rat and wanted to stay out of it.

We were having the usual heavy-drinking bachelor party, but this one was on steroids. Gator could hold his booze. We were up all night, well past our expected end of party time. Gator was wide awake and having a great time of it. We kept looking at each other and at the time. The train was on the way, and we were not.

Everybody came over to have a drink with Gator and they left in worse shape than Gator. Finally, we broke out our ace in the hole. Warrant Officer John Bowden did not drink. We filled an empty bottle of tequila with water and a worm. John challenged Gator to a chug contest. Gator had a full bottle of tequila and took the challenge. The crowd became quiet. They were face-to-face, they stared each other down, and on the count of three they began to chug. Gator was no match for John. Then he passed out. He was gone!

We took him to his room, put his traveling clothes on him and started toward the Yuma train station. I suspected there was a subplot building to put me on the train with him. I locked myself in my trusty Ford pickup. In hindsight, I believe that was a very smart tactical move for me at the time, but a poor strategic move in the scheme of things.

Pat Owen and a few others put Gator on the train. There were a couple of ladies already on there. They thought Gator might be "sick." Pat and others assured them he was OK, but he had to be in Phoenix for his wedding later in the day. Pat asked the ladies, "Could you ladies please make sure he gets off the train in Phoenix? His new bride would really appreciate it!" With a few reservations, they agreed.

With our task completed, we all headed home for the night. It was about 4 a.m. when we left the train station.

About 7 a.m. that morning my phone rang. I answered. The call went something like this. "John this is Shirley. Peter is in Phoenix."

I laughed, full of confidence at a plan well executed, and said, "I know he's in Phoenix. We sent him there. He'll be fine. He'll grab an airplane and be back soon." "John," Shirley replied, "Peter can't talk. He wrote his name on a piece of toilet paper and passed it to the station agent. He asked the agent to call me."

"Oh, shit," I said. Actually, I wondered how he found a pen. Then Shirley said the words that struck fear in my heart. "John, if Pete isn't here for the wedding, you will marry JoAnne. We are having a wedding

216

this afternoon."

I tried to maintain an air of confidence I did not feel at the moment. I told her we would take care of it and had it under control. She was not convinced and, frankly at that point, neither was I. My wife could not believe the story I told her.

The word was quickly passed, and we held an emergency meeting of the co-conspirators. We called Hughes Airwest to get Gator a seat on the first plane to Yuma. We were going to use our credit card to get Gator from the train station to the airport and on the plane. Problem solved.

Somebody called the airport. (Remember this was pre-cellphone days by many years). The word came back, and we were stunned. Hughes had decided to cancel the first flight, and to make matters worse, they canceled the second flight as well.

While we were plotting, Shirley called frequently to obtain an update. We gave her our best "Everything is under control," answer.

A bunch of Marine captains in a crisis can be creative. We called the group CO. He had access to a two-seat TA-4 aircraft. If he would send someone to Luke AFB, we knew we could get Gator from the train station to the base. Gator could be brought back to Yuma, in the TA-4, in no time. The group CO gave that plan about 30 seconds before he made his decision. "No way in hell!"

In the process of this venture, we heard that JoAnne's father's family believed we had this under control, and they thought it was hilarious. Shirley's crowd, on the other hand, thought we did not have any idea about how to get Gator back for the wedding. We sent some obviously false signals to Frank's crowd that we had it well in hand and let them exploit that storyline as much as they could to keep the heat off of us.

Time was passing. It was around 9:30 a.m. or so, and every option we had was exhausted. It was a solid four-hour drive from Phoenix to Yuma, one way. The wedding was at 3p.m. Driving up there and back was out of the question. By now, our wives were not speaking to us because Shirley had put the word out to each wife about what we had done. Skip had the next idea. His brother lived in Phoenix. Skip told us his brother could pick Gator up, take him to the Phoenix airport, and we could charter an aircraft to bring him to Yuma. That idea received a unanimous vote!

Skip spent some time on the phone coordinating the plan with his brother. They found a charter pilot to bring Gator to Yuma, with an estimated landing around 2 p.m. We raided our emergency cash funds and came up with the $200 required for the flight. We met Gator's plane at the terminal. To this day, there is still a question if the pilot actually stopped the plane or just slowed down enough to let Gator slide off the wing. He was air sick all the way to Yuma. We gave the pilot our money and he was gone.

When we met Gator, he seemed to be getting back to his old self. In a hoarse voice, he kept saying, "I love you guys, I love you guys!" Then we helped him climb in the back of my pickup to sit in a rocking chair. I drove him to the BOQ to get him ready for his wedding. He looked a tad rough but was in great spirits. The BOQ is fairly close to the chapel, so we figured we were good for time. There was a sigh of relief, for a while. Once we had Gator in his room, his uniform was not even close to being "ready," as he promised me.

It was determined that I be dispatched to the base chapel. The time was rapidly approaching 3 p.m. The church was essentially full when I arrived. Shirley headed me off, and we discussed the situation. As we spoke, I looked around the church, and gave a conspiratorial thumbs up and a confident grin to the crowd.

While I was in the church, there were three or four Marines helping to get Gator dressed in his dress blue uniform. His uniform was missing many parts. Each of us provided something, from rank insignia to socks, for his wedding. But finally, he was properly dressed for his nuptials. Only Gallo had enough ribbons to equal Pete's, so Pete's uniform contained a little of each of us. It was a love fest as we all were so relieved he was back, alive, and well.

Ten or so minutes after my arrival at the base chapel, the minister began to grill me about what was going on. We were only a few minutes away from start time. I told him the bridegroom was running a few minutes late. He asked. "How many minutes?" I said, "Probably 30." He was incensed. I did my best to keep him in good humor but found avoidance to be my best course of action.

The pianist played to fill the time with music, but she wanted additional money to continue to play for the wedding. I told her that would not be a problem. Now, I know the bride's family is supposed to pay for the wedding expenses, but I felt, given the circumstances, we should cover this expense.

It was probably a couple of minutes past 3:30 p.m. when Major Pete Wallis, UCMC could be pronounced ready for marriage by his fellow Marines.

Gator and I were finally in our positions. Looking over the crowd, I saw a full church, I did not see many happy faces. JoAnne began the march down the aisle on the arm of her father. I won't comment about the look she gave me as she walked up to the altar. But as soon as her gaze left me and went to Gator, I think she thought he was near dead. He looked pretty good to me.

The wedding ceremony went well. Gator held up very well until near the end. He and JoAnne were kneeling on a portable kneeler. I was standing reasonably close to them. When they started to get up, I could read Gator's mind as he contemplated placing his weight on his forearms on the top of the kneeler to assist him as he stood up. I knew what was about to happen. He was going to flip the kneeler. I whispered, "Gator, don't lean on the kneeler!" He looked at me, got the message, and all was well!

The happy couple left the chapel for pictures. Now our mission was complete. The co-conspirators all gathered to debrief the execution of the plan. We were looking forward to the reception starting in an hour or so. Our wives were not even remotely friendly, but that didn't dampen our euphoria of the moment.

The reception was at the best hotel in Yuma and was catered by the best restaurants. We were all on a high. This high was about one-half thankfulness and one-half relief. The crowd in the room was divided. Frank's crowd was cheering us on our success. Shirley's crowd wanted to kill us, and none of our wives were speaking to us. Measured by that standard, we all agreed the plan to be a complete success.

We went to Winterhaven to continue our group debrief and settle up

219

the money we ponied up for the expenses. It came to about $200 apiece and we all believed it was worth every penny. I guess, looking back, it was obvious we were getting a little full of ourselves.

• • •

In July 1977, we sent six aircraft to Twentynine Palms, the Marine Corps' ground training base for the Combined Arms Exercise (CAX). LtCol Hearney, recently promoted, had the same concerns about availability that we experienced in 542. We worked hard to get the planes ready for flight. Gator kept the pressure on our guys to keep aircraft in the air. We were running into parts issues again and they were getting serious. We contacted Col Pieri for help. He was able to send a crew of three from Hawker Siddeley to move to Yuma to help us out. The fellow in charge of the three Brits was Tug Wilson. Tug Wilson and his pals could do anything, and they significantly helped our availability and our in-house maintenance training. This reminds me of an old Marine Corps saying, "We have done so much, with so little, that we can do anything, with nothing." We also had Frank Armanno searching out parts from all available sources. He was able to find bolts from the John Deere dealer that were the exact part number the government supply could not locate and had been on order for over a year. The combination of these efforts really helped keep our planes in the air.

• • •

One of the pilots who recently joined 513 was Capt. Charlie Reed. I believe he had been in the Harrier program longer than most of us. If you just reached into a squadron to find the best representative of the unit, you could not find a better Marine than Chuck Reed. He was a family man, hard worker, and a very good aviator. Another of the "new" opportunities for us in Yuma was being able to send a pilot to the USAF Fighter Weapons School in late summer1977. These quotas had not been readily available to Marine squadrons in the past. Chuck Reed filled our slot.

We were excited when Charlie left for the Fighter Weapons School located at Nellis AFB near Las Vegas. After the required classroom work, he began flying, converting classroom knowledge to actual flight experiences, but on one of these flights, Chuck Reed impacted the ground and died.

I suspect most of us remember the day when the word was passed to the squadron. It was a shock. This type of mishap is oftentimes, pilot error. Charlie was not a pilot who would be expected to make that mistake. The cause was essentially unknown, but it did result in a low altitude audio warning device being added to the plane. This mishap was up close and personal to us. There was no ocean or landmass separating us from this fatal crash. This one was all ours. We grieved for his family and probably took a look in the mirror to remember we were mortal after all. The loss of Chuck Reed turned the squadron mood somber. For most of us, it was the first pilot loss since Rick Briggs' accident in 1974, but one hit us hard because by now we were all highly experienced, tactical Harrier pilots.

A few days after Charlie Reed crashed, Bonnie and I had our second child, a son, Steven Capito. Steve was named after Steve Arps, my friend from flight school. Our first was named Mike after Mike Siepert. There was a lot going on in the Yuma world.

We slowly began to work our way out of the somber mood.

• • •

Red Flag, a combat training exercise, was close on the horizon. The dates were essentially October 13 to November 18. The decision was made to split the squadron into two groups so we could all participate. Bill Callahan, Few, in his words, remembers the start-up for the exercise.

"When we got to Red Flag, at Nellis, we were assigned two remote sites to work from. Our first was Indian Springs AF (Auxiliary field), the second was Bicycle Lake located a short distance from Ft. Irwin. We would launch from Nellis AFB, fly up through the corridors into the restricted areas, recover at Indian Springs, refuel and then back into the restricted areas and recover at Nellis.

Prior to our deployment to Red Flag, Sabs and I, along with two others were sent to Ft. Irwin to inspect Bicycle Lake to make sure it was usable for Harrier operations. Since the airfield was on a dry lakebed, we found that a pad would have to be installed to accommodate Harrier vertical landings. Our DET was tasked to work in conjunction with AF A-10s to provide close air support for the Army units deployed to Ft. Irwin. Since the Harriers were still in the proof-of-concept phase and somewhat in competition with the A-10s, HQMC thought a pad would be a great idea. The pad was constructed, and everything was set for operations out of Ft. Irwin/Bicycle Lake. I am not sure who made the inspection of the pad or even if a Harrier pilot was called on to take a look at it.

The first sortie to be flown into Bicycle Lake was by our skipper, LtCol Rich Hearney. The squadron launched as a section (two aircraft) with everything being normal up to a point prior to touchdown. Prior to a vertical touchdown, the Harrier was engulfed by a sandstorm generated by the nozzle exhaust of the aircraft. Although the aircraft was totally engulfed in sand, the skipper made a perfect landing. I am not sure if the aircraft, after it was inspected, was flown, or trucked out of Bicycle Lake. It seems the site prep was not up to standards. Our DET was then moved to Barstow Daggett Airfield for operations. I know there was a lot of message traffic and paperwork filled out on the incident. The skipper returned to Yuma to deal with HQMC."

The maintenance department knew the heat was on to get the planes up and all systems go for Red Flag. As I remember, there was a lot of jockeying to be one of the first pilots to participate. That was the same issue in maintenance, everybody wanted to be part of another 513 Harrier first. We flew in Red Flag and comported ourselves well both in the air and on the ground. When we left Nellis after the exercise was completed, our goal was to be invited again. We finished out the year going through Thanksgiving and Christmas with the usual flight schedule.

3: 1978

I have tried to place events in calendar sequence, but there are no records available at the Marine Corps Historical Records Branch for VMA-513 from January 1977 to December 1978. So, these experiences will most likely not be in sequential order.

Things began to come unwound in early 1978. Looking back, the clues were subtle, but they were there. My crowd partied way too much. There is not much more to say. The workload seemed to increase. I remember thinking as I left an ops briefing about the upcoming spring and summer deployment schedule that maintenance needed to prepare for the spring offensive. There were other signs.

One of the topics circulating about the squadron concerned the accident rate of the Harrier. In 1977, the Harrier program lost nine aircraft. We lost one and a pilot (Capt. Chuck Reed), 231 and 542 each lost three, and 203 lost two. There was a lot of bad press about the Harrier. For example, one newspaper in North Carolina printed, "If you want to own a Harrier, buy a farm in North Carolina." A name or two that gained popularity was "The widow Maker" or "The Death Machine". It is difficult to say what impact these comments were having on the pilots or their families.

Another topic making the rounds concerned how stagnant the captains were getting in the squadron. Ken Shrum, as an example, was in the original 513. After seven full years as a Harrier pilot, Ken was frustrated as more senior officers were brought to the program. This made him one of the most junior officers in the squadron and he was the pilot with the most Harrier flight time. Ken was our first Marine Air Weapons Training Squadron graduate and became our Weapons Training Instructor (WTI). Ken took his role seriously and was put in charge of the Harrier Tactical Manual (TAC manual). The TAC manual is the official guide to employing the Harrier in combat. He was instrumental in developing the pop-up bomb delivery method from low altitudes that we were starting to use for many of our flights. But he was frustrated as many reasonable inputs were not implemented or were written off at higher headquarters, sometimes by non-Harrier-

223

experienced pilots.

Ken had a unique view of the program. Since he was in the first squadron, he witnessed the political pressure that was often placed on 513 for the first few years. The makeup of that squadron early-on contrasted greatly with the makeup of 542 with Col Stan Lewis as the CO. Ken once told me we introduced humor into 513 when we arrived in Iwakuni. He was also impressed with the extent and intensity of our friendships.

Some of us were beginning to have doubts about where we were going in the program. Three factors -- family concerns about the Harrier, the fact that we were getting tired, and the recently emerging airline pilot hiring spree -- caused some of us to review our long-term commitment to the Harrier program.

CPL Way (facing) and his crew on the frigid Cold Lake, Canada tarmac advises
SSgt Swatosh (right) a jet is ready for a sortie

Canada was where the US went to train aircrews and maintainers to operate in the cold environments. An exercise called Maple Flag, conducted at the air weapons range north of the city of Cold Lake, Alberta. It, like Red Flag, was a top-of-the- line deployment. The weather was cold, the terrain was mostly flat, trees everywhere and lakes galore. Our in-brief (familiarization and indoctrination for the exercise) consisted of the usual course rules, different flight scenarios and living quarters information. There was an O'Club for food, drinks and socializing. We also received a medical brief from the flight surgeon. She was very attractive, so we listened to her every word.

The flying was exciting. Lots of low-level navigation flights with some adversary work. We were a small DET, so we tried to fly twice a day. The Canadians were quite hospitable. There was nothing to do on the base for recreation during the workweek. Over the years, the Canadian pilots had broken the cue sticks, leaving a good pool table with 15 pool balls waiting for a cue stick, which might be slow to arrive. Due to a lack of cue sticks, the Royal Canadian Air Force pilots invented a pool table game called Crud. Crud only uses the cue ball and an object ball, usually a striped pool ball.

Roughly, this game involves guiding, then moving, the cue ball toward the object ball. Once the object ball has been hit and moving, it cannot stop. If it stops, the player letting it stop essentially loses a life, as it is called. Each player has three lives. After the player starts the object ball moving, he moves out of the way to let the other team member sequence in to use the cue ball to keep the object ball moving. It is a fast- paced game with a few more rules. Needless to say, there is a technique of some concern by leaving the opposing player easy access to the cue ball. All shots are to be taken from the ends of the table, not the sides. It is very difficult to switch table ends or climb on the table to get to the cue ball; the only requirement is to keep one foot on the floor when throwing the cue ball. Owen, Sabow and I were playing a good game of crud after lunch. The game was intense and Sabow, chewing on a toothpick, all of a sudden stopped playing. He looked scared and began pointing with his index finger toward his mouth, all the while whispering, "Toothpick; swallowed a toothpick!" He said this over and over.

We grabbed our coats and covers and ran to the van, with Sabow continuing to point toward his mouth. Pat and I could not quit laughing. We were almost unable to drive the van because we were laughing so hard. We drove to the clinic to help Sabs into the waiting room. The flight surgeon had been notified and arrived in short order. Pat and I explained what had happened at the crud game: the XO had swallowed a toothpick and he considered it a life-threatening situation. He kept pointing to his throat and whispering "toothpick." The flight surgeon calmly said, "You're OK. Go ahead and swallow." Sabs looked at her and kept pointing at his throat. She calmly told him again that the toothpick had been swallowed and he was just feeling the bruised area. He could now swallow. He did, and nothing happened. Pat and I were laughing so hard I thought Sabow was going to kill us. In all the years we had together, this is in the top five of most hilarious moments.

We finally had a weekend off and found a ride to Calgary. Sabow, Pat and I rented a suite in a hotel there. We went out on the town, but it was fairly well closed down. We had a beer or two and a meal, then headed back to the hotel for the night. We figured out why the Canadian pilots played crud in Cold Lake instead of going to Calgary in the winter.

· · ·

The great flying continued. One fun commitment was with Top Gun in Miramar, CA. They were receiving the supersonic Northrop F-5 fighters to use as adversary aircraft. 513 was tasked to fly ACM sorties against the Top Gun instructor pilots when they received their new F-5s. We spent a few days working with them and did very well flying against them. I am sure part of our success was due to their lack of flight time in the F-5, but we felt really good about how we conducted simulated air combat in the Harrier against such a formidable foe.

Gator Wallis was tasked with taking 513 DET-B to Iwakuni as the OIC in charge. They left in early April for six months, to return in late September or early October. When he left with the DET, I became the AMO once again.

Bob Snyder was no longer in the squadron. He was the XO of a support squadron, then was sent to the air station as the Clubs Officer; but he continued to fly with us. Since the TRANSPAC flight, Snyds had been much more serious than normal. He did not discuss this much with me, but I know he spoke to Jim Sabow about something on his mind.

• • •

There was an airshow scheduled for Paine Field in Everett, Washington in July 1978. Snyds and I were going to fly it. We were excited to get up there and looked forward to a fun weekend. We launched our two planes and had a glorious view of the mountains from Mt. Hood to St. Helens, Mt. Rainier and to Mt. Baker. We did a little arrival air show on Friday afternoon when we landed. That night there was a huge party for the performers, and we had a great time. It was shades of our Dallas performance a few years earlier. We met everyone from the president of Boeing to the fuel truck drivers. The weather was good Saturday; Snyds was scheduled to fly and I was the narrator. He performed an outstanding airshow, followed by the USAF Thunderbirds flying the Northrup T-38 Talon aircraft.

Saturday night, we returned to the motel where everyone was staying, and Snyds, after clearing it with the airshow managers, began to order "drinks for my friends," all paid for by the airshow. The place went ballistic and everyone had a great time.

It was my turn to fly the Sunday show. There was a lot of moisture on the ground and the cloud cover was fairly low. Prior to leaving Yuma, Dave Clegg, one of our favorite tech reps told us due to a moisture and sand mixture, our Gas Turbine Starters (GTS) might belch some flames when we cranked them, but not to worry about it as it would quickly extinguish itself as the GTS began to achieve RPM. The Thunderbirds canceled their Sunday show due to weather. I told the airshow management I would perform a Harrier low altitude airshow. I was on and Snyds was the narrator.

My Harrier was parked next to the Thunderbirds' T-38s. When I closed my canopy, the moisture prevented me from having a good view of all things around me. I wiped it off, but it came right back. The plane captain gave me the start signal. I cranked the GTS and he immediately gave me a fire signal. I remembered what Dave had told me, and at first, I was not too concerned. The canopy was still covered with moisture and I kept wiping it off with my flight glove. Even with bad visibility I saw the plane captain's fire signal was getting more urgent. I immediately shut down the GTS, opened the canopy, unstrapped, turned around and saw a real fire coming from the area around the GTS.

I jumped down to the ground, grabbed a large fire extinguisher on wheels, pulled it over, extended the hose, placed the nozzle in the GTS access area and pulled the trigger. The fire extinguisher fired off at the valve on the top of the bottle, covering me in fire retardant gases, but not the GTS. I walked out of the cloud and found another medium-size fire extinguisher nearby. I looked over my shoulder to see the crewman from the Thunderbirds pushing the T-38s away. I had my flight gear on and jumped on the starboard wing to get close to the GTS, pointed the nozzle into the GTS and fired. It put the fire right out. The plane captain and I confirmed the fire was out, so I began hatching a plan. Snyds was working the crowd while all this was happening. I still do not know how I made it on top of the wing with a fire extinguisher in hand with all my flight gear on.

I walked toward Snyds, and we talked this over. It was agreed I would fly his Harrier to do the airshow. It was a good feeling to get airborne and fly a modified airshow and to land at Paine Field Sunday afternoon. After it was finished, we called the squadron to let them know what had happened. They started to set up transportation for a crew to bring a new GTS and install it.

Snyds convinced the skipper since he was senior in rank and not in the squadron that his being away would not impact the squadron's daily routine. He volunteered to wait until the Harrier was repaired. The skipper agreed, and I headed to Yuma in Snyds' aircraft late Sunday afternoon.

It took a few days to secure transportation to get the crew with a GTS on a flight to Everett. Snyds and I were in phone contact daily. He told me, "Caps, I've been doing the nightly show in the motel and have a huge crowd every night." He was shouting "drinks for my friends," during happy hour. He made lots of friends and was having a grand time while waiting for the Harrier to be repaired. A few weeks after Snyds returned home, one of the show managers, a lady, called to tell me this was the first time the airshow lost money, that Snyds' big nights put them in the red, but the big nights were the talk of the town, so she did not care one bit. They loved him!

. . .

228

Not long after his return from Everett, Snyds called me to have a talk. We got together, and the first thing he told me was that he had poured out all his booze and suggested I do the same. I was stunned, first because he poured it all out, and second, because he did not offer any of it to us. But Snyds was very serious as he began to tell me a story about what had happened to him on the TRANSPAC.

He was in the flight of four Harriers in front of my division, flying from Hawaii to Oakland. Both divisions had problems tanking. He told me he fell behind the flight when he detached from the KC-130 aircraft after refueling his plane in the rough weather. Apparently, he had used some nozzles (deflecting the thrust from aft to slightly downward, a common Harrier technique to rapidly slow the jet) to keep from overrunning the other planes in the flight. He left the nozzles in a bit too long, causing his Harrier, now heavy with fuel, to slow down too much. Visibility was limited. The other planes in his flight were pulling away far in front of him and becoming small dots on the horizon, making it much more difficult for him to maintain sight.

He was trying to climb to catch them, but it was rough going. He was about flight level 30 or 30,000 feet and the others were level at flight level 33 or 33,000 feet. In a very short time, he noticed a Harrier on his left side. This Harrier appeared to Snyds to be upside down. He spent a few seconds trying to figure out where this Harrier had come from, then he looked at his altimeter. He was in a dive, inverted and was passing 24,000 feet. He thought he was climbing but was actually in a dive. He righted his airplane and began a climb to catch up with the other aircraft in his flight. Snyds then looked for the other Harrier, but it was nowhere in sight. Since he had lost sight of his flight, he contacted our chase plane to find out where his flight was located. They were five miles ahead at one o'clock. He finally joined on the flight and landed at NAS Alameda with low fuel.

Once he was safely on the ground, the plane captain told him he looked pale. Snyds told him, "I just saw the face of God" and walked away. He did not tell anyone else about this experience at first, except maybe Sabow. Slowly, he started going to church. He was aware that he had experienced a supernatural moment in his life. Over the next months, he thought about the social and drinking life he had lived and listened to his strongly supportive wife, Susan. After the Everett airshow and one more he performed in Omaha, NE, Snyds returned to Yuma a changed man. He stopped drinking and began to work on a religious career once he left the Marine Corps. After he retired, he attended a seminary, became an ordained minister and started a successful church in Phoenix, AZ.

...

Since we had access to the ranges when they were not in use by a deploying squadron, we did a lot of bombing and low-level navigation sorties. In Iwakuni, as I remember, Col Gus was probably the best bomber, with maybe Al James close in trail. There were many good bomber pilots in the squadron, but I think those two were the best. Al was still with us, so I suspect Few was the next in line as the best bomber. The ACM crowd consisted of the Skipper, Buc, Ken Shrum, and Mammal. Hands down, the best low-level navigator I ever flew with was Pat Owen. He was like having a human GPS in the other plane. The rest of us were like baseball utility players who could fit right into these groups when required and the flights would lose little, if any, proficiency.

...

One weekend I had been tapped to do a static display at Edwards AFB in California, the home of the USAF test pilot school and many other commands. I arrived Friday afternoon and did the usual warm-up airshow in front of a small crowd. I landed, parked my plane and headed to the O'Club. I spent the night at the BOQ, looking forward to the airshow the next day. I spent the morning touring the planes that landed for the static display. This was a one-day airshow. The flying started with civilian and then military flights. The Blue Angels or the Thunderbirds were not flying.

During the morning briefing the F-16, still undergoing testing, was scheduled to fly the last flight. They did not discuss the flight routine. I spoke to the pilot, a LtCol, and he said they were still working it out before he launched. The F-16 started up and I was able to listen to his radio calls as I was near the base operations vehicle. While he was taxiing for takeoff, the controller of the flight gave the pilot the go ahead for a double Immelmann maneuver on takeoff. That got my attention. The Immelmann is a difficult aerobatic maneuver to reposition the airplane, pioneered by a German pilot in WW I. Most of us had either done or tried to do a double Immelmann in the Harrier, but not after takeoff. I listened as the F-16 became airborne and smartly executed an Immelmann right after takeoff. At the top of the maneuver, the controller confirmed his airspeed, and he gave the pilot the go ahead for the second Immelmann. If you know a little about airplanes, that maneuver is truly impressive; the F-16 had a powerful engine. The F-16 finished a really good air show and landed.

When the airshow was finished, I was ready to return to Yuma. During aircraft refueling and clearing the crowd from the runway, the wind was picking up and approaching 40 knots, 90 degrees to the runway. It took more than an hour to clear the area for a takeoff. I was in base operations filing a flight plan when the senior officer of the airfield shut down flight ops due to the crosswind. I tracked down the officer and told him I wanted to launch for Yuma. We discussed the crosswind and I told him I would like to do a short take off into the wind. The runway was 300 feet wide, and that was plenty of room for a Harrier. He wanted me to call my CO to get approval to takeoff across the runway. The duty officer could not find anyone to okay the takeoff, so he gave me the OK. After a bit more lobbying and explaining the takeoff capability of the Harrier, the officer gave me the go-ahead for takeoff across the active-duty runway. The plane was so light on fuel and the wind so strong I decided to do a rolling vertical takeoff: as the engine passed 99% within a second and a half, you slam the nozzles to 70 degrees. I probably rolled 50 or 60 feet and did my best to reach 1,000 feet of altitude by the time the Harrier crossed the runway.

It was sometimes difficult to make people realize the capabilities of the Harrier. It was one heck of a plane.

• • •

Looking to develop some camaraderie, we decided to reach out to the ground Marines we affectionately called grunts, stationed at Camp Pendleton. We were flying a lot of CAS sorties with them and thought a face-to-face meeting would be helpful for both groups to put faces and names to our Marines. Sabs was the leader of this effort. The plan

231

was to send eight aircraft to Camp Pendleton for a Friday happy hour. The pilots would buy the drinks. Our plan was for each of us to drop a $100 bill on the bar and enjoy the evening discussing all things Marine.

Sabs and another pilot went to Pendleton to set up transportation for us and secure our lodging. The grunts had an open squad bay for us to spend the night in, an older and slightly used barracks. Sabs nixed the squad bay idea and told the Major he met with he would get BOQ rooms at NAS Miramar instead. Friday arrived and we were excited. As I remember it, we wore our finest flight suits adorned with appropriate patches and flew over to have a nice evening with our ground counterparts. We arrived at Pendleton only to have a very few lieutenants and maybe a major show up. We had been stood up. So, we stayed for a reasonable amount of time, then quickly devised a back-up plan. We left Pendleton in our van, provided by the base, and hit Friday happy hour at Miramar, the bar of Top Gun fame. It was one of the best places to be on Friday night when you were on the west coast. We had a great time and returned to Yuma the next morning. Later, the word came back to us that the grunts were not happy with us. They thought that we considered the accommodations at Pendleton were not good enough for us and they felt like we were just lording it over them that we received flight pay. From our viewpoint, these were definitely unintended consequences. We were all disappointed at the turn this venture took.

...

Later in the summer, Denny Greene, a big, tall good looking Texas gent with a call sign of Texan, and I were scheduled to fly an airshow in Dallas. I was pumped because of my friends there, and Denny was excited because he had many family members in Mesquite, a town a few miles east of Dallas. I was scheduled to fly the airshow both days and Denny was to be the announcer. We arrived early Friday and I flew a practice show that afternoon. Friday night we met with a bunch of my Dallas friends and hit the bar. The Dallas reserve unit now had the F-4 Phantoms they were supposed to have had when I was transferred there seven years earlier.

The talk in the bar was of Harrier flying and airline hiring. The airlines were starting to hire again. While Denny and I were drinking with these guys, they began to talk to me about flying with the airlines. A senior pilot with a major airline offered me a slot. He told me I only had to let him know and he would set it up. That was something that at one time I had wanted to do, being an airline pilot and to fly in the reserves. But at that moment I was not quite ready to leave the Marine Corps. I asked for time to consider the offer and would respond to him soon. Denny listened intently to what was being said and jumped on it. He asked me to help him get on with the airlines.

Denny wanted to fly the Saturday airshow since his family was there. I tried to call the OPSO but could not find him to get approval. Denny flew the show and did a good job with it. Being a big, tall, good looking Texan, the crowd mobbed him when he landed. Denny spent Saturday night with his family, and I stayed in the motel. It was an aviation gift for me. I wound up sitting at the bar with Art Scholl and Bob Hoover. Bob was a WWII fighter pilot ace and was considered to be one of the best pilots in America. He was beyond nice. Art Scholl flew in many airshows, putting on a great show, was a wonderful pilot and most pleasant man. It was an honor for me to spend time with them.

I flew the Sunday show and we both left Dallas with a lot on our minds. Once we debriefed, we shared the discussion we had about flying with the airlines with our friends; a lot of airline discussions started in the squadron.

• • •

Few went to Area 51 to fly against a Soviet era fighter. He could not talk about it, as it was top secret. We were excited for him and the Harrier. Joe Gallo was selected to attend Top Gun at Miramar. This was a huge honor for Joe and again the Harrier. The exposure the Harrier was getting just from 513 was gratifying.

Ken Shrum had worked hard on a weapons delivery maneuver called a pop-up. We began flying low altitude ingress training below 500 feet to be completed with a pop-up, rollover delivery, ostensibly to protect us from anti-aircraft guns and missiles.

The air show schedule continued, and we stayed busy. All of us were very comfortable flying the Harrier. I would never say complacent because each of us respected the Harrier. You could not take the plane for granted. My thought then, and is now, that we all felt like we were one with plane. Like any good fighter pilot would say, we did not strap in the plane, we strapped the plane on our ass. The Harrier brought each of us home from some close calls time and time again.

One afternoon while at Yuma I flew a test flight, just a quick out and back. After getting airborne and finishing the checks I headed back to the field. I came into the overhead break, rolled out downwind, put down the landing gear and the nose gear would not come down. The procedure to remedy the problem was to recycle the gear. I did and the nose gear stayed up again. It would not come down. After some discussion, the decision was to raise the landing gear and perform a vertical landing on the concrete. The speed brake remained extended but all else was normal. The aircraft had gun pods on it, so the landing was fairly easy. The problem is that the canopy won't open when the plane is resting on the ground because in normal operation the boarding ladder extends and retracts as the canopy is either opened or closed. Thus, in the case of a gear-up landing, the ladder hits the ground, preventing the canopy from opening. In Yuma it was very hot as usual but the maintenance guys, being the experts they were, had me out in no time. The plane was back up for a test flight by noon the next day.

Gator had taken another DET to WESTPAC in late March or early April. During October there was a lot going on around the squadron. Gator's "Det-B" was returning from Iwakuni and there was a lot of excitement brewing for that event. Gator's Marines were arriving on a C-141 in the early afternoon after having been gone for six months.

• • •

Ken Shrum and I had recently returned from getting our Airline Transport Rating (ATP) at the John Wayne airport in California. On Oct. 2, my first day back in the squadron, Joe Gallo and I were scheduled to fly two early-morning flights to drop practice ordnance. Joe had recently completed Top Gun.

We briefed the first flight, launched and followed the railroad tracks west for a bit, flying a low-level combat spread formation, abeam each other about a half mile apart. Since I knew him so well and had flown with him many times, it was easy to see how much he had learned from the Top Gun course. I even commented to him about it on the way to the target area. Joe was always a good pilot, but now he was a step above some of us after attending Top Gun. We dropped our bombs, and he critiqued our flight on the way back to base. We landed and went to the hangar to get something to drink and to plan and brief our next flight. I told him I could not wait to fly an air-to-air sortie with him so he could show me some tricks. We both laughed.

Getting ready for the next flight, he mentioned he did not feel quite up to par but we both blew it off. Joe was the flight leader. We briefed the pop-up attacks we were going to use for dropping our ordnance. We also discussed doing some air combat training (ACT) after dropping our bombs so he could show me what he had learned at Top Gun. We had a normal takeoff and headed to the Chocolate Mountains for the second time that morning.

The flight out was uneventful. We had flown together so many times there was not much chatter on the radios. As we approached the target area, Joe checked in with the appropriate agencies, then we entered the range area. The pop-up maneuver is designed to commence as a low-level attack with the run-in to the target at about 200 feet altitude, followed by pulling up to a modified wingover maneuver. During the climb to the apex, you acquire the target and roll in for a briefed 10-degree dive bomb run. The goal is to offer minimal time for someone to acquire and lock you up with a shoulder-fired missile or an anti-aircraft gun. There are variations but this is what we had briefed. Our targets were on our right-hand side as we flew into the area. When Gallo pulled up, I took a 20-degree heading change to the left to ensure adequate separation before beginning my pull-up.

Once in the pull-up, I spotted Joe's aircraft in his dive and at the same time I also identified the target. About the time I started to commence my right turn and pull down toward the target, I saw Joe's aircraft heading rapidly toward the ground. The way I saw his plane totally confused me for a second. Then I was frantically shouting, "pull up, pull up," from the time I saw him until his Harrier impacted the ground.

As I gathered my wits about me, I searched for any sign of an ejection, but found none. The picture, which initially confused me, was that of an inverted aircraft flying into the ground. His plane was not flying upright. There was no response from my calls, no wing movement, no heading change, nothing.

I aborted my run of course, then flew immediately toward the crash site at a low altitude still looking for any signs of a parachute. Joe was nowhere to be seen on the ground. There was nothing to see, no Joe, no Harrier, nothing. It was like the plane evaporated. I just witnessed one of the best people I ever met in my life fly an aircraft into the ground...and disappear!

I went up guard frequency, an emergency radio channel to broadcast what had happened. It was important to me to have an overhead aircraft relieve me before heading back to Yuma. I was in shock but had no idea of that at the time. After some time had passed, a Grumman F-14 Tomcat from Miramar heard my call and was heading to relieve me. I called home base to tell them what had happened and to let them know I was staying overhead until relieved on station. When the F-14 arrived, I reluctantly left to start toward Yuma. It was the first time I checked my fuel. I had enough to get home, but no more. I often wondered had the F-14 been a few minutes later if I would have remained on site and been forced to land in El Centro instead of Yuma. My fuel state was the last thing on my mind. But after looking at the fuel remaining on the fuel gauge, it quickly focused me on the task of getting my own Harrier back on the ground in one piece.

Once at the squadron, the awful job of debriefing what I could about the flight began. Joe's wife, Dana, had to be told, and that task fell to the skipper. The XO, Few's wife and others needed to be notified as well. I met a ready room full of pilots and maintenance folks wanting to know the details and I did my best to lay it out for them. It was extremely difficult to say very much because of my state of mind. Joe was gone, the Harrier was gone, and I was the only witness. Gone also was the friend with whom I had totally bonded, respected, admired and had so many good times with, both in the air and on the ground. I was totally devastated.

• • •

We were still waiting for the C-141 to land that was bringing the troops home. I knew what a horrible welcome home that would be for them.

I am certainly not the only one this had happened to while flying. Mike Ryan watched Charlie Reed hit the ground a year earlier. I believe it was the totality of the moment that wiped me out. Joe and I shared a long and intense friendship. I never knew anyone that close who had been killed in an aircraft accident. Even my high school friend who was killed in Vietnam was far away from Kentucky when it happened. Then there was the fact that I was helpless when it was happening. There was absolutely nothing I could do to make a difference to the flight path of a plane in a 10-degree inverted dive, flying approximately 500 knots, to keep it from hitting the ground.

The squadron had suffered a terrible blow. The simple fact about Joe Gallo was, in my opinion, that he was the heart of our squadron and of our Yuma Harrier family. That is a heavy load to give a person, but over the years I have asked many people how they felt about him. They believe he was very special in each of their lives. There was just something about Joe we all recognized. Be you a PFC or a general, you instinctively would be drawn to Joe. He was solid, a one-of-a-kind Marine who worked hard, played hard and was loyal to all. He was loved by the troops. Joe was truly a Marine's Marine.

. . .

Capt. Byron Trapnell, Trapper, had moved to Yuma and was assigned to the Marine Aviation Weapons and Tactics Squadron, (MAWTS). He had recently moved into his house. Fortunately for me, my wife and two kids were visiting her family, so I was by myself. I had to deal with the loss of Joe Gallo in my own way and I was not sure what that way might be. When I got home, Trapper called me to come over to his house. Trapper was a lot like Joe Gallo. He could also be the heart of a squadron. He had lots of charisma and was a great friend. I grabbed a bottle of Chivas Regal scotch, bought when I started flight school, and headed his way. That bottle had been around for 10 years. During that time, I had received my wings, got fighters, went to Vietnam, got married, got Harriers, had kids, and for each of those events not even one of them seemed to be a big enough reason to open that bottle. Now, I had my reason.

It was like the first day Trapper and I met, only this time we drank MY bottle of scotch. I talked, I cried, I was a mess. I walked back home from Trapper's house in the early morning feeling sober enough to pass a blood alcohol test.

When I arrived at the squadron the next morning, I was headed toward ops. I had been scheduled to fly an airshow in Brownsville, TX the coming weekend. I thought that might be the perfect way to get me back on track. The skipper grabbed me before I made it to ops to tell me I was not going on that flight. I was unhappy, but soon realized I was in no shape to fly an airshow. I appreciated that gesture.

The days prior to Joe's memorial service are somewhat a blur to me. The service was at the base chapel, with burial to be in California. I was selected to deliver the eulogy in Yuma.

The skipper had made arrangements with Joe's father and members of his family to attend the memorial service. We were all seated, and the members of Joe's family were not there yet. We were in the chapel waiting for them to arrive and I am sure there was talk of delaying the service to await their arrival. Just a very few minutes prior to the start of the service, Gallo's family walked into the church. They represented the family very well. They had flown from Philadelphia to San Diego, then chartered a plane to Yuma. They were a group of solemn, sad people, just like the rest of us.

During the service, it was difficult for me to concentrate on what was being said. The skipper said a few words about Joe. When it was time for me to come forward to read the eulogy, I could hardly do it. Mike Ryan, sitting right behind me, tapped me on my shoulder, kindly asking if I wanted him to read it for me. I shook my head no. I appreciated his offer, but I owed Joe, and I slowly walked forward to read his eulogy. That was one of the most difficult things I have had to do in my life!

After the service, there was a large gathering to honor and discuss Joe and his life. I met his father and family. Since I had an empty house, I offered to put up Joe's father, and his cousins until they left. We eventually went to the house, continuing to visit for a long time. Joe's father wanted to go to the crash site, so I worked on that with the

238

skipper and we were able to get him there in a helo. I was also allowed to go. It was my first time there on the ground. When we landed at the crash site, there truly was nothing to see. After wandering around looking for anything of value to the investigation, I experienced a loving and difficult life lesson. I watched a father have the moments he needed to tell his son goodbye. I turned away because of the intensity of that moment. The Gallo family soon departed Yuma to go to the burial in California. I did not attend that service. I did return to the crash site a couple of more times to look around. I found a piece of his watch and a quarter. That was it.

...

We returned to business as usual during the next few weeks. The flying continued like always, but in my opinion, there was a slight change in the squadron atmosphere. I believe we were more serious around the squadron. Our exaggerated sense of humor and laid-back outlook on life was missing something. We did not seem as focused as we had been prior to Joe's crash. For the past five years we had escaped mishaps in the Harrier. The other two squadrons had mishaps and fatalities, but not us, not the 542/513 guys. Then we experienced two fatalities about one year apart. That reality hit us hard! We had no doubt we were the better pilots. We also knew we had probably been very lucky.

After we began flying our normal schedule for a couple days, Mike Ryan ejected from another Harrier four days after Gallo had his accident. Mike was OK, but I really believe we were so spent that if he had been injured or killed, it could have shut the squadron down for a period of time. Now our squadron had a mechanical failure to add to our total number of mishaps and fatalities.

I had held firmly to a core belief about squadron life since we had left Beaufort. I believed the strength of the 542/513 pilots was the fact that we had longer than normal tours together in the squadron. By the fall of 1978, many of us had flown together for five or more years. That was similar to what I had experienced with the reserves in Dallas. They flew together for many years and were the best of friends. They flew safely and were extremely well-qualified F-8 pilots.

When Joe died, we lost one of our family members. Suddenly we were no longer the group of pilots in the Harrier program who avoided accidents and Harrier fatalities. We were just like the other squadrons. Two of our best Harrier pilots were dead, killed in a Harrier, about a year apart. I believe Chuck Reed's was gravity-induced loss of consciousness as he maneuvered at high speed near the ground and Joe's was illness. Maybe we were mortal after all. At the time Mike Ryan ejected, if he had been killed, I wondered if we could find any organizational emotion left to offer his family. Speaking for myself, I was spent, and I do not believe I was alone in these feelings.

For the first time in my Harrier career, I began to question my long-held belief of keeping the same people in a squadron for an extended period of time. The very thing I championed and cherished, flying with my best friends, partying and living life together for many years, had possibly become a weakness for the operation of the squadron. The idea of getting too close to one another never entered my mind. But was that a real possibility?

There were other items that kept coming up. Ken Shrum told me about a statement he heard from Few that went something like this: Few talked about us being like a great football team that never played a game, all we did was practice and practice. He said eventually you start to compete on a different level, who has the best uniform, who shined their brass every day, who had the best locker and desk set, etc. I confess I never had those feelings at the time, but I understood his comment. Most of us were promoted to major the month Joe was killed. There would soon be much more expected of us. Our antics as captains would be frowned upon as majors, our flying time would be reduced to make sure junior pilots flew enough to keep their training on schedule. Squadron life was going to change.

Then there was the lure of the airlines calling. Denny Greene had taken my slot as AMO and had just departed Yuma for training in Houston at Continental Air Lines a week or two prior to Gallo's crash. We had been doing the same things in our squadrons for each of the last five-plus years. As a group, we had accomplished about everything you could do with a Harrier. The shipboard work, the CAL sites, the airshows, the deployments, the TRANSPAC, ACM, bombing, Red Flag and Cold Lake exercises, the long hours trying to get airplanes ready for the flight schedule, and the drinking and partying. We had done it all, many times over, by the fall of 1978.

Pat Owen recently said to me, "We were then in our 30s, no longer the hard charging 20-something captains of the previous five years. Maybe we were just tired and needed a change."

After Joe's death, many of us began to fly for the airlines; some stayed in the Marines and transferred to schools or new assignments.

On paper, 1978 was a much safer year for the Harrier program. The program lost three aircraft, two in 513 and one in 542. When you realize "who" you lost in addition to the aircraft, it makes the safer year somehow seem meaningless.

Like 542 when we left Cherry Point for Iwakuni, new pilots and maintainers came to 513, and it eventually became a new squadron and a good squadron. That was the exact way a squadron was designed to function.

The squadron gave up to the civilian world Al James, Mike Siepert, Denny Greene, Toby Griggs, Bill Callahan, Ken Brust, Ken Shrum, and me. Ted Herman went to Spain for an exchange tour with the Spanish Harriers, and Pat Owen transferred to the college degree completion program.

It would be unfair to say all this was because of the loss of Joe Gallo, but in some strange way, his death made us all rethink life a bit. We also had two officers passed over for promotion. One was ready to retire but the other, as well as the ones who left for the airlines, had lots of time left to pursue a professional career. They were as good as anyone in the squadron. Their leaving was a real turnoff for many of us.

My flight time in Yuma was 349 hours, averaging 14 hours a month. I left the Marine Corps with 1,062 total Harrier flight hours. Looking back on our Harrier life together, maybe we did have too much of a good thing!

PART 5 (1979-1983)

<u>NAS Kingsville, TX</u>

Once a Marine, always a Marine

1: I'm Back

When I left 513 in January 1979, I truly believed I had flown my last Harrier flight on January 3. I had 1,062 flight hours in the AV-8A. I left the Marines looking for a second career flying in the airlines. My Braniff connections from the Dallas Marine reserves helped me secure a place at the airline.

Bonnie and I moved to Dallas and I started work late January. It was different but I enjoyed it. I joined the Dallas reserves in a non-flying billet and was able to get together with my mentors and friends once again.

Braniff went through some great times and then some bad ones. I was furloughed in May 1980. Airline flying jobs were difficult to get at the time, but I did have high-level contacts with one other airline, so I was heading in that direction.

One afternoon while all the turmoil was going on, I received a phone call from Col Gustafson asking if I would consider returning to the Marine Corps and back to the Harrier. All of a sudden, it was time to make a decision. Bonnie and I now had three children, Mike, Steven and a very recent arrival, Jocelyn. I really missed the camaraderie, and of course, there was the lure of flying the Harrier, once again.

I signed up.

In a couple months my orders arrived at our home in Irving, TX. Instead of going to a Harrier squadron as I had envisioned, I was headed to NAS Kingsville, TX to become an advanced jet flight instructor in VT-22, flying the TA-4J Skyhawk. Being a flight instructor in the Naval Training Command was the last thing I wanted to do for the next three years of my life. I did some work at Braniff in the training department and that was rewarding, but the TA-4J was not a Harrier! I was bummed about the assignment.

Yet, we all know sometimes the path ahead might not be the one you would choose for yourself, but oftentimes turns out to be the one that gives you the best possible life experience. Being a flight instructor in VT-22 at Kingsville would turn out to be that experience for me.

2: Flight Instructor

I checked into the squadron and was sent to the instructor training school, referred to as charm school, in Pensacola, and slowly began to get used to the idea that I was going to be a flight instructor for the next three years. I began flying very soon after I arrived. The CO discussed the flight time I had in the different aircraft I had flown, then assigned me as the maintenance check pilot after a few flights in the TA-4. In a very short time, I flew as much as I wanted, averaging more than 25 hours a month. I found out quickly why A-4 pilots loved their Skyhawks, even though I was only flying the TA-4J, the trainer, not the single seat A-4M. It was a fun, reliable and very forgiving aircraft.

My good friend Major Bobby Light had been transferred from 513 and was now the operations officer for VT-22. I was unaware of that when I received orders to Kingsville, and it was a real treat for me as I knew no one else on the base. I started as the squadron safety officer and then spent about a year and a half as the AMO. The tour turned out to be two-plus years of learning and professional growth for me. I never tired of teaching Navy ensigns and Marine 2ndLts how much fun it was to fly. The flight students lived, slept, and breathed flying. It was exciting to see them progress through the flight syllabus to receive their wings and go to the fleet. I really enjoyed the tour. While I was unaware of it at the time, it turned out to be the perfect place for me to prepare for my future career.

In Kingsville I met flight students that were being assigned to the fleet hoping to fly the F-18 Hornets, Harriers, F-14 Tomcats, and other high-performance naval aircraft. It was obvious to me these young officers were much different from my generation.

For the most part, they were smarter, much more serious, better prepared, and motivated than we were when I went through flight school. There was intense competition to fly the airplane of choice in the fleet. Just like during my time as a student, the needs of the service dictated the number of slots that came up each week for fighter or attack airplanes. In order to fly the F-18 or Harrier, each student pilot put forth his best effort, every day. The Harrier was a bit of a hard sell to a few

247

students. Marines' other choice was the F-18, so the Harrier had tough competition. Bobby and I worked with students to dispel rumors about the crashes and fatalities that were in the training command's bag of urban legends. I believe we were successful for the most part.

The other huge change I noticed as soon as I walked into the ready room was the attitude of the instructors. It had been over 11 years since I had been in the training command environment. When I attended flight school, many of the instructors were marking time to either get out of the service or return to Vietnam. Many of them did not want to be there, and when I was at NAS Meridian, MS I noticed there was a bit of animosity in the training squadrons.

I found there was a marked change of that attitude when I arrived at VT-22. The instructors I met there were much more student-friendly, gave of their time to work with students to get them through any rough spots, and seemed genuinely happy to be there. The instructors' attitude, the ready room environment, the hard-working students and the desire to put out a good product became evident when you walked into the squadron. I believe much of that portion of the squadron's success was due to the subtle touch of Major Bobby Light. He made the squadron come alive. Bobby and I always told people we were just two country boys, but he was a Naval Academy graduate and one of the smartest people I ever met in the Marines.

3: Aviation Maintenance Officer (AMO)

After almost a year as the safety Officer, I asked the new CO to make me the AMO. He declined. So, I spoke to his boss, the commodore, at the bar one Friday night to tell him my frustrations. I asked him if he would either try to convince the new CO to make me the AMO or allow me to transfer to another squadron where they needed an AMO. That squadron flew the T-2 Buckeye. That conversation earned me a lot of visibility, much of it unwanted. My CO had to eventually replace a Marine major in VT-22 for me to get the job as AMO. It worked out because the major was getting out in about four months and agreed to step down early.

After watching the maintenance department struggle for almost a year, I could not wait to get my hands dirty on the hangar deck. At that point I was in hog heaven as they say. I had been there for about a year and knew where the bodies were buried. It was in that job where I learned to work with people in a much more productive manner than I did in the Harrier program. There is a difference in the Navy culture and the Marine culture. Working with sailors was a different, but very rewarding, experience. In the AV-8A squadrons, we worked the troops all the time, making up for the lack of parts through overworking Marines and massive cannibalization. In Kingsville we had parts availability problems, but they were much more solvable than the Harrier had been. The TA-4 had been around a long time and parts were in the system.

The Navy chiefs in the maintenance department were of the highest caliber and knew how to meet any challenge. The catch to working with Navy chiefs was simple. They had to believe they could trust you to cover them with the command element. Once you earned their trust, they would do anything you asked of them. My chiefs, as I called them, were the best. I knew them well from being the safety officer and hanging around the maintenance department hoping to get the AMO job.

We were off to a rough start, though, because they loved the major who was leaving the job. My first day on the job, the maintenance chief walked into my new office and said, "Major you will never be good enough to replace the AMO." I remember telling him, "I hope you're right chief, I want to be much better. We don't have enough up aircraft."

When I went downstairs, we had about 10 to 12 aircraft flyable for the daily flight schedule. We had 24 TA-4s on hand. The second day I was there, I gave the senior chief seven blank legal pads and told him to gather the chiefs and write down all the things that prevented 100 percent aircraft availability. I told him I wanted no solutions, just problems. He returned in about 90 minutes, after five or so cups of coffee, to proudly hand me seven blank legal pads.

I was excited. It was the Tuesday after Thanksgiving and Christmas leave was coming up. Before I went downstairs to see the senior chief, I convinced the CO to let me cancel Christmas leave if I needed the labor force to work on airplanes. I would not have done that after my experience in 542, but I needed some leverage working with these guys.

When I was handed the blank pads, I said to the senior chief, "That's great. We'll keep working until we get 'em all flying since there are no known issues to prevent that from happening." He immediately mentioned, Christmas leave is coming up. I told him I would cancel leave until we got all the planes flying. He responded, "Sir. You can't do that!" I told him the CO gave me permission to do that very thing. The senior chief asked for the legal pads and took off. It was not long until I had the information I needed to get the maintenance department going. He returned with seven full pads.

It took a bit, but once the chiefs knew they could trust me, they got on board. The incident that made it all happen was memorable for me. One of our Marines, 1stLt, Griz Adams, was a recent graduate of the VT-22 flight program, who was retained in the squadron to be a flight instructor. Griz brought an aircraft back with an engine vibration. The power plants sailors turned it up on the flight line and said it was fine. I decided to fly it on a test flight. I felt the described vibration and returned to the maintenance control area to declare, "Change the engine."

That was not my best move. I had stepped on the toes of the power plants experts by declaring the engine needed removal without

250

discussing it with them. The maintenance senior chief told me I created some issues in the department. The only thing for me to do was double down. I told the maintenance chief if I were wrong, I would buy the maintenance department a few cases of beer to purchase my credibility back. On the other hand, if the engine failed the test at the higher maintenance level, I did not need to know about it. Six weeks later, I received a call from the crew leader checking the engine at the higher maintenance level telling me the engine had serious internal damage. I never heard anything from the maintenance chief about the engine, but the relationship between the chiefs and me took off. I did not have to buy any beer.

The VT-22 maintenance department soon had all 24 aircraft up and flying at various times and maintained an 81 percent availability rate which was 10 percent higher than the entire training command average and significantly higher than previous numbers in the squadron. Because of the effort from the maintenance department, VT-22 flight-hour production increased by 12 percent during the period I was AMO. It was the people/leadership training program I needed to move forward in and enjoy my career. Coming to work there every day was a joy. One of the highlights from those days was an invitation for my assistant, Capt. Jack Harland, and me to join the chiefs for happy hour at the chief's club. That was quite an honor for both of us, as officers were usually not invited there. We felt honored to be there and knew we had developed a strong working relationship with them that benefited all of us.

4: Return to Cherry Point

During my last year in Kingsville, I was selected for promotion to LtCol, and would pin on the rank in the fall of 1983. That sounded good, but being a new LtCol out of his primary aircraft for over four and a half years makes you a target for staff tours or other non-flying assignments. I was that LtCol. I always felt like we were isolated from the east coast Harrier community when I was in Yuma with 513. Two years with an airline and two and a half years in the Navy training command just enhanced that feeling.

Orders to 2nd MAW arrived for the third time in my career. Shortly after the orders arrived, I was in my office when I was told I had a phone call from some colonel in Cherry Point. I took the call. It was Col Fred Ogline, the MAG-32 CO. He had been a flight instructor in my training squadron when I was a flight student and we had been in the Harrier training class together. Col O, as he was called, asked me if I could come to Cherry Point for a visit. I agreed and made plans to go as soon as possible. A bit of maneuvering on my part, coupled with a Marine student wanting to look at the Harrier as his choice of aircraft, provided me with a chance to go to Cherry Point.

I did not know many Marines at Cherry Point so I had no idea what to expect when I arrived. We landed and taxied to the VMAT-203 flight line. When we got out of the airplane, the 203 CO and other pilots met us on the flight line. We visited for a few minutes. I had no idea who these people were, and they knew nothing about me. I was a stranger in their land. After we talked, the CO took me to his office to tell me there were many jobs for a Harrier LtCol on the wing staff, the 2nd Marine Division and other locations. He told me to get a good look at the Harrier while I was parked on the flight line. He assured me that due to the student load, plus refreshers and poor aircraft availability, I would most likely not be flying the Harrier again. He invited me to happy hour at the *Shame* later that afternoon. All I could think of to say was thank you for letting us park our TA-4 on your flight line, Skipper!

Although the walk from 203's hangar to the group CO's office was only 300 yards, it was a long one. I had no idea what I was getting myself into returning to Cherry Point. I did not know Col O well. Through the years I met a few people who knew and worked with him and was told he was a very good and fair Marine officer. He enjoyed the respect of all those he served with during his career. You just knew he was one of the good guys.

I stopped in front of the white MAG-32 headquarters building that I had entered only a few times during my previous tours at Cherry Point. As a captain, I believed the less you hung around the group headquarters, the more you reduced your chances of getting a group job. I walked up the stairs to the second-floor office suite, home of the Group CO, XO and adjutant. I saw LtCol Duke Savage, also a member of my Harrier training class. He was the group XO. We talked for a minute and then went in together to see the Group skipper. Col O was very cordial, friendly and we had the usual conversation about where we had been and what was going on in the group.

My goal during the visit with Col O was to ask to be considered to be assigned as the CO of VMAT-203. During my time in Kingsville, I discovered a love for flight instruction and a passion for figuring out how to coordinate and maximize the effort required to get students out the door, well qualified, and on time. VT-22 was a perfect training ground for the CO's job at 203.

When we got around to my future, Col O began by telling me that he could not give me a gun squadron because there were too many LtCols ahead of me in the queue. He then asked me to think about becoming the CO of VMAT-203. He told me my training command experience uniquely qualified me for the job. I almost leaped across the room to give him a hug. I quickly uttered, "Yes Sir, sign me up!" I told him I had come to plead my case for 203 after spending time in the training squadron. In about 30 minutes, Col O, Duke Savage, and I agreed on my next assignment. I was told to keep this to myself or else it would not happen.

That evening at the bar, I enjoyed meeting a few Harrier pilots and was amazed at the turnover that had taken place in my four short years away from the program. As I left the bar, I suspected they perceived me as another soon-to-be LtCol Harrier pilot who would be quickly assigned to a staff somewhere, never to be seen again.

. . .

The return trip to Kingsville was anxiety-free. It was wonderful knowing where I was headed upon my arrival at Cherry Point. I spent another month in Kingsville and left VT-22 on a high. It had been the best of tours. My good friend and assistant AMO, Capt. Jack Harland and I bought "Whataburger" lunches for the entire maintenance department as we both transferred at the same time. It was some of the best money we ever spent; an offbeat but fun way to say thank you to the people who made it work so well for us.

The journey to my goal of becoming a CO had taken a non-traditional course, but I felt well prepared for the job. My time in the Phantom was of little value to me. The time in Dallas was a game changer. I learned to be myself, for better or worse, and not try to be someone I was not. I learned how much fun it was to fly and make close friends. My time out of the Marine Corps was also very helpful to me. Like some of my close friends, I was burned out in Yuma. The change did me a lot of good. Most likely an assignment somewhere else in the Marines would have been fine. It just did not happen. I think many of us just needed to decompress. In Kingsville, I learned to give credit to the person at the lowest level who performed the job. If a sailor on the flight line caught something the pilot missed during preflight, I made sure he or she was personally recognized. Prior to that tour I would have given the flight line OIC credit for running a good flight line and expected him to tell the plane captain he did a good job. That might not have happened. I watched other officers in VT-22 claim they had done wonderful things that had been accomplished by those working for them. You could see the resentment in the ranks.

To sum it up, it is much better to have many of your sailors or Marines telling others how good you are as their officer in charge rather than you telling the world how well you perform your job. The voices of many are much easier to hear than a voice of one.

I was sad to leave the sailors in the maintenance department, but was beyond excited to be going to Cherry Point to meet the current Harrier pilots, fly the Harrier, and one day become the VMAT-203 CO.

PART 6 (1983-1987)

<u>VMAT-203</u>

What <u>Stays</u> Here <u>Happens</u> Here!!!
A quote from a 203, instructor pilot

1: VMAT-203

Bonnie and I arrived at Cherry Point about eight years after the first time we had come as a family. The housing situation quickly resolved itself. The base and the area had changed for the better and it was a good place to be stationed.

The word quickly spread that I was to become the XO of 203, to move up to CO in two years. This journey would turn out to be the most remarkable experience of my life. LtCol Mike Ryan, my friend from 542/513, was the CO of 203 for two years, from 1983-85. I was scheduled to follow him. Mike began the introduction of the AV-8B, and it continued under my time as CO. I believe being the XO for two years was the perfect path to becoming the squadron commander. I knew everyone in the squadron, but more importantly, they knew me. Now I look back at Col Price being thrown into his job as the CO of 542 without any Harrier flight experience, not knowing anyone in the squadron, and no one in the squadron knowing him. It does not take much thought to realize he had a much more difficult task ahead of him than I did.

When I first arrived in 1983, I still only knew about four people. However, in many ways the Harrier program was still the same. Prior to getting the AV-8B, we had serious aircraft availability problems with the AV-8A and TAV-8A. The maintenance issues were essentially the same as they always had been, that being the problem of parts availability. Now the AV-8A was on its way out of the Marine Corps inventory, so it was not receiving the attention necessary to keep 'em flying.

...

The game changer in the summer of 1983 was the new aircraft coming in January 1984, the AV-8B or Harrier II. The planning and work going on in 203 for the arrival of the AV-8B kept squadron morale high as we looked forward to transitioning to the Harrier II.

While I was the XO, I continued work on the integration of the squadron into a new hangar. One of the 203 pilots, Major Jerry

Fitzgerald, had worked hard with architects to get what we wanted and needed for a training squadron hangar. He was leaving the squadron, so I took this task over. Fitz pretty well had it put together so there was not a lot for me to accomplish, but I was able to help complete the process and oversee the move to the new facility. Going into a brand-new hangar was a first for or me, and I believe, for most of our squadron mates.

Many of the best AV-8A mechanics were tapped to be the first AV-8B mechanics. My other task was to work with the new training program for maintenance Marines. It was called the Fleet Replacement Aircraft Maintenance Program (FRAMP). This program was new to the Marines and was developed in large part by senior staff non-commissioned officers (SNCO) with previous Harrier experience. It was well on the way by the time I arrived. This was a sea change in the way of doing business for training maintainers. The plan was to provide a classroom environment and a dedicated aircraft to the instructors for maintenance training. When a squadron had to dedicate an aircraft for any use other than flying there were always some concerns. I believe this program made good use of the aircraft asset. Once again, my overall involvement was minimal as this effort had rounded the final turn and was headed for the finish line. I was proud of the effort these particular SNCOs put forth to send Harrier gun squadrons a trained maintainer when they completed the training program in VMAT-203.

We did have one glitch, however. Computers were used extensively to create documents, training manuals, parts manuals, etc. As the AV-8B was getting close to arriving in the squadron, the FRAMP SNCOs were ready to print these documents from McDonnell Douglas to make our training aids. We no longer received printed manuals from the manufacturer. We had to print them ourselves and we had enough large printers to do the job. But there was a problem. It turned out the software the contractor had been using for two years or so and had presented to the FRAMP was not compatible with the software the Marine Corps used. We could not print the manuals. After some discussions, I went to St. Louis to visit the contractor to find out how to solve the problem. He told me it was the Marines' fault. I replied that fault or blame did not matter, we needed to get the documents printed to prepare for upcoming classes. We just needed to get it fixed.

For me, the kicker came when the contractor's VP I was working with told me that with a change order for $250,000 they could convert their software to be compatible with what the Marines were using. The gentleman, a retired USAF three-star general and I had a nice discussion. There was no give from either of us during the meeting. I knew I was the low man on the totem pole, as they say, so I told him that was OK. Then as I turned to walk out the door I said, "I'm on my way home to contact Jack Anderson." Jack was well known as a reporter who wrote articles about the federal government being overcharged by vendors. I promised the VP I would use his name in my conversation so there would be no misrepresentation of the facts. The VP looked at me and said, "Colonel, you can't do that." I assured him I could, and I would. Then I left his office and headed back to Cherry Point. By the time I went to the squadron the next day, the software issue had been resolved. We were soon printing our manuals. I had a call from one of the computer workers in the contractor's office a few days later. The cost to do the switch was $15. I doubt that I made a friend at MCAIR, but I was one happy Marine to win this battle.

Me, Major Art Nalls, Col Duke Savage, and McDonnel Douglas test pilot Jack Jackson (Col, USMCR) after my familiarization flight in the new TAV-8B

The arrival of the AV-8B aircraft seemed slow to me at first. We began to transition instructors, then pilots going to VMA-331, the first AV-8B tactical squadron. The CO of that squadron was none other than my good friend LtCol Jim Cranford of VMA-542 and 513 fame.

As more Bs started to arrive, 203 was the perfect place to be a Harrier pilot. We had the TAV-8A, a few AV-8As and were receiving AV-8Bs. Our task was to train new students from the training command to fly either the A or B and to transition current AV-8A and A-4 pilots to the AV-8B when their squadrons stood down to receive their new aircraft. We had great AV-8B maintenance, we had parts, and we had wonderful instructor pilots. As the A's were being sent away it was easier to keep the Ts in the air.

When the A model ground training was completed, instructor pilots had to train new students arriving from flight school to first fly the TAV-8A to learn V/STOL maneuvers. After completion of the V/STOL syllabus, the students went to fly the AV-8B. The TAV-8A and the B cockpits had very little in common, but the B was a more stable bird to fly and the two aircraft had reasonably similar flight characteristics in the vertical flight mode. The student pilots had no problem with the transition between these two aircraft. We had a state-of-the-art AV-8B flight simulator to ensure each student or transition pilot was well prepared to fly the B. TAV-8B trainers did not arrive until the summer of 1987.

Once the AV-8Bs arrived, MAG-32 squadrons were rapidly filled with B pilots and maintenance Marines. We converted all the AV-8A squadrons and one A-4 squadron before I left in 1987. Buc Taber, another 542/513 pilot and good friend, was the CO of the last AV-8A squadron, VMA-542.

Our squadron was a busy place. We had many visitors who came to see the B in person as it was a new and well-advanced Harrier. A lot of Marine Corps aviation pride rested on the successful introduction of this aircraft. During my time as XO, I felt very fortunate to have been able to work with many different agencies to facilitate integration of the B into both 203 and the operational squadrons as quickly and safely as possible. HQMC manpower reps came to discuss manpower requirements, personnel needs, and the training that would be required for a new Harrier transition squadron.

...

NavAirSysCom was very involved in the AV-8B, and I was able to work once again with LtCol Frank Pieri. He was more determined than ever to make the Harrier program successful. I will always believe Frank was the person responsible for the AV-8A turnaround. Now his hard work was invaluable to the successful introduction of the AV-8B into the fleet. Hank Wall from McDonnell Douglas, US manufacturer for the B, worked directly with us to make this aircraft acceptance and transition as smooth as possible. His efforts benefited all of us as we learned while we progressed with how to best take care of our new Harrier.

Representatives from McDonnell Douglas and NAVAIR and I discuss issues with the new AV-8B

The B was fun to fly; it was one of three of the first "electric jets" – F-16, F/A-18, AV-8B. The weapons systems that came with the plane, though primitive compared to the 2018 systems, were awesome for their time. I had my first bombing hop and had 12 direct hits. That was a first for me and I had not had to think about it.

Mike Ryan was scheduled to give a pep talk to the company making the bombing systems as they were slightly behind aircraft production. Mike had to cancel his talk and I was sent as a substitute. I thought I would be speaking in front of a few engineers but had a large cafeteria full of people when I walked in the room. Fortunately, I had my notes on the back of the envelope ready to go. It was easy to brag on this system. I expressed as best I was able to how appreciative we were to have their system in our plane. No matter the name of an attack airplane, the ability to place a bomb on the target is the only reason they are purchased. My experience of bullseyes on my first bombing flight was proof they were putting out a good product. Aerial bombing accuracy was finally reaching new thresholds. We just needed for them to step up production. They soon caught up.

• • •

While still the XO in March of 1985, I had the dubious distinction of being the first person to eject from an AV-8B.

I had been in Massachusetts visiting my close flight school friend Joe Rowland and his family. My wingman was 1stLt Dennis O'Donoghue (Irish, later head test pilot for the Boeing Corporation). I was leading the flight of two at FL240 approaching Long Island Sound when the engine threw a blade, flamed out and all electrical power was lost. I was descending through the clouds, trying to get a relight, knowing full well that was not going to happen. The feeling in the plane was like putting a quarter in a vibrating bed in a cheap motel. It was shaking and shaking. Irish saw the plane was on fire but soon lost sight. I was now in the weather and stayed with the plane until I double-checked it would not relight, and confirmed it was on fire by looking in my mirror.

I transmitted a Mayday call and then without much hesitation, but with much dread and anxiety, I pulled the ejection handle. The sequence of leaving the aircraft started: the canopy being exploded by the mild detonating explosive charges that lined its top, the noise and explosion of the rocket seat firing and propelling me out of the aircraft, the sudden noise and rush of the wind as I met the horrific wind forces, and the sudden jolt of a beautiful canopy opening, and all within just a few seconds, told me the ejection sequence had worked as advertised, even though it left me shaken and terribly disoriented.

As I left the plane, my flight helmet was ripped off. I was in a vicious thunderstorm and battered by hail for a time on the way down. After a nice, well, not so nice, but long parachute ride starting around 15,000 feet I broke out of the clouds at an estimated altitude of 5,000 feet. I landed in Long Island Sound. After two tries, I was safe and secure in my life raft. The air and water temperature were both around 38 degrees. A young fellow heard about the ejection on his new Bearcat scanner and raced to get his father. They flew their Cessna 172 to look for a downed pilot. They located me and contacted the Coast Guard. I was picked up in a Coast Guard cutter, transported to the hospital emergency room and treated for hypothermia. After my release, I spent the night with the John Duell family who found me in the water and called the Coast Guard. It was quite an experience.

Col Duke Savage led the accident investigation and spent a few very cold weeks on Long Island Sound searching for the engine. He finally found it. The investigation determined that I did in fact have a first stage engine blade material failure. The blade broke off and continued through the rest of the engine, causing it to ruin the engine and damage both electrical systems. The "new aircraft" had 150 hours on it.

Even though I believed I followed all procedures correctly, jumping out of a brand-new aircraft less than three months before I was to take command of 203 did give me pause. I was one very happy pilot when the investigation was wrapped up with material failure as the primary cause factor.

Commanding Officer VMAT-203

I became the CO of VMAT-203 in June of 1985, and Col Savage was the new CO of MAG-32. This was the beginning of a two-year time period in my professional life that would never be eclipsed. Duke Savage was always one of the Marine officers I most admired. After two years' time working with him when we were both XOs, I knew I could not have a better mentor or boss. When General Cooke arrived for the change of command, he did not know me and mispronounced my name a couple times as he called me over to tell me to keep it short.

After spending many years in squadrons, getting my own was truly a gift. The first AOM I had, I put forth a list of things I would like the squadron to accomplish. By myself, I could accomplish none of these items. I needed every officer and Marine in the squadron to make that happen. I told them that from the first day. In keeping with my admiration of my reserve pals, I did my best to set a professional, yet casual, environment in the squadron. I believe happy people do great things.

• • •

An early change I was proud of involved cross-country flights. I had always been a cross-country hound and did my best to fly as many as possible anywhere I had been stationed. One problem with turning a few pilots loose on the weekend is that when they returned home the planes usually went into the hangar for repair. I spoke with Col Savage about taking all the planes that were up and going for a one-night cross-country, which we referred to as an Alpha Strike. Col Savage was planning to join us on the first one we flew to Naval Air Station Oceana in Virginia Beach, very soon after the change of command. He had to cancel at the last minute and could not make the flight. Before we left Friday morning, I had flight equipment make a Capt. Duke Savage name tag for every pilot. A lot of people met Capt. Savage that Friday night in Oceana. Duke was not there in the flesh but certainly in spirit. That Friday night helped set the standard for the remainder of our time in 203. Do things right and have fun.

Since I had recently been in the Naval Training Command and had been the 203 XO, I was familiar with the caliber of students we were getting through the door to fly the Harrier. With only a couple of exceptions, each new pilot exceeded our expectations. They studied hard and were well prepared for their flights. The instructors were great. Being an instructor in a tactical jet air group is not something most pilots would like to do. With a lot of help from the captains in the squadron, we were able to create an atmosphere conducive to getting fantastic instructors when needed. In a very short period of time, we all became close friends. The squadron goal was simple: train well-qualified pilots to go to tactical squadrons, do it quickly and do it with a smile.

In the Navy training program, the squadrons deployed to enhance student flight production. When I was in VT-22 we went to NAS El Centro twice a year. Fleet Marine training squadrons such as 203 did not deploy. Even though we were instructing in the B, most of us had never dropped live ordnance during the first year and a half we had been flying the plane. Working with our instructors and Col Savage, we convinced the wing CG the instructors needed to fly this part of the syllabus. The decision was made to send instructors for a heavy weapons deployment to NAS Fallon, NV in October 1985. That was a very beneficial training DET for us. We returned better equipped to instruct students in the flight characteristics of a fully loaded AV-8B.

...

We had only been operating in the new hangar for a short time when I was told the commanding general, Major General Dick Cooke, wanted to hold the Marine Corps birthday ball in our hangar. I was stunned as we would be out of the hangar for more than three weeks in late October and early November. That would severely impact pilot production. I asked Col Savage to help us to find a way out of this commitment. That did not happen. After some brainstorming, it was decided we would "deploy" to an underused runway at Cherry Point and work out of tents. Again, this was a case of something we would never have chosen to do, but it turned out great. Squadron morale was off the charts with bragging rights about working in tents at Cherry Point. The Marine Corps Ball was wonderful. We kept our production rate up. Life was good!!!

...

For the squadron Christmas party, we decided to have a pig picking. Bobby Light and I had a farm not too far from the base and we raised pigs. The 203 Sergeant Major was Joe Rufra. He was also a Kentuckian and had been a force recon Marine. He was well liked by everyone in the squadron. He worked with the pilots and they had a lot of respect for one another. Bobby killed the pig and had it frozen. We brought it to the squadron Friday morning and placed it in a closed room with a Marine Pfc on guard. The captains and the Sgt Major made a bet. The captains would get a high and tight (Marine regulation haircut) if they could not steal the pig, and the Sgt Major would get one if they did.

This became the story of the day on Friday before the party. Eventually the captains convinced the Pfc on guard the Sgt Major wanted to see him. He left his post and the pig fell into the hands of the captains. A ransom note, with photo, was immediately delivered to the

Sgt Major. It took a high and tight to get the pig returned. I called the Pfc to my office. He was scared about what happened. The Sgt Major and I explained the situation to him, and we gave him an attaboy, signed by me, for a job almost well done. I bet he still tells that story, and no one believes him. Sergeant Major Rufra did get the high and tight.

After the events of the day in the squadron, we went to the *Shame* to relive the story. Capt. Dog Davis was in charge of monitoring the cooking of the pig. He was assisted by a student, 1stLt Dan Claney, who was to be there all through the night to make sure the pig was ready for the noon meal. We were feeding well over 200 people at noon. It would seem possible that 1stLt Claney might have been a wee bit tired after happy hour and fell asleep while cooking the pig. Dog went in early Saturday morning and called to report the pig was burning. I told Dog to put it out and it would be OK. Claney received a temporary call sign of Flambo, and the pig was not seriously damaged. It was a great Christmas party for the squadron with a lot of laughs to go with it.

· · ·

In February, Gen Cooke decided to check out in the Harrier. We were getting much better at turning out pilots. Gen Cooke came to the squadron for his first day of lectures. Since he was the CG, we had a captain escort him from his car to the hangar, we had another instructor give him a lecture and for some reason now lost to me, there was a third captain involved with the general on his first day. That tied up three instructors and put a crimp in our flight schedule. I thought about it overnight and the next morning when he came to the ready room, I asked, "Sir, when you finish up today would you mind coming to my office?" He looked at me sort of funny and replied, "Colonel, I usually invite people to my office, not the other way around." I started to answer, but then he said, "I'll see you there."

As I waited for Gen Cooke to arrive, I was not sure how this was going to work out. He came in, took a seat, and asked me what I needed to speak with him about. I explained the instructor situation to him and asked, "Sir, would you like to be treated like a general officer or a squadron pilot while you're here?" He quickly answered, "Squadron pilot." Then he asked, "Anything else, Colonel?" I answered with a quick, "No, sir." The general left and I was breathing much easier.

Gen Cooke was a welcome addition to the ready room. His presence enriched the squadron in every way and that is not exactly what I thought would happen. He took the time to get to know the captains and they enjoyed him being there. One ready exchange was pretty famous around 203. During his FAM stage he would come down to study. As I remember it, the phone rang and now Capt. Dennis O'Donoghue said out loud, "It's probably some fucknuckle from the wing." Gen Cooke turned around in his chair in the front of the ready room, to ask Dennis if he would like to be a fucknuckle from the wing. Things like that seemed to happen all the time while he was assigned us. He would banter with the captains like he was one of them.

There was one Gen Cooke experience that cannot be omitted. I stopped by the squadron one Saturday afternoon when Gen Cooke was still in the AV-8B FAM syllabus. I saw his car in the parking lot as I walked into the hangar. One of the staff sergeants hurried over to me when I walked through the door. He looked nervous. He said, "Sir, Gen Cooke is in that Harrier on the hangar deck." I answered, "That's great. No problem." The SSgt said, "Sir, you don't understand. The general was in civilian clothes and I did not recognize him. I asked him if he was a tech rep when he came to maintenance control to ask if we had a Harrier he could sit in." I assured the SSgt that would be OK.

I walked toward the Harrier that Gen Cooke was sitting in and noticed his head was bent really low in the cockpit, so I assumed he was reading an emergency procedures manual. I climbed quietly up the work stand parked next to his aircraft. When I looked in the plane, Gen Cooke had a small TV in his lap and was watching a Villanova basketball game. He looked up at me and said, "Caps, looks like you caught me." I started laughing and said, "Yes, sir. I did." We both laughed. He was one of a kind, that is for sure.

In March, Gen Cooke accompanied us on an alpha strike to Ft. Bragg, NC to get a briefing from the Delta Force for a future operation we had planned. Getting to know and work with Gen Cooke was a high point for the squadron. We all benefited from that experience.

The senior Navy medical officer showed up in March 1985 to tell me he was assigning a female flight surgeon to 203. Lt. Debbie Lambert checked in later that week. I asked her, "Do you like to fly?" She replied, "Yes." This was on a Wednesday. Friday she was in a T headed to Ft. Bragg on an alpha strike along with Gen Cooke. Debbie was a very important part of our squadron and well thought of by all. It seemed the Harrier squadrons always had good flight surgeons, but Debbie was a cut above.

...

Snacks took some of the original AV-8B pilots trained in 203 to build up VMA-331, and he had some of the best Harrier pilots in the program in his squadron. 331 Harrier operations were going well until there was a mishap at Cherry Point involving 1stLt Ed Jasiewicz. Jas, as he was known, ejected extremely close to the runway in an unfavorable aircraft attitude. The flaps experienced an un-commanded input causing the nose to pitch downward. Had Jas not ejected when he did, he would most likely have been killed in the crash. The investigation found there was a problem with the flap controller; consequently, there was no pilot error causing the crash.

Gen Cooke believed Jas did not handle the situation correctly. He convened a pilot disposition board to determine if Jas should continue flying. In layman's terms, this is referred to as "losing your wings." The board at the wing level determined Jas should lose his wings. The paperwork was forwarded to HQMC to adjudicate the final status of 1stLt Jasiewicz's flying career in the Marine Corps.

Snacks and I strongly disagreed with the findings of the wing board. We asked Col Savage for permission to go to HQMC and testify on Jas's behalf. Col Savage, Snacks and I were convinced that had a more experienced pilot been flying that airplane, he would have stayed with it too long and died in the crash. Jas made the right decision.

Gen Cooke heard about our maneuver and told us before we left for HQMC he never heard of two squadron commanders going to HQMC to testify against the findings of the wing CG. We respected his position but told him we believed Jas did the right thing by ejecting from the plane. We were going to HQMC to do what we believed was the right thing for the two of us to do. We attended the hearing at HQMC, and recommended Jas be returned to the squadron as a Harrier pilot. HQMC concurred with our assessment and Jas kept his wings.

Gen Cooke proved to both Snacks and me what a fine Marine leader he truly was. He was not happy with us about what we did, but neither of us ever heard of the incident again. Jas came back to the squadron, completed his tour, and ultimately found employment with a major airline after he later left the USMC.

Gen Cooke's time as the CG was over and there was to be a change of command. Right before that happened, he called all the 203 pilots to his office and we had a great visit. He and the captains truly bonded with each other. Gen Cooke was replaced as the CG 2nd MAW by Gen Jack Dailey. He also checked out in the Harrier with 203.

• • •

In the fall of 1985, I asked Col Savage if I could throw a Harrier reunion in 1986. We talked it over. It would be a great time to celebrate 15 years of Harrier operations in the Marine Corps and also a chance to show off the B to those who helped build it, test it and fly it. He gave me the OK, so I pressed on to make this happen. We had excellent cooperation from British Aerospace, McDonnell Douglas, and Rolls Royce.

The event was an overwhelming success. With the AV-8B operational, we were able to showcase the plane, not only to pilots and maintainers, but to many people at NavAir, supply people and factories that had a significant part to play in the successful introduction. It was fun to actually meet someone in person you had spoken with many times on the phone. We had a golf tournament, did some sailing on the Neuse River, ran a PFT and had a pig picking, unburned this time, and provided once again by Bobby Light.

• • •

At the midpoint of 1986, we had an 83 percent mission capable rate for the aircraft that allowed us to reduce the conversion training time from 180 days to an average of 75. The FRAMP trained around 600 Marine maintainers to fill the squadrons with highly skilled technicians.

• • •

It was a fast summer and 203 had been nominated for the Commandant's Aviation Efficiency Award. We were selected to receive the award at the 1986 Marine Corps Aviation Association (MCAA) awards ceremony in Dallas, TX. This was an award to highlight the efficiency 203 had embedded in the production of pilots and maintenance Marines during the previous year.

Historically, the CO would receive the award for the squadron. In my mind, this award should go to the person most responsible in the squadron for making it happen. Master Sergeant Jim Dye, the aircraft maintenance chief, accepted the award on behalf of the squadron. I have never been prouder of being a Marine than I was when he accepted that award for VMAT-203. This setting was the best venue available to get in front of a large audience to recognize the SNCOs and maintenance Marines who were doing the hard work in every squadron, day after day.

· · ·

I was given the Bud Baker award at the MCAA in 1986. Col Baker was the CO of VMA-513, the first Harrier squadron, and he was instrumental in the acquisition and acceptance of the aircraft by the Corps, in implementing the V/STOL concept, and for forming the components of that first squadron. This award was given annually to someone who contributed to the advancement of V/STOL. I was grateful for the award, but I knew it was the members of 203 who made all our success happen. During the weekend ceremony, I was able to meet and spend a few minutes with Joe Foss, a famous Marine Corps fighter pilot from WWII. He was one of the pilots my father had watched take off and land at Henderson Field on Guadalcanal. Foss was the all-time USMC leading Acc with 26 kills, all in the Grumman F4F-4 Wildcat. His notable awards included the Medal of Honor, Silver Star, Bronze Star, Distinguished Flying Cross, and a Purple Heart. Needless to say, I was in total awe of his presence and cherished every second with him.

We took all the available pilots to Dallas for the acceptance of the commandant's award and they had an incredibly great time. Fortunately, I did not participate in the after-hours antics, but the stories came out later. This was another milestone bonding experience for all of us and helped continue the atmosphere established from day one. My goal of having the squadron be both professional and casual was still on track after the first year.

...

The availability of the AV-8B, coupled with the support of Col Savage and Gen Cooke and later Gen Dailey, allowed 203 to deploy once a year. In 1985, we sent the instructors to Fallon, NV; in 1986, we went to Patrick AFB, FL; and in 1987 we returned to NAS Fallon. The squadron was able to increase replacement pilot training on these deployments. It was a win-win for the instructors since one of the advantages of being in a gun squadron was the chance to deploy. Now that 203 could deploy, rather than remain home-based, it helped make a tour in the training squadron somewhat more desirable.

As with most things in life, people are what make the difference. We had just such an outstanding group of officers during my two years in 203. I really do not know what else to say about them. Everyone seemed to enjoy their ground jobs and loved the flying. The camaraderie was always over the top. I believe the replacement pilots and students enjoyed their time in the squadron as well. The ready room was a welcoming place. There was usually a line waiting to play Acey Deucy, a dice game played on a Backgammon board; there was laughter, storytelling and usually someone taking heat for something they did or did not do. As noted earlier, the quality of the young officers was most likely superior to many of my generation, but the "fighter pilot" personality was still common to us all.

We did have one incident involving a captain instructor who was newly assigned to 203. He checked in and when he came to my office, he stated in no uncertain terms that he was an AV-8B pilot and would not fly the T model. I chewed on that for a minute and told him that would be OK. I told him there were enough T pilots and we considered that to be a special assignment not offered to everyone. He departed very happy. I knew he was a good pilot with a great reputation and loved to fly the B, so I just let it go. In some ways he reminded me of myself when I may have in the past announced how things were going to be, according to me.

Soon after our discussion, we flew an alpha strike. All instructors flew the B, but the T guys flew the T with a passenger. There was a bit of nostalgia about flying the T. It performed similarly to the A, so maybe that was the reason we enjoyed flying it. The few of us flying the T just loved it. After that trip, one of the captains approached me to ask if I would consider allowing his friend, the pilot who was only there to fly the B, to check out in the T. That request was just too good! I replied, "Send him to see the OPSO". That captain had a fine run and excelled in his duties in 203. He later sat at the helm as CO of his own squadron that was considered to be one of the best at the time. These experiences were so rewarding and so much fun!

. . .

Bonnie did a wonderful job as the CO's wife. She had the squadron wives, most of whom were working at the time, get together on numerous occasions, but no one felt left out. She had no clipboard checking people in, she just enjoyed everyone's company.

We had a good social life in the squadron. When it was time for an officers' dress white uniform inspection, I decided to have a cocktail party with the officers and their wives or girlfriends at our home after the inspection was completed. I think every officer's uniform had been inspected by his wife or significant other prior to arrival for the inspection. No one wanted to flunk the inspection in front of a spouse or significant other. The inspection was over quickly with no discrepancies. The cocktail party began and went on for a couple more hours. It was a throwback to a bygone era and certainly one fond memory for me.

. . .

VMAT-203 had two cases of Marines that had contracted AIDS, which had increased rapidly in the United States in the 1980s. This was a tough time and very early in the AIDS epidemic. There was a great deal of concern from the senior medical officer on base about how to handle these two Marines and how to deal with the facilities they had used in the squadron. One contracted the AIDS virus from a blood transfusion. He passed away, leaving a family behind. The other Marine was single, and he also passed. We were not able to determine how he contracted the disease. These were two good Marines. Since this was at the beginning of public awareness of the AIDS epidemic, it was a serious problem for us to work through. The squadron loss of our Marines was only a harbinger of dreadful times ahead for the rest of our country.

...

One of the things I enjoyed most about being the CO of 203 was the opportunity to do some things out of the ordinary. Having been an instructor in the training command, I knew how important it was for a student aviator to receive his or her set of gold wings. In Kingsville we had a weekly winging ceremony, and it was something I looked forward to attending every Friday. There was always a guest invited to assist with the winging ceremony and it normally was a senior officer.

One day I received a call to be a guest for a winging ceremony at NAS Meridian. I was excited. I worked on a short speech, they are the most appreciated, and was pumped to be involved. The ceremony went off without a hitch. The next step was to head to the O'Club to let the newly designated naval aviators buy drinks.

I had just walked into the bar when I was cornered by a parent of one of the newly designated aviators. He had questions and lots of them. I had never needed to defend my chosen occupation before. This fellow had a very successful business and wanted his son to come onboard after college. Obviously, that did not happen, and he was unhappy. The questions came hard and fast and had an edge to them. He began to disparage the fighter pilot image, the make-believe dogfights, and the whole inefficient military way of life. This was getting a bit testy and we had not even made it to the actual bar. He finally asked his real question. He wanted to know if I thought his son's time in the Navy was a waste of time. That is when I got on my high horse and said, "I believe anyone who receives their wings of gold and spends one tour in the fleet should be equipped to handle almost any situation in a civilian company such as yours. Being a junior officer and a pilot is an exceptional learning experience." He shook his head and wandered off. It was the strangest reaction by a parent to a child receiving their naval wings I had ever witnessed. I have often wondered if his son ever joined the family business.

As I finished the evening, I had enjoyed speaking with all the others and headed to my BOQ room after dinner. Once there, I called my good friend Joe Rowland to tell him one of the two dumbest people to ever fly jets was the guest speaker at a winging ceremony. We both had a good laugh about that. By that time, Joe had built a large aviation insurance business and was extremely successful.

· · ·

Back home, I was doing a bit of reflecting and was thinking that perhaps sometimes pilots can be a bit superstitious. We had a TAV-8A that crashed a few years earlier, then sent to NARF for rework and later returned to the squadron. Unfortunately, it was involved in another mishap. Again, it was returned to NARF and was reworked and restored to flying condition. One day NARF brought it over to the VMAT-203 flight line. There was a rumor going around that not many instructors wanted to fly the plane because of its history. I had flown it, and it was the lowest time T airframe we owned. I thought about the concerns and one Monday morning I had maintenance paint Christine on the aircraft. Nobody made a big deal out of that, but ready room chatter would include comments about flying Christine. It became one of our most productive aircraft. (This, of course, is a reference to the Stephen King book about the car that keeps coming back to life)

· · ·

We had an IG inspection and completed it with a good grade and did not lose a step with production. We continued to meet all our commitments and challenges head-on and kept up with our pilot and maintainer throughput. From my perspective, the squadron ran itself. We had awesome XOs, Rick Priest, Jerry Fitzgerald, and Trapper who significantly contributed to our success.

· · ·

On 203's last deployment to NAS Fallon, MCAIR was marketing AV-8Bs to different countries. The person they chose to introduce the Italians to the B was General Chuck Yeager. Col Savage and I took a TAV-8A from Fallon to Edwards AFB to give the general a ride. MCAIR also brought a TAV-8B to Edwards so the general could fly it to tell the difference in flight characteristics between the two planes. Duke and I enjoyed our time with Gen Yeager. I especially enjoyed my time because Yeager was kind enough to call Joe Rowland around 3 a.m. east coast time and have a discussion with him. The irony of Gen Yeager talking about flying with the two dumbest students to ever fly jets was not lost on either of us. There are some things you never forget!

BGen Chuck Yeager flies a TAV-8A to familiarize him with Harrier flight characteristics for the introduction to the Italian Navy

Another special time for me was when Trapper returned from a staff assignment to check out in the B and become the XO of 203. This was our third time together. He was an exceptionally good friend. In March and April 1987, we checked out Col Sabow and Col Hearney in the B. That was fun! Having these two officers complete the AV-8B transition again pointed out the small size of the Marine Corps Harrier program.

We checked out MajGen Jack Dailey (call sign Zorro), the new 2nd MAW CG, and Brigadier General (BGen) Mike Sullivan (call sign Lancer), still the assistant wing commander. Gen Dailey was well known in Marine Corps aviation. He was a wonderful leader and the perfect CG for 2nd MAW. I do not believe we could have had a better replacement for Gen Cooke if we had selected a general ourselves.

Gen Sullivan was also a legendary Marine pilot. I first heard about him around the time I was leaving Dallas to go to the Harrier program. He was the CO of VMFA-323, an F-4 squadron, and the reserves wanted to send an ACM DET to Yuma to fight the Phantoms. They called me because I was the AMO and asked if we could do it. I promised my guys the Dallas reserves, flying the F-8's, would go to Yuma to fight Gen Sullivan's F-4 squadron. This agreement happened over a couple drinks at the Yuma O'Club between the reserves, LtCol Sullivan and with me on the phone in Dallas. Col Stiver asked how I planned to get enough F-8s up for this "pop-up" deployment. I told him my plan and he told me to make it happen. I had reserves coming in for training days. We had a Capt. James Bailey who had a PhD in radar wave theory, and he helped work on the radars. We had plenty of F-8s up for the deployment, and though I did not get to go myself, I was told by all that it was a success.

Later in his career, Gen Sullivan became the CO of MARTD Dallas. Both Gen Dailey and Gen Sullivan added to the morale of the squadron. They were fun to be around and were very good pilots.

…

Some of the instructor call signs were Bill Jukich (Greyhound), Jon Davis (Dog), Georges Leblanc (Bone), Gary Monroe (Stray Dog), Rick Rodecker (Hagar), Lee Buland (Snake), Russ Currer (Conan), Dennis O'Donoghue (Irish), Jim Lee (Rebel), Denny Snook (Rainbow), Jerry Fitzgerald (Mystic), Jack Kreitzburg (K-9), Pat Wheeler (Wheels), Bill Green (Pilgrim), Ron Wilson (Wiley), Paul Pruitt (Panama), Eddie Holcomb (Carbo), Rick Priest (Hawk), Scott Shogren (Shogun), Jay Rodgers (Rider), Dan Campbell (Indian), Steve Coker (Coke), Kevin Bjorge (BJ), Mark Bebo (Beebs), Ken Star (Blackjack), Kyle Andrews (Bongo), Mike Kelly (Combat), Debbie Lambert (Lady Hawk), Cliff Dunn (Troll) and Byron Trapnell (Whiskey). In spite of these call signs, these were the most professional and productive group of officers I ever had the privilege to serve with in my career. There was never a challenge too great or a moment so serious that I could not count on each one of these guys to deliver. The days in 203 never seemed to be work, just fun.

Flanked by a graduating class of new AV-8B Harrier pilots

It was toward the end of my time as the CO in May of 87. We were in Oceana for the last alpha strike. I came up with a great idea for returning home to Cherry Point. We took our 19 airplanes and flew a tail chase all the way to the Point. I cannot tell you how much fun that was for all of us. It was very safe as you just followed the plane in front without pulling lead on him. That flight still brings a lot of smiles to many people.

Due to the outstanding AV-8B availability, we were able to exceed most of the training goals that were assigned to us. We had captains who developed pilot training schedules and lectures that enhanced our ability to reduce training time. The first year that I was CO, the OPSO was Major Russ Currer. He did a great job keeping things running smoothly. The AMO was Major Rick Rodecker. He had a very smooth-running maintenance department. After about a year in these positions, I called them in one day and told them they were going to switch jobs. I know they were surprised, but nothing changed. The squadron

280

continued to perform as it had the past year. I really liked making that move because it gave each of these fine officers' exposure to the challenges of the other side of the squadron.

Since we were home-based, most of the time we bonded more at work than at the bar. We had a job to do and we did it with fun and professionalism. The instructor and student pilots in 203 would ultimately become the leadership of the AV-8B program in the late 80s through the mid-90s. We had a few pilots leave 203 for the Naval Test Pilot School and we sent one pilot to the Weapons Tactics Instructor Course. One captain went to test pilot school, then to Boeing and was the chief test pilot for their Joint Strike Fighter entry and the winner of the Collier award for Aviation and many other aviation awards. We had six future squadron commanders, some who participated in the Gulf War.

Marines do not use the "L" word much, but I loved those guys. They made my tour as the CO the easiest job I had in my entire career. There was never a day I did not look forward to coming to the squadron. I was fortunate to have been friends with them throughout my life.

$$\cdots$$

Col Savage and I had our changes of command on the same day. The walk to the podium for me was a long trip. I knew I could never duplicate what I was leaving. Being the CO of VMAT-203 was the pinnacle of my career, so the change of command for me was doubly sad. I had lots of pride in what the squadron had accomplished, but the finality of it all was hard for me to take. I think anyone giving up a squadron would list that in the top 10 of the worst days of their Marine Corps lives.

All I could think to say that day was to thank the troops, the officers in the squadron, my good friend Duke Savage and Generals Cooke, Dailey and Sullivan for their support. But the sad fact for me was that it was over.

It has been difficult for me to express in words what I want to say about 203. The time spent there was superlative in every way. Each officer was unique, multitalented, and possessed a great personality. There were daily stories, most in the "you had to be there" or in the

TINS (This Is No Shit) category. I find it interesting the most difficult tour for me to write about was the 203 XO/CO tour. There was no drama, everything worked as advertised, we flew as we were tasked, we enjoyed being in the squadron together, and it was a fairly simple two years. It was awesome, I loved it, so there is not much else to say.

...

When I checked into NAS Pensacola for flight school, I was as green as anyone could ever be when I walked through that door. I had no uniforms, and I had no idea that with very few exceptions, I would meet the best friends of my life over the next 20 years while serving in the Marine aviation community – people I would love and do anything I could for them, and they for me. As many smart people have said before me, "You don't die for your country, you die for the person next to you." I understood that sentiment early in my Marine career.

My education in all things Marine began in Pensacola, continued in Dallas with the reserves, was enhanced at NAS Kingsville, TX and was completed serving in the Harrier program. My learning experience came through years of hard work, observation, and experimentation, and I almost always had a lot of good luck. I asked for assignments, did my best to complete them, became a good pilot and through the years learned how to work with sailors in Kingsville and Marines all the rest of the time. I never thought too much about getting promoted. I figured if I did a good job, I would get promoted like everyone else.

Occasionally throughout my career, I drank too much, partied too much, and disregarded some rules. The post-Vietnam years seemed to be the craziest time of all. I believe the fact that the Harrier community lost many pilots and planes affected each of us to some extent. I spent a year in Vietnam, and we lost one A-4 pilot. In my years in the Harrier program there were a significant number of aircraft lost and pilots killed. The Harrier is a plane you either love or not. It is a pilot's airplane. I doubt there are many Harrier pilots who do not look back fondly on the plane and the many times it brought them home. I know my friends miss flying the plane as much as I do, but we all still have and love the memories.

My service as a pilot in the Marine Corps was a wonderful ride and

I would do it all over again! But today, with my college grades and PFT scores, I would not be qualified to get in the program!!!

Epilogue
A Harrier Pilot

Leading, instructing, flying…it doesn't get any better

If you have ever attended an airshow to watch a Harrier performing, it was exciting to see, it was very noisy and close to the crowd. The plane was constantly maneuvering in all directions, and the show was fairly short. Many times, no matter what other acts were there, Harriers stole the show. The Harrier pilot you watched that day made it look easy.

It was not! Harriers required numerous man-hours to get the plane ready for that particular flight, just like every other flight. The plane required an extraordinary amount of maintenance to keep it in the air. The maintenance troops worked extremely long hours to keep Harriers flying, and most importantly, it took a very professional and talented pilot to perform the maneuvers for the airshow.

Those of us who flew an AV-8A Harrier in the 1970s and early 80s, signed on for something special in the world of military aviation. At that time, other jet pilots in the Marines flew a more combat capable aircraft and logged more flight time annually than a Harrier pilot, but they did not experience the unintended consequences of being a Harrier pilot. The Harrier's unique flight characteristics were a treat unto themselves. But in addition to that, pilots flew airshows, met celebrities, took designated individuals for rides in the TAV-8A, flew flight demonstrations for members of Congress and other dignitaries. Harrier pilots were invited to tell the Harrier story to civilian groups and organizations in communities where we served. Some were on TV, some were featured in international airshows, and a few were written about in newspaper and professional aviation articles and books. Harrier pilots, when on the ground, became Marine ambassadors to the civilian and military communities everywhere we flew.

When I tossed my hat in the ring to fly the Harrier in 1972, I had no idea where the journey would take me. I suspect my fellow Harrier pilots can pretty much say the same thing. As lieutenants and captains, we were just a bunch of young pilots in our early to mid-20s looking for the next big thing. We found it!

There was definitely a bit of mystique about flying the Harrier. When people found out that I was a Harrier pilot, a few began the conversation by telling me how difficult the Harrier is to fly. Others actually asked, "Is the Harrier really hard to fly?" My answer has always been the same. "If it were really hard to fly, I probably couldn't do it!" During the 48 months after receiving my wings, I first transitioned to the F-4 Phantom, then the F-8 Crusader and finally, the Harrier. In my case, bragging rights about flying two famous legacy fighters sounded good but my total flight time was not that great. When I achieved the same amount of flight time in each of these three aircraft, about 300 hours, I can easily say I felt considerably more comfortable in all flight regimens of Harrier flight than I ever did in either the Phantom or Crusader. I also have flight time in the TA-4J and two-seat FAC version. the OA-4M, as well as some in the single-seat A-4M. These were extremely capable, wonderful, forgiving airplanes and easy to fly. But they were not Harriers!

However, after a lot of thought about this through the years, I still believe the Harrier was the easiest aircraft I ever had the opportunity to fly. I do not say that in a boasting manner. The Harrier would treat you well if you respected it and its limitations. In terms of an enjoyable flying experience, the Harrier surpassed every aircraft I have ever flown. And for me, every flight was as rewarding as the first one.

The Harrier, after a few flights, was the aircraft I became one with when I strapped myself into the cockpit. The cockpit was small and intimate in the sense you were closely surrounded by every switch, button or latch you would ever require when you closed the canopy. With a few exceptions, you used them. The seat, the HUD and the gauges became both your home and office when you climbed in the cockpit for a flight. When you became comfortable in the Harrier, the seemingly small cockpit you climbed into on your first flight, became a much larger space to pilot the plane.

About the first three years of actual squadron operations, the Harrier was fatality-free. Then there was a fatality, and all of a sudden Harrier squadrons began to experience an elevated mishap rate. No squadron member, either enlisted or officer, escaped fallout from those events. Almost all Harrier pilots lost a close friend or two who died flying the Harrier. Many people in all areas of naval aviation worked overtime to analyze the cause of these mishaps in an attempt to prevent them. Many were pilot error, many were mechanical failure, some were maintenance error, and some had unknown causes. It was very difficult to identify a specific cause that could be quickly corrected to solve Harrier mishaps.

The price Marine pilots paid to prove the V/STOL concept with the AV-8A, and early AV-8B, was heartbreaking. The largely untold story about the AV-8B Harrier II (second generation of the Harrier) is that it became the go-to warfighter in the 20 plus years since the involvement of the US in Middle East conflicts. Now, due to the efforts of all who went before, the Marine Corps operates the new F-35B STOVL aircraft for future war fighting and CAS missions.

The purchase of the Harrier came at great risk to the Marine Corps. If the Harrier had not worked as intended, the Marine Corps would have wasted a lot of dollars purchasing an aircraft that could not perform the CAS mission. Marines had skin in the game, and failure of the V/STOL concept was not a possibility. That is one of the reasons the tempo of operations never slacked off. The AV-8A was the lead aircraft for the follow-on and much more capable AV-8B. V/STOL had to be done right!

We also agree there seemed to be fewer rules in the Harrier community back in the beginning, and most of the time you could break those rules without major consequences. It was almost always easier to get forgiveness than permission. That became the motto for many of us.

Most of the pilots mentioned in this book have left the service or were discharged/retired from the Marine Corps and have been out of the Harrier and the Harrier community for many years. As some of us discussed, the ideas about this story obviously came from the early-on Harrier pilots who lived in a different time. The war in Vietnam was winding down, then over, and the Cold War was going strong. In the beginning, some, certainly not all, became big drinkers and partiers during our time in the early Harrier squadrons. Some of us became such good friends we would rather go to the O'Club after work to debrief events of the day than go home. A few of us pressed the edge of the envelope one time or another. Some of us pressed the edge of a couple different envelopes at the same time. In the end, we all know that we were, in many ways, very lucky.

We began having Harrier reunions in 1986. There have been seven reunions to this point. All of us found second careers after leaving the Marine Corps. The reunions brought us together for a couple days to appreciate what we were able to accomplish during our time in Marine aviation. The love, camaraderie and friendship for our fellow Harrier pilots and maintainers remains alive and well.

In spite of all the bad press the Harrier received throughout the years, I believe if you were to speak with the average Harrier pilot or maintainer, they would tell you no matter the long hours, hard work and challenges, it was the greatest airplane they ever had the opportunity to fly or work on. In my mind, that is the ultimate endorsement of not only a unique aircraft but also of the bold concept, both of which the Marine Corps gambled on, and won!

SEMPER FIDELIS

CAPS

Appendix A

CALL SIGNS

Al James	Uncle
Andy Boquet	Bucket
Art Nalls	Chaos
Bill Callahan	Few
Bill Green	Pilgrim
Bill Jukich	Greyhound
Bob Reed	Bullet
Bill Spicer	Sugar
Bob Snyder	Diamond
Bobby Light	Flash
Byron Trapnell	Whiskey
Cliff Dunn	Troll
Dan Campbell	Indian
Dan Claney	Flambo, later Clancy
Dick Gustafson	Swede
Debbie Lambert	Lady Hawk
Dennis O'Donoghue	Irish
Denny Snook	Rainbow
Denny Greene	Texan
Duke Savage	Ruby
Eddie Holcomb	Carbo
Gary Monroe	Stray Dog
Georges Leblanc	Bone
Greg Kusniewski	K-9
Jack Kreitzburg	K-9
Jay Rodgers	Rider
Jerry Fitzgerald	Mystic
Joe Gallo	Cobra
Jim Cranford	Snacks
Jim Lee	Rebel
Jim Sabow	Stranger
John Capito	Bambi
John Halleran	Filthy

Jon Davis	Dog
Ken Brust	Bruiser
Ken Starr	Blackjack
Kevin Bjorge	BJ
Kyle Andrews	Bongo
Larry Kennedy	Slug
Larry Wahl	Squid
Lee Buland	Snake
Mark Bebo	Beebs
Mark O'Conner	Nods
Marx Branum	Carrot
Mike Kelly	Combat
Mike Ryan	Rook
Mike Siepert	Mammal
Pat Owen	Peppermint Patty
Pat Wheeler	Wheels
Paul Lowery	Dixie
Paul Pruitt	Panama
Pete Wallis	Gator
Ray Bright	Not So
Rich Hearney	Horse
Rick Priest	Hawk
Rick Rodecker	Hagar
Ron Wilson	Wiley
Russ Currer	Conan
Scott Shogren	Shogun
Skip Klinefelter	Klink
Steve Coker	Coke
Steve Linder	Dwarf
Ted Herman	Mongoose
Toby Griggs	Mongo
Todd Eikenbery	Yobo
Vic Ashford	Sundance
Vic Taber	Buc
Win Rorabaugh	Bag

Appendix B

ACRONYMS:

Administration Officer	AO or S-1
All Officers Meeting	AOM
Airline Transport Rating	ATP
Administrative Office	S-1
Air Combat Tactics or Training	ACT
Aircraft Maintenance Officer	AMO
All Marine Message	ALMAR
Angle of Attack	AOA
Assistant Aircraft Maintenance Officer	AAMO
Batchelor Officers Quarters	BOQ
Board of Inspection and Survey	BIS
Brigadier General	BGen
Captains Protection Association	CPA
Clear And Visibility Unrestricted	CAVU
Close Air Support	CAS
Combined Arms Exercise	CAX
Commanding General	CG
Commanding Officer	CO
Confined Area Landings	CAL
Continental United States	CONUS
Department of Defense	DOD
Detachment	DET
Direct Air Support Center	DASC
Emissions Controlled	EMCON
Executive Officer	XO
Familiarization	FAM
Field Carrier Landing Practice	FCLP
Fleet Marine Force Pacific	FMFPAC
Fleet Replacement Aircraft Maintenance Program	FRAMP
Forward Air Controller	FAC
Gas Turbine Starter	GTS
General Staff Level for Plans and Operations	G-3
Harrier Tactical Manual	TacManual

Head-up Display	HUD
Headquarters Marine Corps	HQMC
Inspector General	IG
Inertial Navigation System	INS
Landing Signal Officer	LSO
Landing Site Supervisor	LSS
Landing Zone	LZ
Major General	MajGen
Marine Aviation Cadet	MarCad
Marine Aircraft Wing	MAW
Marine Aircraft Group	MAG
Marine Air Reserve Training Detachment	MARTD
Marine Corps Air Station	MCAS
Marine Corps Aviation Association	MCAA
Marine Corps Auxiliary Landing Field	MCALF
Marine Corps Recruit Depot	MCRD
Marine Aviation Weapons Tactics Squadron	MAWTS
McDonnell Douglas	MCAIR
Naval Air Rework Facility	NARF
Naval Air Station	NAS
Naval Aviation Depot	NADEP
Naval Aviation Training Command	NATC
Navan Aviation Training and Operations Manual	NATOPS
Officers Club	O'Club
Operation Duty Officer	ODO
Officer in charge	OIC
Operations	S-3
Operations Officer	OPSO
Physical Fitness Test	PFT
Platoon Leaders Class	PLC
Public Affairs Office	PAO
Radar Intercept Officer	RIO
Republic of Vietnam	RVN
Rolling Vertical Takeoff	RVTO
Rolling Vertical Landing	RVL
Royal Air Force	RAF
Staff Non-Commissioned Officer	SNCO
Short take off	STO

Squadron Duty Officer	SDO
Stability Augmentation System	SAS
Staff Non-Commissioned Officer	SNCO
STOVL	Later term for V/STOL
Supervisor of Flying	SOF
Supply and Logistics	S-4
Trans-Pacific	TRANSPAC
Vertical Landing	VL
Vertical Speed Indicator	VSI
Vertical takeoff	VTO
Vertical/Short Take-Off and Landing	V/STOL
Viet Cong	VC
Weapons Tactics Instructor	WTI
Western Pacific	WESTPAC

Straight Up and Out of Control

Printed in Great Britain
by Amazon